THE LIFE
OF
GEORGE WASHINGTON

VOL. III.

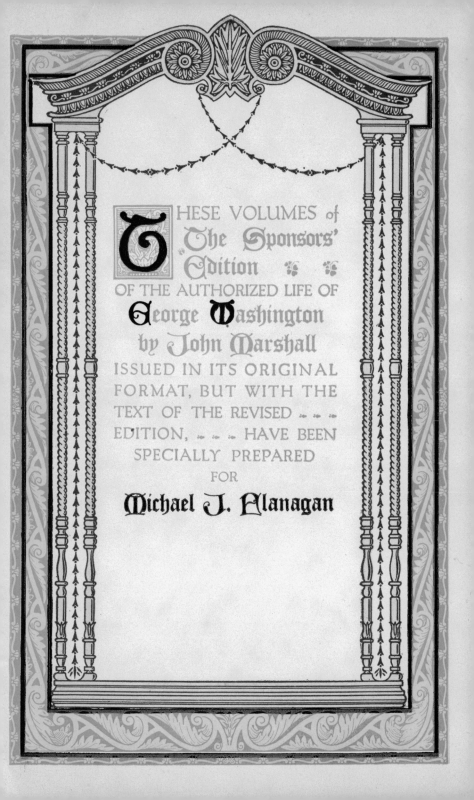

THESE VOLUMES of
The Sponsors' Edition
OF THE AUTHORIZED LIFE OF
George Washington
by John Marshall
ISSUED IN ITS ORIGINAL
FORMAT, BUT WITH THE
TEXT OF THE REVISED
EDITION, HAVE BEEN
SPECIALLY PREPARED
FOR

Michael J. Flanagan

THE

LIFE

OF

GEORGE WASHINGTON,

COMMANDER IN CHIEF

OF THE

AMERICAN FORCES,

DURING THE WAR WHICH ESTABLISHED THE INDEPENDENCE
OF HIS COUNTRY,

AND

FIRST PRESIDENT

OF THE

UNITED STATES.

COMPILED
UNDER THE INSPECTION OF
THE HONOURABLE BUSHROD WASHINGTON,
FROM
ORIGINAL PAPERS
BEQUEATHED TO HIM BY HIS DECEASED RELATIVE, AND NOW IN POSSESSION
OF THE AUTHOR.

TO WHICH IS PREFIXED,

AN INTRODUCTION,

CONTAINING
A COMPENDIOUS VIEW OF THE COLONIES PLANTED BY THE ENGLISH
ON THE
CONTINENT OF NORTH AMERICA,
FROM THEIR SETTLEMENT
TO THE COMMENCEMENT OF THAT WAR WHICH TERMINATED IN THEIR
INDEPENDENCE.

BY JOHN MARSHALL.

VOL. III.

THE CITIZENS' GUILD
OF WASHINGTON'S BOYHOOD HOME
FREDERICKSBURG, VA.

1926

Printed in the U. S. A.

CONTENTS

CHAPTER I.

CHAPTER II.

CHAPTER III.

CHAPTER IV.

CHAPTER V.

CHAPTER VI.

CHAPTER VII.

CHAPTER VIII.

CHAPTER IX.

CHAPTER X.

CHAPTER XI.

THE LIFE
OF
GEORGE WASHINGTON

THE LIFE
OF
GEORGE WASHINGTON

CHAPTER I.

Incursion into Jersey....General Lacy surprised....Attempt on Lafayette at Barren Hill....General Howe resigns the command of the British army....Is succeeded by Sir H. Clinton....He evacuates Philadelphia, and marches through the Jerseys....A council of war which decides against attacking the British on their march....Battle of Monmouth....General Lee arrested ....Sentenced to be suspended for one year....Thanks of congress to General Washington and his army.

THE position at Valley Forge had been taken 1778
for the purposes of covering the country, protecting the magazines, and cutting off all supplies to Philadelphia. Although the intercourse of the inhabitants with that place could not be entirely prevented; the sufferings of the British army from the scarcity of fresh provisions and forage were considerable; and, as the spring opened, several expeditions were undertaken both to relieve their own wants, and to distress the army of the United States.

CHAP. I

1778

About the middle of March, Colonel Mawhood and Major Simcoe, who were detached into Jersey at the head of about twelve hundred men, landed at Salem, nearly opposite Reedy Island, and dispersed the small bodies of militia who were stationed in that part of the country.

General Washington had given early intelligence of this expedition to Governor Livingston; and had requested that he would immediately order out the militia to join Colonel Shreve, whose regiment was detached into Jersey; but the legislature had neglected to make provision for paying them; and the governor could not bring them into the field. Colonel Shreve, on his arrival at Haddonfield, the place at which they had been directed to assemble, found less than one hundred men. Colonel Ellis, their commanding officer, remarked, in a letter to the

March 23.

governor, that "without some standing force, little was to be expected from the militia, who, being alone not sufficient to prevent the incursions of the enemy, each one naturally consults his own safety, by not being found in arms."

Mawhood, of course, was unrestrained; and the devastation committed by his party was wantonly distressing. Its course of destruction was preceded by a summons to Colonel Hand, the commanding officer of the militia, to lay down his arms, which was accompanied with a threat of the consequences to result from his refusal. This threat was too faithfully executed.

After completing his forage, without molestation, Mawhood returned to Philadelphia. During the continuance of this incursion, which lasted six or seven days, not more than two hundred men could be collected to reinforce Colonel Shreve, who was consequently unable to effect any thing, and did not even march to the lower parts of Jersey, which were plundered without restraint.*

May 1.

Not long after this incursion into Jersey, an enterprise was undertaken against General Lacy, who, with a small number of Pennsylvania militia, seldom amounting to six hundred, and sometimes not exceeding fifty, watched the roads leading to Philadelphia on the north side of the Schuylkill, and was generally posted within twenty miles of that town.

General Lacy surprised.

This expedition was entrusted to Colonel Abercrombie and Major Simcoe, who avoided all the posts Lacy had established for his security, and threw a body of troops into his rear before he discovered their approach. After a short resistance, he escaped with the loss of a few men killed, and all his baggage. His corps were entirely dispersed, and he was soon afterwards relieved by General Potter.

To maintain the command of the water as far as was practicable, congress had ordered impediments to be sunk in many of the rivers of common use, so as to obstruct the passage up them,

* See note No. I. at the end of the volume.

CHAP. I

1778

and had constructed frigates, and other smaller vessels, to be employed above those impediments or elsewhere, as the occasion might require. Several of them had been commenced above Philadelphia, but were not completed when the British obtained the command of the river. General Washington then became apprehensive for their safety, and repeatedly expressed his desire that they should be sunk in such a manner as to be weighed with difficulty, should any attempt be made to raise them. The persons, however, who were entrusted by congress with this business, supposed it would be equally secure to put plugs in their bottoms, which might be drawn out on the approach of danger.

Against these vessels, and some stores collected at Bordentown, an expedition was planned which ended in their total destruction. General Dickenson was in the neighbourhood, but his force was too small to interrupt the execution of the design; and General Maxwell, who had been ordered to his assistance, was retarded in his march by a heavy rain, which did not obstruct the movement of the British, who passed up the river in vessels.

May 18.

To cover the country more effectually on the north of the Schuylkill, to form an advance guard for the security of the main army, and to be in readiness to annoy the rear of the enemy, should he evacuate Philadelphia, an event believed to be in contemplation, General Washington detached the Marquis de Lafayette, with more than two thousand choice troops, to take post near the lines. As this corps formed a very valuable part of the army, the Commander-in-chief recommended in his instructions to General Lafayette the utmost attention to its safety; and, particularly, to avoid any permanent station, as a long continuance in one position would facilitate the execution of measures which might be concerted against him.

The Marquis crossed the Schuylkill and took post near Barren Hill church, eight or ten miles in front of the army. Immediate notice * of his arrival was given to Sir William Howe, who reconnoitred his position, and formed a plan to surprise and cut him off.

Attempt on Lafayette at Barren Hill.

On the night of the 19th of May, General Grant with five thousand select troops, took the road which leads up the Delaware, and consequently diverges from Barren Hill. After marching some distance, he inclined to the left, and passing White Marsh, where several roads unite, took one leading to Plymouth meeting-house, the position he was directed to occupy, some-

* General Wilkinson, in his memoirs, says that this notice was given by a person formerly a lieutenant in Proctor's regiment of artillery, who, disgusted at being discarded from the American service, became a spy to Sir William Howe; and, the better to fulfil his new engagements, kept up his acquaintance with his former comrades, and frequently visited the camp at Valley Forge. To avoid the suspicion which would be excited by his going into Philadelphia, a rendezvous had been established on Frankford Creek, where he met a messenger from General Howe, to whom his communications were delivered. This statement is certainly correct.

CHAP. I

1778

May 20.

thing more than a mile in the rear of the Marquis, between him and Valley Forge. He reached his point of destination rather before sunrise. Here the roads fork; the one leading to the camp of Lafayette, and the other to Matron's ford over the Schuylkill.

In the course of the night, General Gray, with a strong detachment, had advanced up the Schuylkill on its south side, along the ridge road, and taken post at a ford two or three miles in front of the right flank of Lafayette, while the residue of the army encamped on Chestnut hill.

Captain M'Clane, a vigilant partisan of great merit, was posted on the lines some distance in front of Barren Hill. In the course of the night, he fell in with two British grenadiers at Three Mile Run, who informed him of the movement made by Grant, and also that a large body of Germans was getting ready to march up the Schuylkill. Immediately conjecturing the object, M'Clane detached Captain Parr, with a company of riflemen across the country to Wanderers hill, with orders to harass and retard the column advancing up the Schuylkill, and hastened in person * to the camp of Lafayette. He arrived soon after daybreak, and communicated the intelligence he had received. It was, not

* Extracts of letters from the adjutant general and the officer of the day to Captain M'Clane.

Camp Valley Forge, May 21st, 1778.

Dear Captain,—I am happy you have with your brave little party conducted with so much honour to yourself. The long afterwards, confirmed by the fire of Parr on the Ridge road, and by an inhabitant who had escaped from White Marsh as the British column passed that place.†

Thus surrounded with danger, Lafayette took with promptitude and decision the only course which could preserve him. He instantly put his troops in motion, and passed over at Matron's ford, which was rather nearer to General Grant, than to himself, without being intercepted by that officer, or sustaining a greater loss than nine men.

General Grant, who reached the ground lately occupied by Lafayette soon after it was abandoned, followed his rear, and appeared at the

---

Marquis effected, owing to your vigilance, a glorious retreat as well as a difficult one.

Signed ALEX. SCAMMELL, *Adj. Gen.*

Camp Valley Forge, May 23d, 1778.

Dear Captain,—I am pleased to hear you are still doing something to distinguish yourself in the eyes of your country. I have the pleasure to inform you that your conduct with the Marquis has been very pleasing to his Excellency and the whole army.

I am your obedient servant,
CHARLES SCOTT, *Brig. Gen. and officer of the day.*

† The danger with which this detachment was threatened, was perceived from the camp at Valley Forge, soon after it had been communicated to Lafayette. Alarm-guns were fired to announce it to him, and the whole army was put under arms, to act as circumstances might require. It has been erroneously stated that General Washington was unapprised of this movement of the British army until its object was defeated. The author was in camp at the time, saw the Commander-in-chief, accompanied by his aids and some of the general officers ride, soon after sun-rise, to the summit of the hill on the side of which the huts were constructed, and look anxiously towards the scene of action through a glass. He witnessed too the joy with which they returned after the detachment had crossed the Schuylkill.

CHAP. I 1778

ford just after the Americans had crossed it; but, finding them advantageously posted, did not choose to attack them; and the whole army returned to Philadelphia, having effected nothing.

He did not escape censure for having allowed the great advantage he had acquired, to slip through his hands unused. He might with the utmost certainty have reached Matron's ford before the Marquis, and have cut off the only retreat which remained for him. But the same skill and address were not displayed in executing this plan as in forming it.*

In the statement of this affair made by General Lafayette, he represents himself to have advanced the head of a column towards Grant, as if to attack him, while the rear filed off rapidly towards the Schuylkill. This movement gained ground even for the front, which, while it advanced towards the enemy, also approached the river, and at the same time induced General Grant to halt, in order to prepare for battle.

While this manœuvre was performing in the face of the detachment under Grant, a small party was thrown into the church yard, on the road towards General Gray, which also gave the appearance of an intention to attack in that quarter. By these dispositions, happily conceived, and executed with regularity, the Mar-

* It has been said that his troops were excessively fatigued by a march of upwards of twenty miles, and that he waited, confident that the Marquis could not escape him, for information that Gray had reached his position.

quis extricated himself from the destruction which had appeared almost inevitable. In a letter to congress, General Washington termed it "a timely and handsome retreat," and certainly the compliment was merited.

It might be supposed that this young nobleman had not displayed the same degree of military talent in guarding against the approach of danger, as in extricating himself from it. But the imputation which generally attaches to an officer who permits an enemy to pass unobserved into his rear, is removed by a circumstance stated by Lafayette. The Pennsylvania militia were posted on his left flank with orders to guard the roads about White Marsh. Without his knowledge, they changed their position, and retired into the rear, leaving that important pass open to the enemy.

General Howe resigns his command and returns to England; is succeeded by Sir Henry Clinton.

This was the last enterprise attempted by Sir William Howe. He resigned the command of the army into the hands of Sir Henry Clinton, and embarked for Great Britain. About the same time, orders were received for the evacuation of Philadelphia. The part it was now evident France was about to take in the war, and the naval force which had been prepared by that power before she declared herself, rendered that city a dangerous position, and determined the administration to withdraw the army from the Delaware.

CHAP. I

1778

The preparations for this movement could not be made unobserved; but they indicated equally an embarkation of the whole army, or an intention to march to New York through Jersey. The last was believed by the American chief to be most probable; and he made every exertion to take advantage of the movement. His detachments were called in, and the state governments were pressed to expedite the march of their levies.

In the mean time Sir Henry Clinton hastened his preparations for the evacuation of Philadelphia; and the opinion that he intended to reach New York through Jersey, gained ground.

General Maxwell, with the Jersey brigade, was ordered over the Delaware to take post at Mount Holly, and to join Major General Dickenson, who was assembling the militia of that state for the purpose of co-operating with the continental troops, in breaking down the bridges, felling trees in the roads, and otherwise embarrassing the march of the British General.

June 17.

In this state of things intelligence was received that a great part of the British army had crossed the Delaware, and that the residue would soon follow.

The opinion of the general officers was required on the course now to be pursued. General Lee, who had been lately exchanged, and whose experience gave great weight to his opinions, was vehement against risking either a general or partial engagement. The British army was computed at ten thousand effective men, and that of the Americans amounted to between ten and eleven thousand. General Lee was decidedly of opinion that, with such an equality of force, it would be "criminal" to hazard an action. He relied much on the advantageous ground on which their late foreign connexions had placed the United States, and contended that defeat alone could now endanger their independence. To this he said the army ought not to be exposed. It would be impossible he thought to bring on a partial action, without risking its being made general, should such be the choice of the enemy, since the detachment which might engage must be supported, or be cut to pieces. A general action ought not to be fought unless the advantage was manifestly with the American army. This at present was not the case. He attributed so much to the superior discipline of the enemy as to be of opinion that the issue of the engagement would be, almost certainly, unfavourable.

General Du Portail, a French officer of considerable reputation, maintained the same opinions; and the Baron de Steuben concurred in them. The American officers seem to have been influenced by the councils of the Europeans; and, of seventeen generals, only Wayne and Cadwallader were decidedly in favour of attacking the enemy. Lafayette appeared inclined to that

CHAP. I

1778

opinion without openly embracing it; and General Greene was inclined to hazard more than the councils of the majority would sanction. The country, he thought, must be protected; and if, in doing so, an engagement should become unavoidable, it would be necessary to fight.

The British army evacuate Philadelphia and march through the Jerseys.

On the morning of the 18th, Philadelphia was evacuated; * and, by two in the afternoon, all the British troops were encamped on the Jersey shore, from Cooper's Creek to Red Bank. Although they availed themselves to a great extent of the transportation by water, yet their line of march was so lengthened and encumbered by baggage, and the weather was so intensely hot, that they were under the necessity of proceeding slowly. Indeed their movements wore the appearance of purposed delay; and were calculated to favour the opinion that Sir Henry Clinton was willing to be overtaken, and wished for a general engagement.

As his line of march, until he passed Crosswicks, led directly up the Delaware, General Washington found it necessary to make an extensive circuit, and to cross the river at Coryell's Ferry; after which he kept possession of the high grounds in Jersey, thereby retaining the choice of bringing on, or avoiding an action.

* As the British army moved down Second street, Captain M'Lane, with a few light horse and one hundred infantry, entered the city, and cut off, and captured one Captain, one Provost Marshal, one guide to the army, and thirty privates, without losing a man.

CHAP. I

1778

June 24.

As Sir Henry Clinton encamped at, and about, Allentown, the main body of the American army lay in Hopewell township, about five miles from Princeton, Major General Dickenson, with about one thousand militia, and Maxwell's brigade, hung on Sir Henry Clinton's left flank. General Cadwallader, with Jackson's regiment and a few militia, was in his rear; and Colonel Morgan with a regiment of six hundred men watched his right.

Council of war called by General Washington; decide against attacking the enemy on the march.

Notwithstanding the almost concurrent opinion of his general officers against risking an action, Washington appears to have been strongly inclined to that measure. He could not be persuaded that, with an army rather superior in point of numbers to his enemy, too much was hazarded by fighting him. The situation of the two armies was, therefore, once more submitted to the consideration of the general officers, who were asked whether it would be adviseable, of choice, to hazard a general action? And, if it would, whether it should be brought on by an immediate general attack, by a partial attack, or by taking such a position as must compel the enemy to become the assailants?

If the council should be of opinion that it was unadviseable to hazard an engagement, then he asked what measures could be taken with safety to the army, to annoy the enemy in his march, should he proceed through the Jerseys?

CHAP. I

1778

The proposition respecting a general action was decidedly negatived. But it was proposed to strengthen the corps on the left flank of the enemy with a reinforcement of fifteen hundred men, and to preserve, with the main body of the army, a relative position which would enable it to act as circumstances might require.

In pursuance of this opinion, the troops on the lines were strengthened with a detachment of fifteen hundred select men, commanded by General Scott; and the army moved forward the next day to Kingston.

The opinion of the general against this decision.

Though the council had been almost unanimous against a general action, several officers, whose opinions were highly valued, secretly wished for something more than light skirmishing. Knowing this, General Washington, who was still in favour of an engagement, determined to take his measures on his own responsibility. As the British army moved towards Monmouth court-house, he ordered Brigadier General Wayne, with an additional detachment of one thousand select men, to join the advanced corps. As the continental troops, now constituting the front division, amounted to at least four thousand men, he deemed it proper that they should be commanded by a major general. Lee had a right to claim this tour of duty; but, as he had declared himself openly and strongly against hazarding even a partial engagement, and supposed that nothing further would be at-

June 25.

1778

tempted than merely to reconnoitre the enemy, and restrain plundering parties, he showed no inclination to assert his claim. Unintentionally promoting the private wishes of General Washington, that the command should be given to an officer whose view of the service comported more with his own, Lee yielded this important tour of duty to Lafayette. The orders given to this general were, to proceed immediately with the detachment; and, after forming a junction with General Scott, and taking command of the troops on the lines, to gain the enemy's left flank and rear; give him every practicable annoyance; and attack by detachment, or with his whole force, as the occasion might require.

These dispositions and orders could scarcely fail to bring on an engagement. Wayne had openly supported that measure; and Lafayette, though against seeking a general action, had been in favour of a partial one. Of consequence, should any proper occasion offer, he would certainly attack with his whole force, which would as certainly produce such a state of things as would render it proper to support him with the whole army.

Immediately after the march of this detachment, General Washington moved to Cranberry, that he might be in readiness to support his front division. June 26.

The intense heat of the weather; a heavy storm; and a temporary want of provisions, pre-

CHAP. I

1778

vented the army from continuing its march that day. The advanced corps had pressed forward, and taken a position about five miles in rear of the British army, with the intention of attacking it next morning on its march. Thinking this corps too remote to be supported in case of action, General Washington ordered the Marquis to file off by his left towards Englishtown. These orders were executed early in the morning of the twenty-seventh.

June 27.

Lafayette had scarcely taken command of the advanced party, when General Lee began to regret having yielded it to him. He perceived that, in the opinion of all the general officers, great importance was attached to it, and that his reputation was in danger of being impaired by connecting his strenuous opposition to even a partial action, with his declining the command of a very strong detachment, which, it was believed, would engage the rear of the enemy. He therefore solicited earnestly for the command he had before declined.

To relieve the feelings of Lee, without wounding those of Lafayette, General Washington detached him with two additional brigades to Englishtown, to support the Marquis. He would, of course, have the direction of the whole front division, which would now amount to five thousand continental troops; but it was expressly stipulated, that if any enterprise had been already formed by Lafayette, it should be carried into execution, as if the commanding officer had not been changed. Lee acceded to this condition; and, with two additional brigades, joined the front division of the army, encamped at Englishtown. The rear division also moved forward, and encamped about three miles in his rear. Morgan's corps still hovered on the right flank of the British, and General Dickenson on their left.

Sir Henry Clinton occupied the high grounds about Monmouth court-house, having his right flank in the skirt of a small wood, while his left was secured by a very thick one, and a morass running towards his rear. His whole front was also covered by a wood, and for a considerable distance towards his left, by a morass.

This position seemed unassailable; and the British were within twelve miles of the high grounds about Middletown, after reaching which they would be perfectly secure.

Under these circumstances, General Washington ordered Lee to attack the British rear the moment it should move from its ground.

June 28.

About five in the morning, intelligence was received from General Dickenson that the front of the enemy was in motion. The troops were immediately put under arms, and Lee was ordered to attack the rear, "unless there should be powerful reasons to the contrary." He was at the same time informed that the rear division would be on its march to support him.

CHAP. I

1778

Sir Henry Clinton had observed the appearances on his flanks and rear on the twenty-seventh; and, conjecturing that the American army was in his neighbourhood, had changed the order of his march. The baggage was placed under the care of General Knyphausen, while the strength and flower of his army, entirely unincumbered, formed the rear division, under the particular command of Lord Cornwallis, who was accompanied by the Commander-in-chief.

To avoid pressing on Knyphausen, Cornwallis remained on his ground until about eight; and then, descending from the heights of Freehold into an extensive plain, took up his line of march in rear of the front division.*

General Lee had made dispositions for executing the orders given the preceding evening, and repeated in the morning; and, soon after the British rear had moved from its ground, prepared to attack it. General Dickenson had been directed to detach some of his best troops, to take such a position as to co-operate with him; and Morgan was ordered to act on the right flank.

Lee appeared on the heights of Freehold soon after Lord Cornwallis had left them; and, following the British into the plain, ordered General Wayne to attack the rear of their covering party with sufficient vigour to check it, but not to press it so closely as either to force it up to the main body, or to draw reinforcements to its

* Letter of Sir Henry Clinton.

Martha Washington

From the portrait by Gilbert Stuart

After studying under Benjamin West, the American painter who succeeded Sir Joshua Reynolds as (second) president of the Royal Academy in London, Gilbert Stuart established a studio in Philadelphia where he met and painted the first of his famous portraits of George Washington. This one of Martha Washington, the best known likeness of her in existence, was painted in the city of Washington, where the artist had a studio between 1800 and 1802. She gave him several sittings at Mount Vernon.

aid. In the mean time, he intended to gain the front of this party by a shorter road, and, intercepting its communication with the line, to bear it off before it could be assisted.

While in the execution of this design, a gentleman in the *suite* of General Washington came up to gain intelligence; and Lee communicated to him his present object.

Before he reached the point of destination, there was reason to believe that the British rear was much stronger than had been conjectured. The intelligence on this subject being contradictory, and the face of the country well calculated to conceal the truth, he deemed it adviseable to ascertain the fact himself.

Sir Henry Clinton, soon after the rear division was in full march, received intelligence that an American column had appeared on his left flank. This being a corps of militia was soon dispersed, and the march was continued. When his rear guard had descended from the heights, he saw it followed by a strong corps, soon after which a cannonade was commenced upon it; and, at the same time, a respectable force showed itself on each of his flanks. Suspecting a design on his baggage, he determined to attack the troops in his rear so vigorously, as to compel a recall of those on his flanks; and, for this purpose, marched back his whole rear division. This movement was in progress as Lee advanced for

CHAP. I 1778

the purpose of reconnoitring. He soon perceived his mistake respecting the force of the British rear, but still determined to engage on that ground, although his judgment disapproved the measure; there being a morass immediately in his rear, which would necessarily impede the reinforcements which might be advancing to his aid, and embarrass his retreat should he be finally overpowered.

This was about ten. While both armies were preparing for action, General Scott (as stated by General Lee) mistook an oblique march of an American column for a retreat; and, in the apprehension of being abandoned, left his position, and repassed the ravine in his rear.

Being himself of opinion that the ground was unfavourable, Lee did not correct the error he ascribed to Scott, but ordered the whole detachment to regain the heights. He was closely pressed, and some slight skirmishing ensued without much loss on either side.

As soon as the firing announced the commencement of the action, the rear division of the army advanced rapidly to the support of the front. As they approached the scene of action, General Washington, who had received no intelligence from Lee giving notice of his retreat, rode forward, and, to his utter astonishment and mortification, met the advanced corps retiring before the enemy, without having made a single effort to maintain its ground. The troops he first saw neither understood the motives which had governed General Lee, nor his present design; and could give no other information than that, by his orders, they had fled without fighting.

General Washington rode to the rear of the division, where he met General Lee, to whom he spoke in terms of some warmth, implying disapprobation of his conduct.

Orders were immediately given to Colonel Stewart and Lieutenant Colonel Ramsay to form their regiments for the purpose of checking the pursuit; and General Lee was directed to take proper measures with the residue of his force to stop the British column on that ground. The Commander-in-chief then rode back to arrange the rear division of the army.

He attacks the enemy at Monmouth Court-house.

These orders were executed with firmness; and, when forced from his ground, Lee brought off his troops in good order, and was directed to form in the rear of Englishtown.

This check afforded time to draw up the left wing and second line of the American army on an eminence, covered by a morass in front. Lord Stirling, who commanded the left wing, brought up a detachment of artillery under Lieutenant Colonel Carrington, and some field pieces, which played with considerable effect on a division of the British which had passed the morass, and was pressing on to the charge. These pieces,

CHAP. I

1778

The action severe but not decisive.

with the aid of several parties of infantry, effectually stopped the advance of the enemy.

Finding themselves warmly opposed in front, the British attempted to turn the left flank of the American army, but were repulsed. They then attempted the right with as little success. General Greene had advanced a body of troops with artillery to a commanding piece of ground in his front, which not only disappointed the design of turning the right, but enfiladed the party which yet remained in front of the left wing. At this moment, General Wayne was advanced with a body of infantry to engage them in front, who kept up so hot and well directed a fire, that they soon withdrew behind the ravine, to the ground on which the action had commenced immediately after the arrival of General Washington.*

The position now taken by the British army was very strong. Both flanks were secured by thick woods and morasses; and their front was accessible only through a narrow pass. The day had been intensely hot, and the troops were much fatigued. Notwithstanding these circumstances, General Washington resolved to renew the engagement. For this purpose he ordered

* General Lafayette, in a communication made to the author respecting this battle, expresses himself thus: "Never was General Washington greater in war than in this action. His presence stopped the retreat. His dispositions fixed the victory. His fine appearance on horseback, his calm courage, roused by the animation produced by the vexation of the morning, (le depit de la matinée) gave him the air best calculated to excite enthusiasm."

Brigadier General Poor, with his own and the North Carolina brigade, to gain their right flank, while Woodford with his brigade should turn their left. At the same time the artillery was ordered to advance, and play on their front. These orders were obeyed with alacrity; but the impediments on the flanks of the British were so considerable that, before they could be overcome, it was nearly dark. Farther operations were therefore deferred until next morning; and the brigades which had been detached to the flanks of the British army continued on their ground through the night, and the other troops lay on the field of battle with their arms in their hands. General Washington passed the night in his cloak in the midst of his soldiers.

The British employed the early part of the night in removing their wounded; and, about midnight, marched away in such silence that their retreat was not perceived until day.

As it was certain that they must gain the high grounds about Middletown before they could be overtaken; as the face of the country afforded no prospect of opposing their embarkation; and as the battle already fought had terminated in a manner to make a general impression favourable to the American arms; it was thought proper to relinquish the pursuit, leaving a detachment to hover about the British rear, the main body of the army moved towards the Hudson.

CHAP. I

1778

The Commander-in-chief was highly gratified with the conduct of his troops in this action. Their behaviour, he said, after recovering from the first surprise occasioned by the unexpected retreat of the advanced corps, could not be surpassed. General Wayne was particularly mentioned; and the artillery were spoken of in terms of high praise.

The loss of the Americans in the battle of Monmouth was eight officers and sixty-one privates killed, and about one hundred and sixty wounded. Among the slain were Lieutenant Colonel Bonner of Pennsylvania, and Major Dickenson of Virginia, both of whom were much regretted. One hundred and thirty were missing; but a considerable number of these afterwards rejoined their regiments.

In his official letter, Sir Henry Clinton states his dead and missing at four officers, and one hundred and eighty-four privates. His wounded at sixteen officers and one hundred and fifty-four privates. This account, so far as respects the dead, can not be correct, as four officers and two hundred and forty-five privates were buried on the field by persons appointed for the purpose, who made their report to the Commander-in-chief; and some few were afterwards found, so as to increase the number to nearly three hundred. The uncommon heat of the day proved fatal to several on both sides.

As usual, when a battle has not been decisive, both parties claimed the victory. In the early part of the day, the advantage was certainly with the British; in the latter part, it may be pronounced with equal certainty to have been with the Americans. They maintained their ground, repulsed the enemy, were prevented only by the night, and by the retreat of the hostile army from renewing the action, and suffered less in killed and wounded than their adversaries.

It is true that Sir Henry Clinton effected what he states to have been his principal object,—the safety of his baggage. But when it is recollected that the American officers had decided against hazarding an action, that this advice must have trammeled the conduct, and circumscribed the views of the Commander-in-chief, he will be admitted to have effected no inconsiderable object in giving the American arms that appearance of superiority which was certainly acquired by this engagement.

Independent of the loss sustained in the action, the British army was considerably weakened in its march from Philadelphia to New York. About one hundred prisoners were made, and near one thousand soldiers, chiefly foreigners, deserted while passing through Jersey.

The conduct of Lee was generally disapproved. As however he had possessed a large share of the confidence and good opinion of the

CHAP. I
1778

Commander-in-chief, it is probable that explanations might have been made which would have rescued him from the imputations that were cast on him, and have restored him to the esteem of the army, could his haughty temper have brooked the indignity he believed to have been offered him on the field of battle. General Washington had taken no measures in consequence of the events of that day, and would probably have come to no resolution concerning them without an amicable explanation, when he received from Lee a letter expressed in very unbecoming terms, in which he, in the tone of a superior, required reparation for the injury sustained "from the very singular expressions" said to have been used on the day of the action by the Commander-in-chief.

June 30.

This letter was answered by an assurance that, so soon as circumstances would admit of an inquiry, he should have an opportunity of justifying himself, to the army, to America, and to the world in general; or of convincing them that he had been guilty of disobedience of orders, and misbehaviour before the enemy. On his expressing a wish for a speedy investigation of his conduct, and for a court-martial rather than a court of inquiry, he was arrested.

General Lee arrested for his behavior in this action, and afterwards to the commander-in-chief.

First. For disobedience of orders in not attacking the enemy on the 28th of June, agreeably to repeated instructions.

Secondly. For misbehaviour before the enemy on the same day, in making an unnecessary, disorderly, and shameful retreat.

Thirdly. For disrespect to the Commander-in-chief in two letters.

Before this correspondence had taken place, strong and specific charges of misconduct had been made against General Lee by several officers of his detachment, and particularly by Generals Wayne and Scott. In these, the transactions of the day, not being well understood, were represented in colours much more unfavourable to Lee, than facts, when properly explained, would seem to justify. These representations, most probably, induced the strong language of the second article in the charge. A court-martial, over which Lord Stirling presided, after a tedious investigation, found him guilty of all the charges exhibited against him, and sentenced him to be suspended for one year. This sentence was, afterwards, though with some hesitation, approved, almost unanimously, by congress. The court softened, in some degree, the severity of the second charge, by finding him guilty, not in its very words, but "of misbehaviour before the enemy, by making an unnecessary, and, in some few instances, a disorderly retreat."

Court-martial appointed to try him. Sentenced to be suspended for one year.

Lee defended himself with his accustomed ability. He proved that, after the retreat had

CHAP. I 1778

commenced, in consequence of General Scott's repassing the ravine, on the approach of the enemy, he had designed to form on the first advantageous piece of ground he could find; and that, in his own opinion, and in the opinion of some other officers, no safe and advantageous position had presented itself until he met General Washington; at which time it was his intention to fight the enemy on the very ground afterwards taken by that officer. He suggested a variety of reasons in justification of his retreat, which, if they do not absolutely establish its propriety, give it so questionable a form as to render it probable that a public examination never would have taken place, could his proud spirit have stooped to offer explanation instead of outrage, to the Commander-in-chief.

His suspension gave general satisfaction through the army. Without being masters of his conduct as a military man, they perfectly understood the insult offered to their general by his letters; and, whether rightly or not, believed his object to have been to disgrace Washington, and to obtain the supreme command for himself. So devotedly were all ranks attached to their general, that the mere suspicion of such a design, would have rendered his continuance in the army extremely difficult.

Whatever judgment may be formed on the propriety of his retreat, it is not easy to justify,

CHAP. I

1778

either the omission to keep the Commander-in-chief continually informed of his situation and intentions, or the very rude letters written after the action was over.

The thanks of congress presented to General Washington and his army for their conduct in the battle at Monmouth.

The battle of Monmouth gave great satisfaction to congress. A resolution was passed unanimously, thanking General Washington for the activity with which he marched from the camp at Valley Forge, in pursuit of the enemy; for his distinguished exertions in forming the line of battle, and for his great good conduct in the action; and he was requested to signify the thanks of congress to the officers and men under his command, who distinguished themselves by their conduct and valour in the battle.

After remaining a few days on the high grounds of Middletown, Sir Henry Clinton proceeded to Sandy Hook, whence his army passed over to New York. July 5.

CHAPTER II.

Count D'Estaing arrives with a French fleet....Meditates an attack on the British fleet in New York harbour....Relinquishes it....Sails to Rhode Island....Lord Howe appears off Rhode Island....Both fleets dispersed by a storm....General Sullivan lays siege to Newport....D'Estaing returns....Sails for Boston....Sullivan expresses his dissatisfaction in general orders....Raises the siege of Newport....Action on Rhode Island....The Americans retreat to the Continent....Count D'Estaing expresses his dissatisfaction with Sullivan in a letter to congress....General Washington labours successfully to heal these discontents....Lord Howe resigns the command of the British fleet....Colonel Baylor's regiment surprised....Captain Donop defeated by Colonel Butler....Expedition of the British against Egg Harbour....Pulaski surprised.

1778 July.

Count D'Estaing arrives on the coast of Virginia with a French fleet under his command.

BEFORE General Washington could reach the ground he designed to occupy, intelligence was received that a powerful French fleet, under the command of the Count D'Estaing, had appeared off Chingoteague inlet, the northern extremity of the coast of Virginia.

The Count had sailed from Toulon on the 13th of April, with twelve ships of the line and six frigates, having on board a respectable body of land forces. His destination was the Delaware; and he hoped to find the British fleet in that river, and their army in Philadelphia. An uncommon continuance of adverse winds, protracted his voyage across the Atlantic to the extraordinary length of eighty-seven days. This

CHAP. II

1778

unusual circumstance saved the British fleet and army.

He meditates an attack on the British fleet at New York, but is obliged to relinquish it.

On reaching the capes of the Delaware, the Count announced his arrival to congress; and, having failed in accomplishing his first object, proceeded along the coast to New York, in the hope of being able to attack the British fleet in the harbour of that place.

Sir Henry Clinton was again indebted to some fortunate incidents for his safety.

The violent storms of the preceding winter had broken through the narrow isthmus by which Sandy Hook was connected with the continent, and had converted the peninsula into an island. This rendered it necessary for the army to pass from the main to the Hook on a bridge of boats, which would have been impracticable, if obstructed by a superior fleet. It was effected the very day on which D'Estaing appeared off Chingoteague inlet.

July 13.

At Paramus, in Jersey, General Washington received a letter from the president of congress, advising him of this important event, and requesting that he would concert measures with the Count for conjoint and offensive operations.

The next day he received a second letter on the same subject, enclosing two resolutions, one directing him to co-operate with the French admiral, and the other authorizing him to call on the states from New Hampshire to New Jersey

CHAP. II 1778

inclusive, for such aids of militia as he might deem necessary for the operations of the allied arms.

He determined to proceed immediately to the White Plains, whence the army might co-operate with more facility in the execution of any attempt which might be made by the fleet, and despatched Lieutenant Colonel Laurens, one of his aids de camp, with all the information relative to the enemy, as well as to his own army, which might be useful to D'Estaing. Lieutenant Colonel Laurens was authorized to consult on future conjoint operations, and to establish conventional signals for the purpose of facilitating the communication of intelligence.

The French admiral, on arriving off the Hook, despatched Major de Choisi, a gentleman of his family, to General Washington, for the purpose of communicating fully his views and his strength. His first object was to attack New York. If this should be found impracticable, he was desirous of turning his attention to Rhode Island. To assist in coming to a result on these enterprises, General Washington despatched Lieutenant Colonel Hamilton with such farther communications as had been suggested, by inquiries made since the departure of Lieutenant Colonel Laurens.

Fearing that the water on the bar at the entrance of the harbour was not of sufficient depth to admit the passage of the largest ships of the

French fleet without much difficulty and danger, General Washington had turned his attention to other objects which might be, eventually, pursued. General Sullivan, who commanded the troops in Rhode Island, was directed to prepare for an enterprise against Newport; and the Marquis de Lafayette was detached with two brigades to join him at Providence. The next day Lieutenant Colonel Hamilton returned to camp with the final determination of the Count D'Estaing to relinquish the meditated attack on the fleet in the harbour of New York, in consequence of the impracticability of passing the bar. July 21.

General Greene was immediately ordered to Rhode Island, of which state he was a native; and Lieutenant Colonel Laurens was directed to attach himself to the French admiral, and to facilitate all his views by procuring whatever might give them effect; after which he was to act with the army under Sullivan.

Sails out to Rhode Island and arrives off Newport.

The resolution being taken to proceed against Rhode Island, the fleet got under way, and, on the 25th of July, appeared off Newport, and cast anchor about five miles from that place, just without Brenton's ledge; soon after which, General Sullivan went on board the Admiral, and concerted with him a plan of operations for the allied forces. The fleet was to enter the harbour, and land the troops of his Christian Majesty on the west side of the island, a little to the

CHAP. II

1778

north of Dyer's island. The Americans were to land at the same time on the opposite coast, under cover of the guns of a frigate.

Although the appearance of the French fleet had animated the whole country, and had produced a considerable degree of alacrity for the service; although the success of the enterprise essentially depended on maintaining a superiority at sea, which there was much reason to apprehend would soon be wrested from them; yet such are the delays inseparable from measures to bring husbandmen into the field as soldiers, that the operations against Newport were suspended for several days on this account.

As the militia of New Hampshire and Massachusetts approached, General Sullivan joined General Greene at Tiverton, and it was agreed with the Admiral that the fleet should enter the main channel immediately, and that the descent should be made the succeeding day. The ships of war passed the British batteries and entered the harbour, without receiving or doing any considerable damage.

August 8.

The militia not arriving precisely at the time they were expected, General Sullivan could not hazard the movement which had been concerted, and stated to the Count the necessity of postponing it till the next day. Meanwhile, the preparations for the descent being perceived, General Pigot drew the troops which had been

1778

stationed on the north end of the island into the lines at Newport.

On discovering this circumstance the next morning, Sullivan determined to avail himself of it, and to take immediate possession of the works which had been abandoned. The whole army crossed the east passage, and landed on the north end of Rhode Island. This movement gave great offence to the Admiral, who resented the indelicacy supposed to have been committed by Sullivan in landing before the French, and without consulting him.

August 9.

Unfortunately, some difficulties, on subjects of mere punctilio, had previously arisen. The Count D'Estaing was a land as well as sea officer; and held the high rank of lieutenant general in the service of France. Sullivan being only a major general, some misunderstanding on this delicate point had been apprehended; and General Washington had suggested to him the necessity of taking every precaution to avoid it. This, it was supposed, had been effected in their first conference, in which it was agreed that the Americans should land first, after which the French should land, to be commanded by the Count D'Estaing in person. The motives for this arrangement are not stated; but it was most probably made solely with a view to the success of the enterprise. Either his own after-reflections or the suggestions of others dissatisfied the Count with it, and he insisted that the descent

CHAP. II 1778 should be made on both sides of the island precisely at the same instant, and that one wing of the American army should be attached to the French, and land with them. He also declined commanding in person, and wished the Marquis de Lafayette to take charge of the French troops as well as of the Americans attached to them.

It being feared that this alteration of the plan might endanger both its parts, D'Estaing was prevailed on to reduce his demand from one wing of the American army to one thousand militia. When, afterwards, General Sullivan crossed over into the island before the time to which he had himself postponed the descent, and without giving previous notice to the Count of this movement, some suspicions seem to have been excited, that the measure was taken with other views than were avowed, and no inconsiderable degree of excitement was manifested. The Count refused to answer Sullivan's letter, and charged Lieutenant Colonel Fleury, who delivered it, with being more an American than a Frenchman.

At this time a British fleet appeared, which, after sailing close into the land, and communicating with General Pigot, withdrew some distance, and came to anchor off point Judith, just without the narrow inlet leading into the harbour.

After it had been ascertained that the destination of the Count D'Estaing was America, he was followed by a squadron of twelve ships of the line under Admiral Byron, who was designed to relieve Lord Howe, that nobleman having solicited his recall. The vessels composing this squadron meeting with weather unusually bad for the season, and being separated in different storms, arrived, after lingering through a tedious passage, in various degrees of distress, on different and remote parts of the American coast. Between the departure of D'Estaing from the Hook on the 23d of July, and the 30th of that month, four ships of sixty-four and fifty guns arrived at Sandy Hook.

This addition to the British fleet, though it left Lord Howe considerably inferior to the Count D'Estaing, determined him to attempt the relief of Newport. He sailed from New York on the 6th of August; and, on the 9th, appeared in sight of the French fleet, before intelligence of his departure could be received by the Admiral.

Sails to attack Lord Howe, who appears off Rhode Island.

August 10.

At the time of his arrival the wind set directly into the harbour, so that it was impossible to get out of it; but it shifted suddenly to the north-east the next morning, and the Count determined to stand out to sea, and give battle. Previous to leaving port, he informed General Sullivan that, on his return, he would land his men as that officer should advise.

Not choosing to give the advantage of the weather-gage, Lord Howe also weighed anchor

CHAP. II

1778

and stood out to sea. He was followed by D'Estaing; and both fleets were soon out of sight.

The militia were now arrived; and Sullivan's army amounted to ten thousand men. Some objections were made by Lafayette to his commencing operations before the return of D'Estaing. That officer advised that the army should be advanced to a position in the neighbourhood of Newport, but should not break ground until the Count should be in readiness to act in concert with them. It was extremely desirable to avoid whatever might give offence to the great ally on whose assistance so much depended; but time was deemed of such importance to an army which could not be kept long together, that this advice was overruled, and it was determined to commence the siege immediately.

August 12.

Before this determination could be executed, a furious storm blew down all the tents, rendered the arms unfit for immediate use, and greatly damaged the ammunition, of which fifty rounds had just been delivered to each man. The soldiers, having no shelter, suffered extremely; and several perished in the storm, which continued three days. On the return of fair weather the siege was commenced, and continued without any material circumstance for several days.

Fifteenth.

General Sullivan lays siege to Newport.

As no intelligence had been received from the Admiral, the situation of the American army was becoming very critical. On the evening of the 19th, their anxieties were relieved for a moment by the reappearance of the French fleet.

The two Admirals, desirous the one of gaining, and the other of retaining the advantage of the wind, had employed two days in manœuvring, without coming to action. Towards the close of the second, they were on the point of engaging, when they were separated by the violent storm which had been felt so severely on shore, and which dispersed both fleets. Some single vessels afterwards fell in with each other, but no important capture was made; and both fleets retired in a very shattered condition, the one to the harbour of New York, and the other to that of Newport.

Both fleets dispersed by a storm.

A letter was immediately despatched by D'Estaing to Sullivan, informing him that, in pursuance of orders from the King, and of the advice of all his officers, he had taken the resolution to carry the fleet to Boston. His instructions directed him to sail for Boston should his fleet meet with any disaster, or should a superior British fleet appear on the coast.

D'Estaing returns to Newport, and against the solicitations of Sullivan, sails for Boston.

This communication threw Sullivan and his army into despair. General Greene and the Marquis de Lafayette were directed to wait on the Admiral with a letter from Sullivan remonstrating against this resolution, and to use their utmost endeavors to induce him to change it.

CHAP. II

1778

They represented to him the certainty of carrying the garrison if he would co-operate with them only two days, urged the impolicy of exposing the fleet at sea, in its present condition, represented the port of Boston as equally insecure with that of Newport, and added that the expedition had been undertaken on condition that the French fleet and army should co-operate with them; that confiding in this co-operation, they had brought stores into the island to a great amount, and that to abandon the enterprise in the present state of things, would be a reproach and disgrace to their arms. To be deserted at such a critical moment would have a pernicious influence on the minds of the American people, and would furnish their domestic foes, as well as the common enemy, with the means of animadverting severely on their prospects from an alliance with those who could abandon them under circumstances such as the present. They concluded with wishing that the utmost harmony and confidence might subsist between the two nations, and especially between their officers; and entreated the Admiral, if any personal indiscretions had appeared in conducting the expedition, not to permit them to prejudice the common cause.

Whatever impression these observations may have made on the Count, they could not change the determination he had formed.

General Greene, in his representation of this conversation, stated that the principal officers on board the fleet were the enemies of D'Estaing. He was properly a land officer, and they were dissatisfied with his appointment in the navy. Determined to thwart his measures, and to prevent, as far as could be justified, his achieving any brilliant exploit, they availed themselves of the letter of his instructions, and unanimously persevered in advising him to relinquish the enterprise, and sail for Boston. He could not venture, with such instructions, to act against their unanimous opinion; and, although personally disposed to re-enter the harbour, declined doing so, and sailed from the island.

On the return of Greene and Lafayette, Sullivan made yet another effort to retain the fleet. He addressed a second letter to the Admiral, pressing him, in any event, to leave his land forces. The bearer of this letter was also charged with a protest signed by all the general officers in Rhode Island except Lafayette, the only effect of which was to irritate D'Estaing, who proceeded, without delay, on his voyage to Boston.

Thus abandoned by the fleet, Sullivan called a council of general officers, who were in favour of attempting an assault if five thousand volunteers who had seen nine months service could be obtained for the enterprise; but the departure of the fleet had so discouraged the militia, that

CHAP. II

1778

In consequence of the departure of the French fleet, Sullivan raises the siege of Newport.

this number could not be procured; and, in a few days, the army was reduced by desertion to little more than five thousand men. As the British were estimated at six thousand, it was determined to raise the siege, and retire to the north end of the island, there to fortify, and wait the result of another effort to induce D'Estaing to return.

August 28.

In the night of the 28th, the army retired by two roads leading to the works on the north end of the island, having its rear covered by Colonels Livingston and Laurens, who commanded light parties on each.

August 29.

Early next morning the retreat was discovered by the British, who followed in two columns, and were engaged on each road by Livingston and Laurens, who retreated slowly and kept up the action with skill and spirit until the English were brought into the neighbourhood of the main body of the Americans, drawn up in order of battle on the ground of their encampment. The British formed on Quaker Hill, a very strong piece of ground, something more than a mile in front of the American line.

Sullivan's rear was covered by strong works; and in his front, rather to the right, was a redoubt. In this position, the two armies cannonaded each other for some time, and a succession of skirmishes was kept up in front of both lines until about two in the afternoon, when the British advanced in force, attempted to turn the right flank, and made demonstrations of an intention to carry the redoubt in front of the right wing. General Greene, who commanded that wing, advanced to its support, and a sharp engagement was continued for about half an hour, when the British retreated to Quaker Hill. The cannonade was renewed, and kept up intermingled with slight skirmishing until night.

Action between Sullivan and the British army.

According to the return made by General Sullivan, his loss in killed, wounded and missing was two hundred and eleven. That of the British, as stated by General Pigot, amounted to two hundred and sixty.

August 30.

The next day, the cannonade was renewed, but neither army was inclined to attack the other. The British waited for reinforcements, and Sullivan had at length determined to retire from the island.

The Commander-in-chief had observed some movements among the British transports indicating the embarkation of troops, and had suggested to Sullivan the necessity of securing his retreat. A fleet of transports soon put to sea with a large body of troops, of which immediate notice was given to Sullivan in a letter recommending his retreat to the continent. This reinforcement, which consisted of four thousand men, commanded by Sir Henry Clinton in person, was delayed by adverse winds until the letter of General Washington was received, and the resolution to evacuate the island was taken. The

CHAP. II

1778

whole army passed over to the continent unobserved by the enemy, and disembarked about Tiverton by two in the morning.

Sullivan retreats with his army to the continent.

Never was retreat more fortunate. Sir Henry Clinton arrived the next day; and the loss of the American army would have been inevitable.

The complete success of this expedition had been confidently anticipated throughout America; and the most brilliant results had been expected from the capture of so important a part of the British army as the garrison of Newport. The chagrin produced by disappointment was proportioned to the exaltation of their hopes. In general orders issued by Sullivan, soon after the departure of D'Estaing, he permitted some expressions to escape him which were understood to impute to the Count D'Estaing, and to the French nation, an indisposition to promote the interests of the United States. These insinuations wounded the feelings of the French officers, and added, in no small degree, to the resentments of the moment. In subsequent orders, the General sought to correct this indiscretion; and alleged that he had been misunderstood by those who supposed him to blame the Admiral, with whose orders he was unacquainted, and of whose conduct he was, consequently, unable to judge. He also stated explicitly the important aids America had received from France, aids of which he ought not to be unmindful under any

Sullivan, in one of his general orders, makes use of expressions which offend the count.

disappointment; and which should prevent a too sudden censure of any movement whatever.

Count D'Estaing expresses to congress his dissatisfaction with General Sullivan.

The Count D'Estaing, on his part, addressed a letter to congress containing a statement of all the movements of his fleet subsequent to its arrival on the coast, in which his chagrin and irritation were but ill concealed.

In congress, after approving the conduct of Sullivan and his army, an indiscreet proposition was made to inquire into the causes of the failure of the expedition; but this was set aside by the previous question.

In the first moments of vexation and disappointment, General Sullivan had addressed some letters to the governor of Rhode Island, complaining bitterly of being abandoned by the fleet. These despatches were transmitted by the governor to the speaker of the assembly, and were on the point of being submitted publicly to the house, when they were fortunately arrested by General Greene, who had been introduced on the floor, and placed by the side of the chair; and to whom they were shown by the speaker.

The discontent in New England generally, and in Boston particularly, was so great as to inspire fears that the means of repairing the French ships would not be supplied. To guard against the mischief which might result from this temper, as well as for other objects, General Hancock had repaired from camp to Bos-

CHAP. II

1778

ton, and Lafayette had followed him on a visit to D'Estaing.

General Washington labours to heal these discontents, in which he succeeds.

The consequences to be apprehended from this unavailing manifestation of ill temper, soon induced all reflecting men to exert themselves to control it. In the commencement of its operation, General Washington, foreseeing the evils with which it was fraught, had laboured to prevent them. He addressed letters to General Sullivan, to General Heath, who commanded at Boston, and to other individuals of influence in New England, urging the necessity of correcting the intemperance of the moment, and of guarding against the interference of passion with the public interest.

Soon after the transmission of these letters, he received a resolution of congress, directing him to take every measure in his power to prevent the publication of the protest entered into by the officers of Sullivan's army. In his letter communicating this resolution, he said, "the disagreement between the army under your command and the fleet, has given me very singular uneasiness. The continent at large is concerned in our cordiality, and it should be kept up by all possible means, consistent with our honour and policy. First impressions, you know, are generally longest retained, and will serve to fix, in a great degree, our national character with the French. In our conduct towards them, we should remember that they are a people old in war, very strict in military etiquette, and apt to take fire when others scarcely seem warm. Permit me to recommend in the most particular manner, the cultivation of harmony and good agreement, and your endeavours to destroy that ill humour which may have found its way among the officers. It is of the utmost importance too, that the soldiers and the people should know nothing of this misunderstanding, or, if it has reached them, that means may be used to stop its progress, and prevent its effects." In a letter to General Greene, after expressing his fears that the seeds of dissension and distrust might be sown between the troops of the two nations, he added, "I depend much on your temper and influence, to conciliate that animosity which, I plainly perceive by a letter from the Marquis, subsists between the American and French officers in our service. This, you may be assured, will extend itself to the Count, and to the officers and men of his whole fleet, should they return to Rhode Island, unless a reconciliation shall have taken place. The Marquis speaks kindly of a letter from you to him on this subject. He will therefore take any advice from you in a friendly way; and, if he can be pacified, the other French gentlemen will, of course, be satisfied; since they look up to him as their head. The Marquis grounds his complaint on a general order of the 24th of August, and upon the

CHAP. II
1778

universal clamour that prevailed against the French nation.

"I beg you will take every measure to keep the protest entered into by the general officers from being made public. Congress, sensible of the ill consequences that will flow from our differences being known to the world, have passed a resolve to that purpose. Upon the whole, my dear sir, you can conceive my meaning,* better than I can express it, and I therefore fully depend on your exerting yourself to heal all private animosities between our principal officers and the French, and to prevent all illiberal expressions and reflections that may fall from the army at large."

The General also seized the first opportunity to recommence his correspondence with the Count; and his letters, without noticing the disagreement which had taken place, were calculated to soothe every angry sensation which might have been excited. A letter from the admiral stating the whole transaction, was answered by General Washington in a manner so perfectly satisfactory, that the irritation which threatened such serious mischief, appears to have entirely subsided.

Congress also, in a resolution which was made public, expressed their perfect approbation of the conduct of the Count, and directed the presi-

* Alluding, it is presumed, to the delicacy of suggesting to General Sullivan the mischief to be apprehended from any intemperate expressions.

dent to assure him, in the letter which should transmit it, that they entertained the highest sense of his zeal and attachment.

These prudent and temperate measures restored harmony to the allied armies.

The storm under which the French fleet had suffered so severely did considerable damage also to that of Lord Howe. The British, however, had sustained less injury than the French, and were soon in a condition to put again to sea. Having received information that the Count D'Estaing had made for Boston, Lord Howe sailed for the same port, in the hope of reaching it before him. But in this he was disappointed. On entering the bay he found the French fleet already in Nantasket Road, where such judicious dispositions had been made for its defence, that he relinquished the idea of attacking it, and returned to New York; where he resigned the command to Admiral Gambier, who was to retain it till the arrival of Admiral Byron.

Lord Howe resigns command of the British fleet.

Finding that General Sullivan had retreated to the continent, Sir Henry Clinton returned to New York, leaving the command of the troops on board the transports with Major General Gray, who was directed to conduct an expedition to the eastward, as far as Buzzards bay.

September 5.

Gray entered Acushnet River, where he destroyed a number of privateers with their prizes, and some merchant vessels. He also reduced part of the towns of Bedford and Fairhaven to

CHAP. II

1778

ashes, in which some military and naval stores had been collected. The troops re-embarked the next day, before the militia could be assembled in sufficient force to oppose them, and sailed to Martha's Vineyard, where they destroyed several vessels, and some salt works, and levied a heavy contribution of live stock on the inhabitants.

While so large a detachment from the British army was depredating the coasts of New England, preparations were making in New York for some distant expedition; and many were of opinion that the French fleet was its object. To be in readiness to oppose a combined attack by sea and land on the fleet, General Gates was directed with three brigades, to proceed by easy marches as far as Danbury, in Connecticut. And Washington moved northward to Fredericksburg; while General Putnam was detached with two brigades to the neighbourhood of West Point, and General M'Dougal, with two others, to join General Gates at Danbury.

September 22.

Soon after the return of General Gray from New England, the British army moved up the North River on each side in great force. The column on the west side, commanded by Lord Cornwallis, consisting of about five thousand men, took a position with its right on the river, and its left extending to Newbridge, on the Hackensack; while the other division, which was commanded by General Knyphausen, consisting of about three thousand men, was advanced about the same distance on the east side of the Hudson. The command of the river enabled these two columns to communicate freely with each other; and, at any time, to reunite. Although General Washington conjectured that this movement was made for the purpose of foraging, yet it was possible that the passes in the Highlands might be its object; and orders were given to the detachments on the lines to hold themselves in readiness to anticipate the execution of such a design.

Colonel Baylor, with his regiment of cavalry, had crossed the Hackensack early in the morning of the 27th of September, and taken quarters at Taupaun, or Herringtown, a small village near New Taupaun, where some militia were posted. Immediate notice of his position was given to Lord Cornwallis, who formed a plan to surprise and cut off both the cavalry and militia. The party designed to act against Colonel Baylor was commanded by General Gray, and that against the militia, by Lieutenant Colonel Campbell.

That part of the plan which was to be executed by Campbell was defeated by delays in passing the river, during which a deserter gave notice of his approach, and the militia saved themselves by flight. But the corps commanded by General Gray, guided by some of the country people, eluded the patrols, got into the rear of

September 28.

CHAP. II

1778

Colonel Baylor's regiment surprised.

the sergeant's guard which had been posted at a bridge over the Hackensack, cut it off without alarming Baylor, and completely surprised his whole regiment. The British troops rushed into a barn where the Americans slept; and, refusing to give quarter, bayoneted for a time all they saw. Of one hundred and four privates, sixty-seven were killed, wounded, and taken. The number of prisoners, amounting to about forty, is stated to have been increased by the humanity of one of Gray's captains, who, notwithstanding his orders, gave quarter to the whole of the fourth troop. Colonel Baylor and Major Clough, who were both wounded with the bayonet, the first dangerously, the last mortally, were among the prisoners.

September 30.

Captain Donop, with his corps, attacked by Colonel Butler, and defeated.

Three days after this affair, Colonel Richard Butler, with a detachment of infantry, assisted by Major Lee with a part of his cavalry, fell in with a small party of chasseurs and yagers under Captain Donop, which he instantly charged, and, without the loss of a man, killed ten on the spot, and took the officer commanding the chasseur, and eighteen of the yagers, prisoners. Only the extreme roughness of the country, which impeded the action of the cavalry, and prevented part of the infantry from coming up, enabled a man of the enemy to escape. Some interest was taken at the time in this small affair, because it seemed, in some measure, to revenge the loss of Colonel Baylor.

After completing their forage, the British army returned to New York.

Expedition of the British against Egg Harbour.

This movement had been, in part, designed to cover an expedition against Little Egg Harbour, which was completely successful; and the works and store-houses at the place, as well as the merchandise and vessels, were entirely destroyed.

It has been already stated that Count Pulaski had been appointed general of the American cavalry. The dissatisfaction given by this appointment to the officers, had induced him to resign his commission; but, thirsting for military fame, and zealous in the American cause, he obtained permission to raise a legionary corps, which he officered chiefly with foreigners, and commanded in person. In this corps, one Juliet, a deserter, had been admitted as an officer. The Count had been ordered to march from Trenton towards Little Egg Harbour, and was lying eight or ten miles from the coast, when this Juliet again deserted, carrying with him intelligence of Pulaski's strength and situation. A plan was formed to surprise him, which succeeded completely so far as respected his infantry, who were put to the bayonet. The British accounts of this expedition assert that the whole corps was destroyed. Pulaski stated his loss at about forty; and averred that on coming up with his cavalry to the relief of his infantry, he repulsed the enemy. It is probable that the

Pulaski surprised, and his infantry cut off.

CHAP. II

1778

one account diminishes the importance of this enterprise as much as the other magnifies it.

Admiral Byron reached New York, and took command of the fleet about the middle of September. After repairing his shattered vessels, he sailed for the port of Boston. Soon after his arrival in the bay, fortune disconcerted all his plans. A furious storm drove him out to sea, and damaged his fleet so much that he found it necessary to put into the port of Rhode Island to refit. This favourable moment was seized by the Count D'Estaing, who sailed, on the 3d of November, for the West Indies.

October 12.

Thus terminated an expedition from which the most important advantages had been anticipated. A variety of accidents had defeated plans judiciously formed, which had every probability in their favour.

The Marquis de Lafayette, ambitious of fame on another theatre, was desirous of returning to France. Expecting war on the continent of Europe, he was anxious to tender his services to his king, and to his native country.

From motives of real friendship as well as of policy, General Washington was desirous of preserving the connexion of this officer with the army, and of strengthening his attachment to America. He therefore expressed to congress his wish that Lafayette, instead of resigning his commission, might have unlimited leave of absence, to return when it should be convenient to himself; and might carry with him every mark of the confidence of the government. CHAP. II 1778

This policy was adopted by congress in its full extent. The partiality of America for Lafayette was well placed. Never did a foreigner, whose primary attachments to his own country remained undiminished, feel more solicitude for the welfare of another, than was unceasingly manifested by this young nobleman, for the United States.

There being no prospect of an active winter campaign in the northern or middle states, and the climate admitting of military operations elsewhere, a detachment from the British army, consisting of five thousand men commanded by Major General Grant, sailed, early in November, under a strong convoy, for the West India Islands; and, towards the end of the same month, another embarkation was made for the southern parts of the continent. This second detachment was commanded by Lieutenant Colonel Campbell, who was escorted by Commodore Hyde Parker, and was destined to act against the southern states.

As a force sufficient for the defence of New York yet remained, the American army retired into winter quarters. The main body was cantoned in Connecticut, on both sides the North River, about West Point, and at Middlebrook. Light troops were stationed nearer the lines; and the cavalry were drawn into the interior to re- December.

CHAP. II

1778

cruit the horses for the next campaign. The distribution, the protection of the country, the security of important points, and a cheap and convenient supply of provisions, were consulted.

The troops again wintered in huts; but they were accustomed to this mode of passing that inclement season. Though far from being well clothed, their condition in that respect was so much improved by supplies from France, that they disregarded the inconveniences to which they were exposed.

CHAPTER III.

Arrival of the British commissioners....Terms of conciliation proposed....Answer of congress to their propositions....Attempts of Mr. Johnson to bribe some members of congress....His private letters ordered to be published....Manifesto of the commissioners, and counter-manifesto of congress....Arrival of Monsieur Girard, minister plenipotentiary of France....Hostilities of the Indians....Irruption into the Wyoming settlement....Battle of Wyoming....Colonel Dennison capitulates for the inhabitants....Distress of the settlement....Colonel Clarke surprises St. Vincent....Congress determines to invade Canada....General Washington opposes the measure....Induces congress to abandon it.

ABOUT the time that Commodore Parker sailed for the southern states, the commissioners appointed to give effect to the late conciliatory acts of Parliament, embarked for Europe. They had exerted their utmost powers to effect the object of their mission, but without success. Great Britain required that the force of the two nations should be united under one common sovereign; and America was no longer disposed, or even at liberty to accede to this condition. All those affections, which parts of the same empire should feel for each other, had been eradicated by a distressing war; the great body of the people were determined, at every sacrifice, to maintain their independence; and the treaty with France had pledged the honour and the faith of 1778

CHAP. III

1778

the nation, never to consent to a reunion with the British empire.

Arrival of the British commissioners.

The commissioners arrived in Philadelphia while that place was yet in possession of their army, and are understood to have brought positive orders for its evacuation. Their arrival was immediately announced to General Washington by Sir Henry Clinton, who was joined with them in the commission, and a passport was requested for their secretary, Doctor Ferguson, as the bearer of their first despatches to congress. The Commander-in-chief declined granting this passport until he should receive the instructions of his government; on which a letter addressed "To the president and other the members of congress," was forwarded in the usual manner. Copies of their commission, and of the acts of Parliament on which it was founded, together with propositions conforming to those acts, drawn in the most conciliatory language, were transmitted with this letter.

Terms of conciliation proposed.

Some observations having been introduced into it reflecting on the conduct of France,* the reading was interrupted, and a motion made to proceed no farther in consequence of this offensive language to his most Christian Majesty. This motion producing some debate, an adjournment was moved and carried. When congress

* The offensive words were "insidious interposition of a power which has, from the first settlement of the colonies, been actuated with enmity to us both; and notwithstanding the pretended date or present form of the French offers."

reassembled, the warmth of the preceding day had not entirely subsided; but, after several ineffectual motions to prevent it, the letter was read and committed. The answer which was reported by the committee, and transmitted to the commissioners, declared that "nothing but an earnest desire to spare the farther effusion of human blood, could have induced them to read a paper containing expressions so disrespectful to his most Christian Majesty, the good and great ally of these states, or to consider propositions so derogatory to the honour of an independent nation.

Answer of Congress to these propositions.

"That the acts of the British Parliament, the commission from their sovereign, and their letter, supposed the people of the United States to be subjects of the crown of Great Britain, and were founded on the idea of dependence, which is totally inadmissible.

"That congress was inclined to peace, notwithstanding the unjust claims from which this was originated, and the savage manner in which it was conducted. They would therefore be ready to enter upon the consideration of a treaty of peace and commerce, not inconsistent with treaties already subsisting, when the King of Great Britain should demonstrate a sincere disposition for that purpose. The only solid proof of this disposition would be an explicit acknowledgment of the independence of these states, or the withdrawing his fleets and armies."

CHAP. III

1778

July 13.

On the 13th of July, after arriving at New York, the commissioners addressed a second letter to congress, expressing their regrets that any difficulties were raised which must prolong the calamities of war; and reviewing the letter of congress in terms well calculated to make an impression on those who had become weary of the contest, and to revive ancient prejudices in favour of England and against France.

This letter being read, congress resolved that, as neither the independence of the United States was explicitly acknowledged, nor the fleets and armies withdrawn, no answer should be given to it.

It would seem that the first letter of congress must have convinced the British commissioners that no hope could be indulged of restoring peace on any other terms than the independence of the United States. Congress must have been equally certain that the commissioners were not empowered to acknowledge that independence, or to direct the fleets and armies of Great Britain to be withdrawn. The intercourse between them therefore, after the first communications were exchanged, and all subsequent measures, became a game of skill, in which the parties played for the affections and passions of the people; and was no longer a diplomatic correspondence, discussing the interests of two great nations with the hope of accommodation.

CHAP. III

1778

Attempts of Mr. Johnson to bribe influential members of congress.

The first packet addressed by the commissioners to congress, contained several private letters, written by Governor Johnson to members of that body, in which he blended, with flattering expressions of respect for their characters and their conduct, assurances of the honours and emoluments to which those would be entitled who should contribute to restore peace and harmony to the two countries and to terminate the present war.

A few days before the receipt of the letter of the 13th of July, congress passed a resolution requiring that all letters of a public nature received by any member from any subject of the British crown, should be laid before them. In compliance with this resolution, the letters of Governor Johnson were produced; and, some time afterwards, Mr. Read stated, in his place, a direct offer which had been made him by a third person, of a considerable sum of money, and of any office in the gift of the crown, as an inducement to use his influence for the restoration of harmony between the two countries.

Congress orders the publication of the private letters from Johnson to the members of that body.

Congress determined to communicate these circumstances to the American people, and made a solemn declaration, in which, after reciting the offensive paragraphs of the private letters, and the conversation stated by Mr. Read, they expressed their opinion "that these were direct attempts to corrupt and bribe the congress of the United States, and that it was incompatible with

CHAP. III

1778

their honour to hold any manner of correspondence or intercourse with the said George Johnson, Esquire, especially to negotiate with him upon affairs in which the cause of liberty is interested." After an unsuccessful attempt to involve the other commissioners in the same exclusion, this declaration was transmitted to them while they were expecting an answer to a remonstrance on the detention of the army of General Burgoyne.

On receiving it, Mr. Johnson withdrew from the commission, declaring that he should be happy to find congress inclined to retract their former declaration, and to negotiate with others on terms equally conducive to the happiness of both countries. This declaration was accompanied by one signed by the other commissioners, in which, without admitting the construction put by congress on his letters, or the authority of the person who held the conversation with Mr. Read, they denied all knowledge of those letters or of that conversation. They at the same time detailed the advantages to be derived by America from the propositions they had made, "advantages," they added, "decidedly superior to any which could be expected from an unnatural alliance with France, only entered into by that nation for the purpose of prolonging the war, after the full knowledge on their part of the liberal terms intended to be offered by Great Britain." With this declaration was transmitted a copy of the former remonstrance * against the detention of the convention troops, without the signature of Governor Johnson, and an extract from the instructions given by the Secretary of State to Sir Henry Clinton, authorizing him to demand, in express terms, a performance of the convention made with General Burgoyne, and, if required, to renew and ratify all its conditions in the name of the king.

All the publications of the British commissioners indicate an opinion that they could be more successful with the people than with congress; and, not unfrequently betray the desire that the constituents of that body might be enabled to decide on the measures taken by their representatives.

On the part of congress, it was decreed of the utmost importance to keep the public mind correct, and to defeat all attempts to make unfavourable impressions on it. Several members of that body entered the lists as disputants, and employed their pens with ability and success, as well in serious argument, as in rousing the various passions which influence the conduct of men. The attempt to accomplish the object of the mission by corruption was wielded with great effect; and it was urged with equal force

* Some expressions having been used in the letter, respecting the convention troops, which were deemed disrespectful, no other reply was made to it than that "congress gave no answer to insolent letters."

CHAP. III
1778

that should the United States now break their faith with France, and treat on the footing of dependence, they would sacrifice all credit with foreign nations, would be considered by all as faithless and infamous, and would forfeit all pretensions to future aid from abroad; after which the terms now offered might be retracted, and the war be recommenced. To these representations were added the certainty of independence, and the great advantages which must result from its establishment. The letters of the commissioners were treated as attempts to sow divisions among the people of which they might afterwards avail themselves, and thus effect by intrigue, what had been found unattainable by arms.

These essays were read with avidity, and seem to have produced all the effect which was expected from them among the friends of the revolution.

The commissioners appear still to have cherished the hope, that a complete knowledge of the terms they had offered, operating on the disappointment of the extravagant hopes which had been founded on the arrival of a French fleet, would make a great impression on a large portion of the American people. This opinion induced them, before their departure, to publish a manifesto, addressed, not only to congress, but to all the provincial assemblies, and all the inhabitants of the colonies of whatever denomina-

October 3.

Manifesto of the commissioners, and counter-manifestos by congress.

tion, briefly recapitulating the several steps they had taken to accomplish the object of their mission, and the refusal of congress even to open a conference with them. They declared their readiness still to proceed in the execution of the powers contained in their commission, and to treat either with deputies from all the colonies conjointly, or with any provincial assembly or convention individually, at any time within the space of forty days from the date of their manifesto. They also proclaimed a general pardon for all treasons and rebellious practices committed at any time previous to the date of their manifesto, to such as should, within the term of forty days, withdraw from their opposition to the British government, and conduct themselves as faithful and loyal subjects. To enable all persons to avail themselves of this proffered pardon, thirteen copies of the manifesto were executed, one of which was transmitted by a flag of truce to each state. A vast number of copies were printed, and great exertions were made by flags and other means to disperse them among the people.

On being informed of these proceedings, congress, without hesitation, adopted the course which the government of an independent nation is bound to pursue, when attempts are made by a foreign power to open negotiations with unauthorized individuals. They declared the measure "to be contrary to the law of nations,

CHAP. III
1778

and utterly subversive of that confidence which could alone maintain those means which had been invented to alleviate the horrors of war; and, therefore, that the persons employed to distribute such papers, were not entitled to the protection of a flag." They recommended it to the executive departments in the respective states, "to secure, in close custody, every person who, under the sanction of a flag, or otherwise, was found employed in circulating those manifestoes." At the same time, to show that these measures were not taken for the purpose of concealment, they directed a publication of the manifesto in the American papers. Care, however, was taken to accompany it with comments made by individuals, calculated to counteract its effect. A vessel containing a cargo of these papers being wrecked on the coast, the officers and crew were made prisoners; and the requisition of Admiral Gambier for their release, in consequence of the privilege afforded by his flag, was answered by a declaration that they had forfeited that privilege by being charged with seditious papers.

October 30.

Not long after the publication of this paper, a counter-manifesto was issued by congress, in which, after touching on subjects which might influence the public mind, they "solemnly declare and proclaim, that if their enemies presume to execute their threats, or persist in their present course of barbarity, they will take such exemplary vengeance as shall deter others from a like conduct."

Thus ended this fruitless attempt to restore a connexion which had been wantonly broken, the reinstatement of which had become impracticable. With the war, and with independence, a course of opinion had prevailed in America, which not only opposed great obstacles to a reunion of the two countries under one common sovereign, but, by substituting discordant materials in the place of the cement which formerly bound them together, rendered such an event undesirable even to the British themselves. The time was arrived when the true interest of that nation required the relinquishment of an expensive war, the object of which was unattainable, and which, if attained, could not be long preserved; and the establishment of those amicable relations which reciprocal interests produce between independent states, capable of being serviceable to each other by a fair and equal interchange of good offices.

This opinion, however, was not yet embraced by the cabinet of London; and great exertions were still to be made for the reannexation of the American states to the British empire. Even the opposition was not united against a continuance of the war for the object now proposed; and the Earl of Chatham, who had endeavoured first to prevent the conflict, and afterwards to produce conciliation, closed his splendid life in unavail-

CHAP. III

1778

July 14.

Arrival of Girard, minister plenipotentiary from the King of France.

ing efforts to prevent that dismemberment which had become inevitable.*

In the midst of these transactions with the commissioners of Great Britain, the Sieur Girard arrived at Philadelphia, in the character of Minister Plenipotentiary of his Most Christian Majesty.

The joy produced by this event was unbounded; and he was received by congress with great pomp.

While these diplomatic concerns employed the American cabinet, and while the war seemed to languish on the Atlantic, it raged to the west in its most savage form.

---

* The author has been favoured by his estimable friend, Major General Scott, with the perusal of an introduction written by Mr. L. De Sevelinges, to Botta's "History of the war of the independence of the United States of America," translated into French.

Mr. De Sevelinges professes to have received the most precious explanations, relative to incidents and motives, from a gentleman equally distinguished for his knowledge and his character, whose situation enabled him to become acquainted with facts which were concealed from the public. Speaking of the attempt made by Mr. Johnson, he says, p. 19, it was essential "to break off all communication with the agents of the British minister. Mr. Girard directed all his efforts to this object, and had the good fortune to effect it.

"But the English faction of tories subsisted. It was powerful from the credit of its chiefs."

In a note on this passage, he says, "The most influential were Samuel Adams and Richard Lee, (Richard H. Lee,) the brother of Arthur Lee, one of the deputies of congress in France. He was convicted of having secret intelligence with the British minister."

It would be injustice to the memoirs of these distinguished patriots to attempt their vindication against this atrocious and unfounded calumny. A calumny supported by no testimony, nor by a single circumstance wearing even the semblance of probability, and confuted by the whole tenour of their lives. The annals of the American revolution do not furnish two names more entirely above suspicion than

The difficulties which the inability of the American government to furnish the neighbouring Indians with those European articles which they were accustomed to use, opposed to all the efforts of congress to preserve their friendship, have already been noticed. Early in 1778, there were many indications of a general disposition among those savages to make war on the United States; and the frontiers, from the Mohawk to the Ohio, were threatened with the tomahawk and the scalping knife. Every representation from that country supported the opinion that a war with the Indians should never be defensive; and that, to obtain peace, it must be carried into

---

Samuel Adams and Richard Henry Lee. With the first gentleman the author was not personally acquainted. With the last he was; and can appeal with confidence to every man who knew him, to declare the conviction, that he died as he lived, a pure and devoted, as well as enlightened friend of American independence. The same character was maintained by Mr. Adams.

In casting about for the foundation of this calumny, the author is inclined to look for it in the opinions entertained by these gentlemen, on subjects connected with the negotiations for peace.

Since the publication of the secret journals of congress, it is generally known that France countenanced the claim of Spain to circumscribe the western boundary of the United States, by the line prescribed in the royal proclamation of 1763, for settlement of vacant lands. After Great Britain had consented to acknowledge the independence of the United States, it was understood by those who were acquainted with the views of the belligerents, that a disposition existed on the part of France and Spain, to continue the war for objects in which the United States felt no interest,—among others, for Gibraltar and Jamaica. Some American statesmen, and the Lees were of the number, probably Mr. Adams also, were extremely apprehensive that the miseries of their country would be prolonged for these objects. It is not impossible that the sentiments of these gentlemen on these subjects, being in opposition to the views of France, might, though founded entirely in American policy, be attributed to British intrigues,

CHAP. III

1778

their own country. Detroit, whose governor was believed to have been particularly active in exciting hostilities, was understood to be in a defenceless condition; and congress resolved on an expedition against that place. This enterprise was entrusted to General M'Intosh, who commanded at Pittsburg, and was to be carried on with three thousand men, chiefly militia, to be drawn from Virginia. To facilitate its success, the resolution was also taken to enter the country of the Senecas at the same time, by the way of the Mohawk. The officer commanding on the east of the Hudson was desired to take measures for carrying this resolution into execution; and the commissioners for Indian affairs, at Albany, were directed to co-operate with him.

June 11.

Unfortunately, the acts of the government did not correspond with the vigour of its resolutions. The necessary preparations were not made, and the inhabitants of the frontiers remained without sufficient protection, until the plans against them were matured, and the storm which had been long gathering, burst upon them with a fury which spread desolation wherever it reached.

Colonel John Butler, with a party of Indians, breaks into the Wyoming settlement.

About three hundred white men, commanded by Colonel John Butler, and about five hundred Indians, led by the Indian chief Brandt, who had assembled in the north, marched late in June against the settlement of Wyoming. These troops embarked on the Chemung or Tyoga, and descending the Susquehanna, landed at a place called the Three Islands, whence they marched about twenty miles, and crossing a wilderness, and passing through a gap in the mountain, entered the valley of Wyoming near its northern boundary. At this place a small fort called Wintermoots had been erected, which fell into their hands without resistance, and was burnt. The inhabitants who were capable of bearing arms assembled on the first alarm at Forty fort, on the west side of the Susquehanna, four miles below the camp of the invading army.

The regular troops, amounting to about sixty, were commanded by Colonel Zebulon Butler; * the militia by Colonel Dennison. Colonel Butler was desirous of awaiting the arrival of a small reinforcement under Captain Spalding, who had been ordered by General Washington to his aid on the first intelligence of the danger which threatened the settlement; but the militia generally, believing themselves sufficiently strong to repel the invading force, urged an immediate battle so earnestly, that Colonel Butler yielded to their remonstrances, and on the 3d of July marched from Forty fort at the head of near four hundred men to attack the enemy.

The British and Indians were prepared to receive him. Their line was formed a small distance in front of their camp, in a plain thinly

* This gentleman is stated not to have been of the same family with the leader of the invading army.

CHAP. III

1778

covered with pine, shrub oaks, and under growth, and extended from the river about a mile to a marsh at the foot of the mountain. The Americans advanced in a single column, without interruption, until they approached the enemy, when they received a fire which did not much mischief. The line of battle * was instantly

* The representation of this battle, and of the circumstances attending the destruction of the Wyoming settlement, have been materially varied from the statement made of them in the first edition. The papers of General Washington furnished allusions to the transaction, but no particular account of it. The author therefore relied on Mr. Gordon and Mr. Ramsay, whose authority was quoted. Soon after the work was published, he received a letter from a gentleman then residing in that country, (Mr. Charles Miner,) who asserted with confidence that the statement was incorrect, and gave himself a minute detail of events, collected from persons who were in the settlement at the time, and witnessed them.

The author has been since indebted to the same gentleman for a statement of the battle, and of the events which followed it, drawn up by one of the descendants of Colonel Zebulon Butler, to which the certificates of several gentlemen are annexed, who were engaged in the action. These documents, with one which will be mentioned, convince him that the combined treachery and savage ferocity which have been painted in such vivid colours, in the narratives that have been given of this furious and desolating irruption, have been greatly exaggerated. Historic truth demands that these misstatements should be corrected.

The other document alluded to, is a letter from Zebulon Butler to the board of war, making his report of the transaction. The letter has been lately found among his papers, and is copied below.

Grandenhutten, Penn Township, July 10th, 1778.

Honoured Sir,—On my arrival at Westmoreland, (which was only four days after I left Yorktown,) I found there was a large body of the enemy advancing on that settlement. On the first of July we mustered the militia, and marched towards them by the river above the settlement,—found and killed two Indians at a place where the day before they had murdered nine men engaged in hoeing corn. We found some canoes, &c. but finding we were above their main body, it was judged prudent to return. And as every man had to go to his own house for his provision, we could not muster again till the 3d of July. In the mean time, the enemy had got possession of two forts, one of which we had reason to believe was designed for them, though they burnt them both. The informed, and the action commenced with spirit. The Americans rather gained ground on the right where Colonel Butler commanded, until a large body of Indians passing through the skirt of the marsh turned their left flank, which was composed of militia, and poured a heavy and most destructive fire on their rear. The word "re-

CHAP. III

1778

habitants had seven forts for the security of their women and children, extending about ten miles on the river, and too many men would stay in them to take care of them; but after collecting about three hundred of the most spirited of them, including Captain Hewitt's company, I held a council with the officers, who were all agreed that it was best to attack the enemy before they got any farther. We accordingly marched,—found their situation,—formed a front of the same extension of the enemy's, and attacked from right to left at the same time. Our men stood the fire well for three or four shots, till some part of the enemy gave way; but unfortunately for us, through some mistake, the word *retreat* was understood from some officer on the left, which took so quick that it was not in the power of the officers to form them again, though I believe, if they had stood three minutes longer, the enemy would have been beaten. The utmost pains were taken by the officers, who mostly fell. A lieutenant colonel, a major and five captains, who were in commission in the militia, all fell. Colonel Durkee, and Captains Hewitt and Ransom were likewise killed. In the whole, about two hundred men lost their lives in the action on our side. What number of the enemy were killed is yet uncertain, though I believe a very considerable number. The loss of these men so intimidated the inhabitants, that they gave up the matter of fighting. Great numbers ran off, and others would comply with the terms that I had refused. The enemy sent flags frequently—the terms you will see in the enclosed letter. They repeatedly said they had nothing to do with any but the inhabitants, and did not want to treat with me. Colonel Dennison, by desire of the inhabitants, went and complied,—which made it necessary for me and the little remains of Captain Hewitt's company to leave the place. Indeed it was determined by the enemy to spare the inhabitants after their agreement, and that myself and the few continental soldiers should be delivered up to the savages. Upon which I left the place, and came scarcely able to move, as I have had no rest since I left Yorktown. It has not been in my power to find a horse or man to wait on the board till now. I must submit to the board what must be the next step. The little remains of Hewitt's company (which are about fifteen) are gone to Shamoken, and Captain Spalding's company, I have heard,

CHAP. III

1778

treat" was pronounced by some person, and the efforts of the officers to check it were unavailing. The fate of the day was decided, and a flight commenced on the left which was soon followed by the right. As soon as the line was broken, the Indians, throwing down their rifles and rushing upon them with the tomahawk, completed the confusion. The attempt of Colonel Butler and of the officers to restore order were unavailing, and the whole line broke and fled in confusion. The massacre was general, and the cries for mercy were answered by the tomahawk. Rather less than sixty men escaped, some to Forty fort, some by swimming the river, and some to the mountain. A very few prisoners were made, only three of whom were preserved alive, who were carried to Niagara.

Colonel Dennison capitulates for the inhabitants.

Further resistance was impracticable, Colonel Dennison proposed terms of capitulation, which

---

are on the Delaware. Several hundred of the inhabitants are strolling in the country destitute of provisions, who have large fields of grain and other necessaries of life at Westmoreland. In short, if the inhabitants can go back, there may yet be saved double the quantity of provisions to support themselves, otherwise they must be beggars, and a burthen to the world.

I have heard from men that came from the place since the people gave up, that the Indians have killed no person since, but have burnt most of the buildings, and are collecting all the horses they can, and are moving up the river. They likewise say the enemy were eight hundred, one-half white men. I should be glad that, if possible, there might be a sufficient guard sent for the defence of the place, which will be the means of saving thousands from poverty—but must submit to the wisdom of congress. I desire farther orders from the honourable board of war with respect to myself, and the soldiers under my direction.

I have the honour to be

Your Honour's most obedient, humble servant,

ZEBULON BUTLER.

were granted to the inhabitants. It being understood that no quarter would be allowed to the continental troops, Colonel Butler with his few surviving soldiers fled from the valley.

Distress of the settlement.

The inhabitants generally abandoned the country, and, in great distress, wandered into the settlements on the Lehigh and the Delaware. The Indians, as is the practice of savages, destroyed the houses and improvements by fire, and plundered the country. After laying waste the whole settlement, they withdrew from it before the arrival of the continental troops, who were detached to meet them.

To cover every part of the United States would have required a much greater number of men than could be raised. Different districts were therefore unavoidably exposed to the calamities ever to be experienced by those into the bosom of whose country war is carried. The militia in every part of the Union, fatigued and worn out by repeated tours of duty, required to be relieved by continental troops. Their applications were necessarily resisted; but the danger which threatened the western frontier had become so imminent; the appeal made by its sufferings to national feeling was so affecting, that it was determined to spare a more considerable portion of the army for its defence, than had been allotted to that part of the Union, since the capture of Burgoyne. On the first intelligence of the destruction of Wyoming, the

CHAP. III

1778

July 15.

regiments of Hartley and Butler, with the remnant of Morgan's corps, commanded by Major Posey, were detached to the protection of that distressed country. They were engaged in several sharp skirmishes, made separate incursions into the Indian settlements, broke up their nearest villages, destroyed their corn, and by compelling them to retire to a greater distance, gave some relief to the inhabitants.

While the frontiers of New York and Pennsylvania were thus suffering the calamities incident to savage warfare, a fate equally severe was preparing for Virginia. The western militia of that state had made some successful incursions into the country north-west of the Ohio, and had taken some British posts on the Mississippi. These were erected in the county of Illinois; and a regiment of infantry, with a troop of cavalry, were raised for its protection. The command of these troops was given to Colonel George Rogers Clarke, a gentleman whose courage, hardihood, and capacity for Indian warfare, had given repeated success to his enterprises against the savages.

This corps was divided into several detachments, the strongest of which remained with Colonel Clarke at Kaskaskia. Colonel Hamilton, the Governor of Detroit, was at Vincennes with about six hundred men, principally Indians, preparing an expedition, first against Kaskaskia, and then up the Ohio to Pittsburg; after which

1778

he purposed to desolate the frontiers of Virginia. Clarke anticipated and defeated his design by one of those bold and decisive measures, which, whether formed on a great or a small scale, mark the military and enterprising genius of the man who plans and executes them.

He was too far removed from the inhabited country to hope for support, and was too weak to maintain Kaskaskia and the Illinois against the combined force of regulars and Indians by which he was to be attacked so soon as the season for action should arrive. While employed in preparing for his defence, he received unquestionable information that Hamilton had detached his Indians on an expedition against the frontiers, reserving at the post he occupied only about eighty regulars, with three pieces of cannon and some swivels. Clarke instantly resolved to seize this favourable moment. After detaching a small galley up the Wabash with orders to take her station a few miles below Vincennes, and to permit nothing to pass her, he marched in the depth of winter with one hundred and thirty men, the whole force he could collect, across the country from Kaskaskia to Vincennes. This march, through the woods, and over high waters, required sixteen days, five of which were employed in crossing the drowned lands of the Wabash. The troops were under the necessity of wading five miles in water, frequently up to their breasts. After subduing

1779 February.

CHAP. III

1779

Colonel Clarke surprises St. Vincents, and takes possession of it.

these difficulties, this small party appeared before the town, which was completely surprised, and readily consented to change its master. Hamilton, after defending the fort a short time, surrendered himself and his garrison prisoners of war. With a few of his immediate agents and counsellors, who had been instrumental in the savage barbarities he had encouraged, he was, by order of the executive of Virginia, put in irons, and confined in a jail.

This expedition was important in its consequences. It disconcerted a plan which threatened destruction to the whole country west of the Alleghany mountains; detached from the British interest many of those numerous tribes of Indians south of the waters immediately communicating with the great lakes; and had, most probably, considerable influence in fixing the western boundary of the United States.

We have already seen that congress, actuated by their wishes rather than governed by a temperate calculation of the means in their possession, had, in the preceding winter, planned a second invasion of Canada, to be conducted by the Marquis de Lafayette; and that, as the generals only were got in readiness for this expedition, it was necessarily laid aside. The design, however, seems to have been suspended, not abandoned. The alliance with France revived the latent wish to annex that extensive territory to the United States. That favourite subject

Congress determine to attack Canada, and the other British possessions in North America.

was resumed; and, towards autumn, a plan was completely digested for a combined attack to be made by the allies on all the British dominions on the continent, and on the adjacent islands of Cape Breton and Newfoundland. This plan was matured about the time the Marquis de Lafayette obtained leave to return to his own country, and was ordered to be transmitted by that nobleman to Doctor Franklin, the minister of the United States at the court of Versailles, with instructions to induce, if possible, the French cabinet to accede to it. Some communications respecting this subject were also made to the Marquis, on whose influence in securing its adoption by his own government, much reliance was placed; and, in October, 1778, it was, for the first time, transmitted to General Washington, with a request that he would inclose it by the Marquis, with his observations on it, to Doctor Franklin.

This very extensive plan of military operations for the ensuing campaign, prepared entirely in the cabinet, without consulting, so far as is known, a single military man, consisted of many parts.

Two detachments, amounting, each, to sixteen hundred men, were to march from Pittsburg and Wyoming against Detroit, and Niagara.

A third body of troops, which was to be stationed on the Mohawk during the winter, and to be powerfully reinforced in the spring, was

CHAP. III
1779

to seize Oswego, and to secure the navigation of Lake Ontario with vessels to be constructed of materials to be procured in the winter.

A fourth corps was to penetrate into Canada by the St. Francis, and to reduce Montreal, and the posts on Lake Champlain, while a fifth should guard against troops from Quebec.

Thus far America could proceed unaided by her ally. But, Upper Canada being reduced, another campaign would still be necessary for the reduction of Quebec. This circumstance would require that the army should pass the winter in Canada, and, in the mean time, the garrison of Quebec might be largely reinforced. It was therefore essential to the complete success of the enterprise, that France should be induced to take a part in it.

The conquest of Quebec, and of Halifax, was supposed to be an object of so much importance to France as well as to the United States, that her aid might be confidently expected.

It was proposed to request his Most Christian Majesty to furnish four or five thousand troops, to sail from Brest, the beginning of May, under convoy of four ships of the line and four frigates; the troops to be clad as if for service in the West Indies, and thick clothes to be sent after them in August. A large American detachment was to act with this French army; and it was supposed that Quebec and Halifax might be reduced by the beginning or middle of

October. The army might then either proceed immediately against Newfoundland, or remain in garrison until the spring, when the conquest of that place might be accomplished.

It had been supposed probable that England would abandon the farther prosecution of the war on the continent of North America, in which case the government would have a respectable force at its disposal, the advantageous employment of which had engaged in part the attention of the Commander-in-chief. He had contemplated an expedition against the British posts in Upper Canada as a measure which might be eventually eligible, and which might employ the arms of the United States to advantage, if their troops might safely be withdrawn from the sea board. He had, however, considered every object of this sort as contingent. Having estimated the difficulties to be encountered in such an enterprise, he had found them so considerable as to hesitate on the extent which might safely be given to the expedition, admitting the United States to be evacuated by the British armies.

In this state of mind, he received the magnificent plan already prepared by congress. He was forcibly struck with the impracticability of executing that part of it which was to be undertaken by the United States, should the British armies continue in their country; and with the serious mischief which would result to the common cause, as well from diverting so consider-

CHAP. III

1779

able a part of the French force from other objects to one which was, in his opinion, so unpromising, as from the ill impression which would be made on the court and nation by the total failure of the American government to execute its part of a plan originating with itself; a failure which would, most probably, sacrifice the troops and ships employed by France.

On comparing the naval force of England with that of France in the different parts of the world, the former appeared to him to maintain a decided superiority, and consequently to possess the power of shutting up the ships of the latter which might be trusted into the St. Lawrence. To suppose that the British government would not avail itself of this superiority on such an occasion, would be to impute to it a blind infatuation, or ignorance of the plans of its adversary, which could not be safely assumed in calculations of such serious import.

General Washington urges reasons against the plan.

A plan too, consisting of so many parts, to be prosecuted both from Europe and America, by land and by water; which, to be successful, required such a harmonious co-operation of the whole, such a perfect coincidence of events, appeared to him to be exposed to too many accidents, to risk upon it interests of such high value.

In a long and serious letter to congress, he apologized for not obeying their orders to deliver the plan with his observations upon it to the Marquis; and, entering into a full investigation

George Washington

From the portrait by John Trumbull

Colonel Trumbull, whose portraits of Washington, Hamilton, Jay, Adams, George Clinton and other Revolutionary contemporaries form a notable gallery, was General Washington's aide-de-camp at the outbreak of the War for Independence, and during its progress became a pupil of Benjamin West, in London. The news of André's execution fastened upon him the suspicion of being a spy, and he spent eight months in an English prison. Returning to America he painted this and other portraits of Washington, as well as a number of historical pictures, including the "Resignation of Washington at Annapolis," which hangs in the Capitol at Washington.

of all its parts, demonstrated the mischiefs, and the dangers, with which it was replete. This letter was referred to a committee, whose report admits the force of the reasons urged by the Commander-in-chief against the expedition, and their own conviction that nothing important could be attempted unless the British armies should be withdrawn from the United States; and that, even in that event, the present plan was far too complex.

Men, however, recede slowly and reluctantly from favourite and flattering projects on which they have long meditated; and the committee, in their report, proceeded to state the opinion that the posts held by the British in the United States would probably be evacuated before the active part of the ensuing campaign; and that, therefore, eventual measures for the expedition ought to be taken.

This report concludes with recommending "that the general should be directed to write to the Marquis de Lafayette on that subject; and also to write to the minister of these states at the court of Versailles very fully, to the end that eventual measures may be taken, in case an armament should be sent from France to Quebec, for co-operating therewith, to the utmost degree, which the finances and resources of these states will admit."

This report also was approved by congress, and transmitted to the Commander-in-chief;

CHAP. III

1779

who felt himself greatly embarrassed by it. While his objections to the project retained all their force, he found himself required to open a correspondence for the purposes of soliciting the concurrence of France in an expedition he disapproved, and of promising a co-operation he believed to be impracticable. In reply to this communication, he said, "The earnest desire I have strictly to comply in every instance, with the views and instructions of congress, can not but make me feel the greatest uneasiness, when I find myself in circumstances of hesitation or doubt, with respect to their directions. But the perfect confidence I have in the justice and candour of that honourable body, emboldens me to communicate, without reserve, the difficulties which occur in the execution of their present order; and the indulgence I have experienced on every former occasion, induces me to imagine that the liberty I now take will not meet with disapprobation."

After reviewing the report of the committee, and stating his objections to the plan, and the difficulties he felt in performing the duty assigned to him, he added, "But if congress still think it necessary for me to proceed in the business, I must request their more definitive and explicit instructions, and that they will permit me, previous to transmitting the intended despatches, to submit them to their determination.

"I could wish to lay before congress more minutely the state of the army, the condition of our supplies, and the requisites necessary for carrying into execution an undertaking that may involve the most serious events. If congress think this can be done more satisfactorily in a personal conference, I hope to have the army in such a situation before I can receive their answer, as to afford me an opportunity of giving my attendance."

Induces Congress to abandon it.

Congress acceded to his request of a personal interview; and, on his arrival in Philadelphia, a committee was appointed to confer with him, as well on this particular subject as on the general state of the army and of the country.

The result of these conferences was, that the expedition against Canada was entirely, though reluctantly,* given up, and every arrangement recommended by the Commander-in-chief, received the attention to which his judgment and experience gave all his opinions the fairest claim.

* See note No. II. at the end of the volume.

CHAPTER IV.

Divisions in Congress....Letters of General Washington on the state of public affairs....Invasion of Georgia.... General Howe defeated by Colonel Campbell....Savannah taken....Sunbury surrenders....Georgia reduced....General Lincoln takes command of the Southern army....Major Gardiner defeated by General Moultrie....Insurrection of the Tories in South Carolina....They are defeated by Colonel Pickens.... Ash surprised and defeated....Moultrie retreats.... Prevost marches to Charleston....Lincoln attacks the British at Stono Ferry unsuccessfully....Invasion of Virginia.

1779 AFTER the relinquishment of that extensive plan of conquest which had been meditated against Canada, no other object seemed to call forth the energies of the nation, and a general languor appeared to diffuse itself through all the civil departments. The alliance with France was believed to secure independence; and a confidence that Britain could no longer prosecute the war with any hope of success—a confidence encouraged by communications from Europe—prevented those exertions which were practicable, but which it was painful to make. This temper was seen and deplored by the Commander-in-chief, who incessantly combated the opinion that Britain was about to relinquish the contest, and insisted that great and vigorous exertions on the part of the United States were still necessary to bring the war to a successful termination.

It being no longer practicable to engage soldiers by voluntary enlistment, and government not daring to force men into the service for three years, or during the war, the vacant ranks were scantily supplied with drafts for nine, twelve, and eighteen months. A great proportion of the troops were discharged in the course of each year; and, except that the old officers remained, almost a new army was to be formed for every campaign.

Although the Commander-in-chief pressed congress and the state governments continually and urgently, to take timely measures for supplying the places of those who were leaving the service, the means adopted were so slow and ineffectual in their operation, that the season for action never found the preparations completed; and the necessity of struggling against superior numbers was perpetual.

The pleasing delusion that the war was over, to which the public mind delighted to surrender itself, made no impression on the judgment of Washington. Viewing objects through a more correct medium, he perceived that Great Britain had yet much to hope, and America much to fear, from a continuance of hostilities. He feared that the impression which the divisions, and apparent inertness of the United States had made on the British commissioners, would be

CHAP. IV 1779

communicated to their government; and this consideration increased his anxiety in favour of early and vigorous preparations for the next campaign. Yet it was not until the 23d of January that congress passed the resolution, authorizing the Commander-in-chief to re-enlist the army, nor, until the 9th of March, that the requisition was made on the several states for their quotas. The bounty offered by the first resolution being found insufficient, the government was again under the necessity of resorting to the states. Thus, at a season when the men ought to have been in camp, the measures for raising them were still to be adopted.

About this period, several circumstances conspired to foment those pernicious divisions and factions in congress, which, in times of greater apparent danger, patriotism would have suppressed.

The ministers of the United States, in Europe, had reciprocally criminated each other, and some of them had been recalled. Their friends in congress supported their respective interests with considerable animation; and, at length, Mr. Deane published a manifesto, in which he arraigned at the bar of the public, the conduct not only of those concerned in foreign negotiations, but of the members of Congress themselves.

Divisions in congress.

The irritation excited by these and other contests was not a little increased by the appearance, in a New York paper, of an extract from a letter written by Mr. Laurens, the president of congress, to Governor Huiston, of Georgia, which, during the invasion of that state, was found among his papers. In this letter, Mr. Laurens had unbosomed himself with the unsuspecting confidence of a person communicating to a friend the inmost operations of his mind. In a gloomy moment, he had expressed himself with a degree of severity, which even his own opinion, when not under the immediate influence of chagrin, would not entirely justify, and had reflected on the integrity and patriotism of members, without particularizing the individuals he designed to censure.

These altercations added much to the alarm with which General Washington viewed that security which had insinuated itself into the public mind; and his endeavours were unremitting to impress the same apprehensions on those who were supposed capable of removing the delusion. In his confidential letters to gentlemen of the most influence in the several states, he represented in strong terms the dangers which yet threatened the country, and earnestly exhorted them to a continuance of those sacrifices and exertions which he still deemed essential to the happy termination of the war. The dissensions in congress; the removal of individuals of the highest influence and character from the councils of the nation to offices in the respective states; the depreciation of the currency; the destructive

CHAP. IV

1779

spirit of speculation which the imaginary gain produced by this depreciation had diffused throughout the Union; a general laxity of principles; and an unwillingness to encounter personal inconvenience for the attainment of the great object, in pursuit of which so much blood and treasure had been expended; were the rocks on which, he apprehended, the state vessel might yet split, and to which he endeavoured, incessantly, to point the attention of those whose weight of political character enable them to guide the helm.

Letters from General Washington on the state of public affairs.

"I am particularly desirous of a free communication of sentiments with you at this time," says the General in a letter written to a gentleman of splendid political talents, "because I view things very differently, I fear, from what people in general do, who seem to think the contest at an end, and that to make money, and get places, are the only things now remaining to be done. I have seen without despondency, even for a moment, the hours which America has styled her gloomy ones; but I have beheld no day since the commencement of hostilities, when I have thought her liberties in such imminent danger as at present. Friends and foes seem now to combine to pull down the goodly fabric we have hitherto been raising at the expense of so much time, blood, and treasure."

After censuring with some freedom the prevailing opinions of the day, he added, "To me it appears no unjust simile to compare the affairs of this great continent to the mechanism of a clock, each state representing some one or other of the smaller parts of it, which they are endeavouring to put in fine order, without considering how useless and unavailing their labour is, unless the great wheel, or spring, which is to set the whole in motion, is also well attended to, and kept in good order. I allude to no particular state, nor do I mean to cast reflections upon any one of them, nor ought I, it may be said, to do so on their representatives; but, as it is a fact too notorious to be concealed, that congress is rent by party; that much business of a trifling nature and personal concernment, withdraws their attention from matters of great national moment at this critical period; when it is also known that idleness and dissipation take place of close attention and application, no man who wishes well to the liberties of this country, and desires to see its rights established, can avoid crying out—where are our men of abilities? Why do they not come forth to save their country? Let this voice, my dear sir, call upon you, Jefferson, and others. Do not, from a mistaken opinion that we are to sit down under our vine and our own fig-tree, let our hitherto noble struggle end in ignominy. Believe me when I tell you there is danger of it. I have pretty good reasons for thinking that administration, a little while ago, had resolved to give the matter

CHAP. IV 1779

up, and negotiate a peace with us upon almost any terms; but I shall be much mistaken if they do not now, from the present state of our currency, dissensions, and other circumstances, push matters to the utmost extremity. Nothing I am sure will prevent it but the intervention of Spain, and their disappointed hope from Russia."

The circumstances in the situation and temper of America, which made so deep an impression on the Commander-in-chief, operated with equal force on the British commissioners, and induced them to think that, by continuing the war, more favourable terms than were now demanded might be obtained. They seem to have taken up the opinion that the mass of the people, fatigued and worn out by the complicated calamities of the struggle, sincerely desired an accommodation on the terms proposed by Great Britain; and that the increasing difficulties resulting from the failure of public credit, would induce them to desert congress, or compel that body to accede to those terms. These opinions, when communicated to the government, most probably contributed to protract the war.

The narrative of military transactions will now be resumed.

The British arms had heretofore been chiefly directed against the northern and middle states. The strongest parts of the American continent were pressed by their whole force; and, with the exception of the attempt on Sullivan's island in

1776, no serious design had yet been manifested to make an impression in the south. Entertaining the most confident hopes of recovering all the colonies, the British government had not prosecuted the war with a view to partial conquest. But the loss of the army commanded by Burgoyne, the alliance of America with France, and the unexpected obstinacy with which the contest was maintained, had diminished their confidence; and, when the pacific propositions made in 1778 were rejected, the resolution seems to have been taken to change, materially, the object of their military operations; and, maintaining possession of the islands of New York, to direct their arms against the southern states, on which, it was believed, a considerable impression might be made.

It was not unreasonable to suppose that the influence of this impression might extend northward; but, however this might be, the actual conquest and possession of several states would, when negotiations for a general peace should take place, give a complexion to those negotiations, and afford plausible ground for insisting to retain territory already acquired. The most active and interesting operations therefore of the succeeding campaigns, were in the southern states.

Lieutenant Colonel Campbell, who sailed from the Hook about the last of November, 1778, escorted by a small squadron commanded by Com-

CHAP. IV

1779

modore Hyde Parker, reached the isle of Tybee, near the Savannah, on the 23d of December; and, in a few days, the fleet and the transports passed the bar, and anchored in the river.

The command of the southern army, composed of the troops of South Carolina and Georgia, had been committed to Major General Robert Howe, who, in the course of the preceding summer, had invaded East Florida.* The diseases incident to the climate made such ravages among his raw soldiers, that, though he had scarcely seen an enemy, he found himself compelled to hasten out of the country with considerable loss. After this disastrous enterprise, his army, consisting of between six and seven hundred continental troops, aided by a few hundred militia, had encamped in the neighbourhood of the town of Savannah, situated on the southern bank of the river bearing that name. The country about the mouth of the river is one tract of deep marsh, intersected by creeks and cuts of water, impassable for troops at any time of the tide, except over causeways extending through the sunken ground.

Invasion of Georgia.

Without much opposition, Lieutenant Colonel Campbell effected a landing on the 29th, about three miles below the town; upon which Howe formed his line of battle. His left was secured by the river; and along the whole extent of his

* So early as January, 1776, congress had recommended the reduction of St. Augustine to the southern colonies.—*Secret Journals of Congress, page* 38.

front was a morass which stretched to his right, and was believed by him to be impassable for such a distance, as effectually to secure that wing.

After reconnoitring the country, Colonel Campbell advanced on the great road leading to Savannah; and, about three in the afternoon, appeared in sight of the American army. While making dispositions to dislodge it, he accidentally fell in with a negro, who informed him of a private path leading through the swamp, round the right of the American lines to their rear. Determining to avail himself of this path, he detached a column under Sir James Baird, which entered the morass unperceived by Howe.

General Howe defeated by the British under Colonel Campbell, who takes possession of Savannah.

As soon as Sir James emerged from the swamp, he attacked and dispersed a body of Georgia militia, which gave the first notice to the American general of the danger which threatened his rear. At the same instant, the British troops in his front were put in motion, and their artillery began to play upon him. A retreat was immediately ordered; and the continental troops were under the necessity of running across a plain, in front of the corps which had been led into their rear by Sir James Baird, who attacked their flanks with great impetuosity, and considerable effect. The few who escaped, retreated up the Savannah; and, crossing that river at Zubly's ferry, took refuge in South Carolina.

CHAP. IV

1779

The victory was complete, and decisive in its consequences. About one hundred Americans were either killed in the field, or drowned in attempting to escape through a deep swamp. Thirty-eight officers, and four hundred and fifteen privates, were taken. Forty-eight pieces of cannon, twenty-three mortars, the fort with all its military-stores, a large quantity of provisions collected for the use of the army, and the capital of Georgia, fell into the hands of the conqueror. These advantages were obtained at the expense of only seven killed, and nineteen wounded.

No military force now remained in Georgia, except the garrison of Sunbury, whose retreat to South Carolina was cut off. All the lower part of that state was occupied by the British, who adopted measures to secure the conquest they had made. The inhabitants were treated with a lenity as wise as it was humane. Their property was spared, and their persons protected. To make the best use of victory, and of the impression produced by the moderation of the victors, a proclamation was issued, inviting the inhabitants to repair to the British standard, and offering protection to those who would return to their allegiance.

The effect of these measures did not disappoint those who adopted them. The inhabitants flocked in great numbers to the royal standard; military corps for the protection of the country were formed; and posts were established for a considerable distance up the river.

CHAP. IV

1779

Sunbury surrenders to General Prevost.

The northern frontier of Georgia being supposed to be settled into a state of quiet, Colonel Campbell turned his attention towards Sunbury, and was about to proceed against that place, when he received intelligence that it had surrendered to General Prevost.

Sir Henry Clinton had ordered that officer to co-operate from East Florida, with Colonel Campbell. On hearing that the troops from the north were off the coast, he entered the southern frontier of Georgia, and invested Sunbury, which, after a slight resistance, surrendered at discretion. Having placed a garrison in the fort, he proceeded to Savannah, took command of the army, and detached Colonel Campbell with eight hundred regulars and a few provincials to Augusta, which fell without resistance, and thus the whole state of Georgia was reduced.

The State of Georgia reduced.

While the expedition conducted by Lieutenant Colonel Campbell was preparing at New York, congress was meditating the conquest of East Florida.

The delegates of South Carolina and Georgia, anxious that a general of more experience than Howe should command in the southern department, had earnestly pressed that he should be recalled, and that General Lincoln, whose military reputation was high, should be appointed to succeed him. In compliance with their solicita-

CHAP. IV

1779

tions, Howe was ordered in September, 1778, to repair to the head quarters of General Washington, and Lincoln was directed to proceed immediately to Charleston, in South Carolina, in order to take command in the southern department. In pursuance of this resolution, General Lincoln repaired to Charleston, where he found the military affairs of the country in a state of utter derangement. Congress had established no continental military chest in the southern department. This omission produced a dependence on the government of the state for supplies to move the army on any emergency, and consequent subjection of the troops in continental service to its control. The militia, though taken into continental service, considered themselves as subject only to the military code of the state. These regulations threatened to embarrass all military operations, and to embroil the general with the civil government.

General Lincoln takes the command of the southern army.

While Lincoln was labouring to make arrangements for the ensuing campaign, he received intelligence of the appearance of the enemy off the coast. The militia of North Carolina, amounting to two thousand men, commanded by Generals Ash and Rutherford, had already reached Charleston; but were unarmed, and congress had been unable to provide magazines in this part of the Union. These troops were, therefore, entirely dependent on South Carolina for every military equipment; and arms were not delivered to them until it was too late to save the capital of Georgia.

So soon as it was ascertained that the British fleet had entered the Savannah river, General Lincoln proceeded with the utmost expedition towards the scene of action. On his march, he received intelligence of the victory gained over General Howe; and was soon afterwards joined by the remnant of the defeated army at Purysburg, a small town on the north side of the Savannah, where he established his head quarters.

The regular force commanded by General Prevost must have amounted to at least three thousand effective men; and this number was increased by irregulars who had joined him in Georgia. The American army rather exceeded three thousand six hundred men, of whom not quite two thousand five hundred were effective. Something more than one thousand were continental troops, part of whom were new levies; the rest were militia.

Major Gardiner defeated by General Moultrie.

The theatre of action was so well adapted to defensive war, that, although General Prevost was decidedly superior to his adversary, it was difficult to extend his conquests into South Carolina. With the view of entering that state by the way of the sea coast, he detached Major Gardiner with about two hundred men, to take possession of the island of Port Royal. That officer, soon after reaching his place of destina-

CHAP. IV

1779

tion, was attacked by General Moultrie, and compelled to retreat with considerable loss. This repulse checked the designs of Prevost on South Carolina.

From the commencement of the war, a considerable proportion of the western inhabitants of the three southern states had been attached to the royal cause. The first successes of the British were soon communicated to them, and they were invited to assemble and join the king's standard at Augusta. About seven hundred embodied themselves on the frontiers of South Carolina, and began their march to that place. They were overtaken by Colonel Pickens at the head of the neighbouring militia, near Kittle Creek, and defeated with considerable loss. Colonel Boyd, their leader, was among the slain; and several of those who escaped were apprehended, tried, and five of them executed as traitors. About three hundred reached the British outposts, and joined the royal standard. This defeat broke the spirits of the Tories for a time; and preserved quiet in the west.

Insurrection of the Tories in South Carolina, who are defeated by Colonel Pickens.

As the American army gained strength by reinforcements of militia, General Lincoln began to contemplate offensive operations. A detachment had been stationed nearly opposite to Augusta under General Ash, and he purposed joining that officer so soon as a sufficient force could be collected, and attempting to recover the upper parts of Georgia. Before he was able to execute this plan, General Prevost withdrew his troops from Augusta to Hudson's Ferry. Ash was then ordered to cross the Savannah, and take post near the confluence of Briar Creek with that river. This camp was thought unassailable. Its left was covered by a deep swamp, and by the Savannah. The front was secured by Briar Creek, which is unfordable several miles, and makes an acute angle with the river.

Having determined to dislodge the Americans from this position, Prevost kept up the attention of General Lincoln by the semblance of a design to cross the Savannah; and, at the same time amused General Ash with a feint on his front, while Lieutenant Colonel Prevost made a circuit of about fifty miles, and, crossing Briar Creek fifteen miles above the ground occupied by Ash, came down, unperceived and unsuspected, on his rear. Ash, unused to the stratagems of war, was so completely engaged by the manœuvres in his front, that Lieutenant Colonel Prevost was almost in his camp before any intelligence of his approach was received. The continental troops under General Elbert were drawn out to oppose him, and commenced the action with great gallantry; but most of the militia threw away their arms and fled in confusion. As they precipitated themselves into the swamp and swam the river, not many of them were taken. General Elbert and his small band of continental troops, aided by one regiment of North Carolina

Ash surprised and defeated by Prevost.

CHAP. IV 1779

militia, were soon overpowered by numbers, and the survivors were compelled to surrender themselves prisoners of war. The killed and taken amounted to between three and four hundred men. General Elbert and Colonel M'Intosh were among the latter. But the loss sustained by the American army was much more considerable. The dispersed militia returned to their homes; and not more than four hundred and fifty of them could be reassembled.

This victory was supposed to give the British such complete possession of Georgia, that a proclamation was issued the succeeding day by General Prevost, establishing civil government, and appointing executive and judicial officers to administer it.

These disasters, instead of terrifying South Carolina into submission, animated that state to greater exertions. Mr. John Rutledge, a gentleman of great talents and decision, was elected governor; and the legislature passed an act empowering him and the council to do every thing that appeared to him and them necessary for the public good. All the energies of the state were drawn forth. The militia were called out in great numbers, and the laws for their government were rendered more severe.*

Thus reinforced, General Lincoln resumed his plan for recovering the upper parts of Georgia;

* Ramsay.

and marched the main body of his army up the Savannah.

This river was now swelled greatly beyond its usual limits; and the swamps, marshes, and creeks which intersect the country being full, seemed to present an almost impassable barrier to an invading army. A small military force being deemed sufficient to arrest the progress of an enemy through a route which, if at all practicable, was so difficult, about eight hundred of the state militia, aided by two hundred continental troops, were left with General Moultrie for the defence of the country.

Prevost compels Moultrie to retreat.

Aware of the importance of this movement, and hoping to recall Lincoln by alarming him for the safety of Charleston, General Prevost suddenly crossed the Savannah with three thousand men; and, advancing rapidly on General Moultrie, obliged him to retreat with precipitation. The militia could not be prevailed on to defend the passes with any degree of firmness; and Moultrie, instead of drawing aid from the surrounding country, sustained an alarming diminution of numbers by desertion.

On the passage of the river by Prevost, an express had been despatched to Lincoln with the intelligence. Persuaded that the British general could meditate no serious attempt on Charleston, and that the real object was to induce him to abandon the enterprise in which he was engaged, he detached a reinforcement of three hundred

CHAP. IV

1779

light troops to aid Moultrie, and crossing the Savannah himself, continued his march down the south side of that river towards the capital of Georgia.

Though the original purpose of General Prevost had been limited to the security of Georgia, the opposition he encountered was so much less than he had expected; the tenour of the country was so apparent; the assurances of those who flocked to his standard; of the general disposition of the people to terminate the calamities of war by submission, were so often and so confidently repeated, that he was emboldened to extend his views, and to hazard the continuation of his march to Charleston.

Prevost marches to Charleston.

On receiving intelligence of this threatening aspect of affairs in South Carolina, Lincoln recrossed the Savannah, and hastened to the relief of that state.

The situation of Charleston was extremely critical. The inhabitants, entirely unapprehensive of an attack by land, had directed their whole attention to its protection against an invasion by sea. Had Prevost continued his march with the rapidity with which it was commenced, the place must have fallen. But, after having gained more than half the distance, he halted, and consumed two or three days in deliberating on his future measures. While his intelligence determined him to proceed, and assured him of a state of things which rendered success almost certain, that state of things was rapidly changing. Fortifications on the land side were commenced and prosecuted with unremitting labour; the neighbouring militia were drawn into the town; the reinforcements detached by General Lincoln, and the remnant of the legion of Pulaski arrived; and the governor also entered the city, at the head of some troops which had been stationed at Orangeburg.

The next morning Prevost crossed Ashly River, and encamped just without cannon shot of the works. The town was summoned to surrender, and the day was spent in sending and receiving flags. The neutrality of South Carolina during the war, leaving the question whether that state should finally belong to Great Britain or the United States, to be settled in the treaty of peace, was proposed by the garrison, and rejected by Prevost; who required that they should surrender themselves prisoners of war. This proposition being also rejected, the garrison prepared to sustain an assault. But an attempt to carry the works by storm was too hazardous to be made; and Prevost came to the prudent resolution of decamping that night, and recrossing Ashly River.

The British army passed into the island of St. James, and thence to that of St. John's, which lies south of Charleston harbour; soon after which General Lincoln encamped in the neighbourhood, so as to confine them in a great degree

CHAP. IV

1779

to the island they occupied. This island is separated from the main land by an inlet, to which the name of Stono River has been given; and the communication is preserved by a ferry. A British post was established upon the main land at this ferry, and works were thrown up in front for its defence. When Prevost commenced his retreat, and the troops were moving from island to island, the occasion seemed a fair one for attacking it. Only eight hundred men, commanded by Lieutenant Colonel Maitland, defended it; but a large corps still lay on the island. To prevent these troops from supporting those on the main land, General Moultrie, who commanded in Charleston, was ordered to pass over a body of militia into James's island, who should amuse the enemy in St. John's, while a real attack should be made on the post at the ferry. About seven in the morning, General Lincoln commenced this attack with about one thousand men; and continued it with great spirit, until he perceived that strong reinforcements were crossing over from the island; when he called off his troops, and retreated, unmolested, to his old ground.

Lincoln attacks the British at the ferry but without success.

General Moultrie had been unable to execute that part of the plan which devolved on him. Boats were not in readiness to convey the men into James's island, and consequently the feint on St. John's was not made.

The loss of the Americans, in killed and wounded, amounted to twenty-four officers, and one hundred and twenty-five privates. That of the British was stated to be rather less.

Three days after this action, the posts at Stono and St. John's were evacuated. The heat now became too excessive for active service; and the British army, after establishing a post on the island contiguous to Port Royal and St. Helena, retired into Georgia and St. Augustine.

The American militia dispersed, leaving General Lincoln at the head of about eight hundred men; with whom he retired to Sheldon, where his primary object was to prepare for the next campaign, which it was supposed would open in October.

The invasion of the southern states wore so serious an aspect, that Bland's regiment of cavalry, and the remnant of that lately Baylor's, now commanded by Lieutenant Colonel Washington, with the new levies of Virginia, were ordered to repair to Charleston, and to place themselves under the command of General Lincoln. The execution of these orders was for a time suspended by the invasion of Virginia.

An expedition against that state had been concerted in the spring between Sir Henry Clinton and Sir George Collier, the Commander-in-chief of the British naval force on the American station. The land troops assigned to this service were commanded by General Matthews. The

CHAP. IV

1779

Invasion of Virginia by General Matthews.

transports, on board of which they embarked, were convoyed by the Admiral in person. On the 9th of May the fleet entered the Chesapeake, and the next day anchored in Hampton Roads.

Virginia had raised a regiment of artillery for the performance of garrison duty in the state, which had been distributed along the eastern frontier; and slight fortifications had been constructed in the most important situations, which were defensible on the side of the water, but were not tenable against a military force strong enough to act on land. Fort Nelson, on the west side of Elizabeth river, garrisoned by about one hundred and fifty soldiers, commanded by Major Matthews, was designed to protect the towns of Norfolk and Portsmouth, which were on each side of the river just above it; and the town of Gosport, which lies still higher up on a point of land intervening between two branches of the river. Norfolk and Portsmouth were places of the most considerable commerce in Virginia. Large supplies for the army were deposited in them; and the state government had established at Gosport a marine yard, where ships of war and other vessels were building, for which naval stores were collected to a very great amount. The destruction of these vessels and stores, constituted the principal object of General Matthews.

On the morning of the tenth, the fleet entered Elizabeth river, and the troops were landed about three miles below the fort, without opposition. Foreseeing that the works would be attacked the next morning on the land side, the garrison evacuated the fort in the night, and took refuge in a deep and extensive swamp, called the Dismal, which could not be penetrated without difficulty, even by single persons.

The whole sea-board, on the south side of James' river, being now in possession of General Matthews, he fixed his head quarters at Portsmouth, whence small parties were detached to Norfolk, Gosport, Kemps' landing, and Suffolk, where military and naval stores to a great amount, and several vessels richly laden, fell into his hands.

This invasion was of short duration. General Matthews, after destroying the magazines which had been collected in the small towns near the coast, and the vessels in the rivers, was ordered by Sir Henry Clinton to return to New York, where he arrived towards the last of May.

The Admiral and General were both so impressed with the importance of Portsmouth as a permanent station, that they united in representing to the Commander-in-chief the advantages to be derived from keeping possession of it. But, in the opinion of Sir Henry Clinton, the army did not at that time admit of so many subdivisions; and, with a view to more interesting objects, Portsmouth was evacuated.

CHAPTER V.

Discontents in a part of the American army....Letter from General Washington on the subject....Colonel Van Schaick destroys an Indian settlement....Expedition against the Indians meditated....Fort Fayette surrendered to the British....Invasion of Connecticut.... General Wayne storms Stony Point....Expedition against Penobscot....Powles Hook surprised by Major Lee....Arrival of Admiral Arbuthnot....Of the Count D'Estaing....Siege of Savannah....Unsuccessful attempt to storm that place....Siege raised....Victory of General Sullivan at Newtown....Spain offers her mediation to the belligerents....Declares war against England....Letter from General Washington to congress respecting the annual formation of the army.... The army goes into winter quarters.

1779 THE barbarities committed by the Indians, in the course of the preceding year, on the inhabitants of the western frontiers, had added motives of mingled resentment and humanity to those of national interest, for employing a larger force in the protection of that part of the Union than had heretofore been devoted to it.

General Washington had always believed that it was impossible to defend the immense western frontier by any chain of posts which could be established; and that the country would be protected much more certainly by offensive than by defensive war. His plan was to penetrate into the heart of the Indian settlements with a force competent to the destruction of their towns; and also to reduce the British post at Niagara, which gave its possessors an almost irresistible influence over the six nations. This plan constituted one of the various subjects of conference with the committee of congress in Philadelphia, and received the entire approbation of that body.

The state governments also took a strong interest in the protection of their western settlements. Connecticut, New York, and Pennsylvania, applied, severally, to congress, urging the adoption of such vigorous measures as would secure the frontiers against a repetition of the horrors which had been already perpetrated. These papers were referred to the committee which had been appointed to confer with General Washington, in conformity with whose report it was resolved, "that the Commander-in-chief be directed to take efficient measures for the protection of the inhabitants, and chastisement of the savages."

The Six Nations had made some advances towards acquiring the comforts of civilized life. Several comfortable houses were to be seen in their populous villages; and their fertile fields and orchards yielded an abundant supply of corn and fruit. Some few of their towns were attached to the United States; but, in general, they were under the influence of the British. Many of the loyalists had taken refuge among them, and had added to their strength without

CHAP. V

1779

diminishing their ferocity. It was determined to lead a force into these villages, sufficient to overpower any numbers they could possibly bring into the field, and to destroy the settlements they had made. To guard against reinforcements from Canada, means were used to inspire that colony with fears for itself.

Discontents in a part of the American army.

As the army destined for this expedition was about to move, alarming symptoms of discontent appeared in a part of it. The Jersey brigade, which had been stationed during the winter at Elizabethtown, was ordered early in May, to march by regiments. This order was answered by a letter from General Maxwell, stating that the officers of the first regiment had delivered a remonstrance to their Colonel, addressed to the legislature of the state, declaring that, unless their complaints on the subjects of pay and support should obtain the immediate attention of that body, they were, at the expiration of three days, to be considered as having resigned; and requesting the legislature, in that event, to appoint other officers to succeed them. They declared, however, their readiness to make every preparation for obeying the orders which had been given, and to continue their attention to the regiment until a reasonable time should elapse for the appointment of their successors. "This," added the letter of General Maxwell, "is a step they are extremely unwilling to take, but it is such as I make no doubt they will all take; nothing but necessity—their not being able to support themselves in time to come, and being loaded with debts contracted in time past, could have induced them to resign at so critical a juncture."

The intelligence conveyed in this letter made a serious impression on the Commander-in-chief. He was strongly attached to the army and to its interests; had witnessed its virtue and its sufferings; and lamented sincerely its present distresses. The justice of the complaints made by the officers could no more be denied, than the measure they had adopted could be approved. Relying on their patriotism and on his own influence, he immediately wrote a letter to General Maxwell, to be laid before them, in which, mingling the sensibility of a friend with the authority of a general, he addressed to their understanding and to their love of country, observations calculated to invite their whole attention to the consequences which must result from the step they were about to take.

Letter from General Washington on this subject.

"The patience and perseverance of the army," proceeds the letter, "have been, under every disadvantage, such as to do them the highest honour both at home and abroad, and have inspired me with an unlimited confidence of their virtue, which has consoled me amidst every perplexity and reverse of fortune, to which our affairs, in a struggle of this nature, were necessarily exposed. Now that we have made so great a progress to

CHAP. V

1779

the attainment of the end we have in view, so that we can not fail without a most shameful desertion of our own interests, any thing like a change of conduct would imply a very unhappy change of principles, and a forgetfulness, as well of what we owe to ourselves, as to our country. Did I suppose it possible this could be the case, even in a single regiment of the army, I should be mortified and chagrined beyond expression. I should feel it as a wound given to my own honour, which I consider as embarked with that of the army at large. But this I believe to be impossible. Any corps that was about to set an example of the kind, would weigh well the consequences; and no officer of common discernment and sensibility would hazard them. If they should stand alone in it, independent of other consequences, what would be their feelings on reflecting that they had held themselves out to the world in a point of light inferior to the rest of the army. Or if their example should be followed, and become general, how could they console themselves for having been the foremost in bringing ruin and disgrace upon their country. They would remember that the army would share a double portion of the general infamy and distress, and that the character of an American officer would become as infamous as it is now glorious.

"I confess the appearances in the present instance are disagreeable, but I am convinced they seem to mean more than they really do. The Jersey officers have not been outdone by any others in the qualities either of citizens or soldiers; and I am confident, no part of them would seriously intend any thing that would be a stain on their former reputation. The gentlemen can not be in earnest; they have only reasoned wrong about the means of obtaining a good end, and, on consideration, I hope and flatter myself they will renounce what must appear to be improper. At the opening of a campaign, when under marching orders for an important service, their own honour, duty to the public and to themselves, and a regard to military propriety, will not suffer them to persist in a measure which would be a violation of them all. It will even wound their delicacy, coolly to reflect that they have hazarded a step, which has an air of dictating terms to their country, by taking advantage of the necessity of the moment.

"The declaration they have made to the state, at so critical a time, that unless they obtain relief in the short period of three days, they must be considered out of the service, has very much that aspect; and the seeming relaxation of continuing until the state can have a reasonable time to provide other officers, will be thought only a superficial veil. I am now to request that you will convey my sentiments to the gentlemen concerned, and endeavour to make them sensible that they are in an error. The service for which

CHAP. V

1779

the regiment was intended will not admit of delay. It must at all events march on Monday morning, in the first place to camp, and farther directions will be given when it arrives. I am sure I shall not be mistaken in expecting a prompt and cheerful obedience."

The representations of this letter did not completely produce the desired effect. The officers did not recede from their claims. In an address to the Commander-in-chief, they expressed their unhappiness that any act of theirs should give him pain, but proceeded to justify the step they had taken. Repeated memorials had been presented to their legislature, which had been received with promises of attention, but had been regularly neglected. "At length," said they, "we have lost all confidence in our legislature. Reason and experience forbid that we should have any. Few of us have private fortunes; many have families who already are suffering every thing that can be received from an ungrateful country. Are we then to suffer all the inconveniences, fatigues, and dangers of a military life, while our wives and our children are perishing for want of common necessaries at home;—and that without the most distant prospect of reward, for our pay is now only nominal? We are sensible that your excellency can not wish nor desire this from us.

"We are sorry that you should imagine we meant to disobey orders. It was and still is our determination to march with our regiment, and to do the duty of officers until the legislature should have a reasonable time to appoint others, but no longer.

"We beg leave to assure your Excellency, that we have the highest sense of your ability and virtues;—that executing your orders has ever given us pleasure;—that we love the service, and we love our country;—but when that country gets so lost to virtue and justice as to forget to support its servants, it then becomes their duty to retire from its service."

This letter was peculiarly embarrassing. To adopt a stern course of proceeding might hazard the loss of the Jersey line, an event not less injurious to the service, than painful to himself. To take up the subject without doing too much for the circumstances of the army, would be doing too little for the occasion. He therefore declined taking any other notice of the letter, than to declare through General Maxwell that, while they continued to do their duty in conformity with the determination they had expressed, he should only regret the part they had taken, and should hope they would perceive its impropriety.

The legislature of New Jersey, alarmed at the decisive step taken by the officers, was at length induced to pay some attention to their situation; they consenting, on their part, to withdraw their remonstrance. In the meantime, they continued to perform their duty; and their

CHAP. V 1779 march was not delayed by this unpleasant altercation.

In communicating this transaction to congress, General Washington took occasion to remind that body of his having frequently urged the absolute necessity of some general and adequate provision for the officers of the army. "I shall only observe," continued the letter, "that the distresses in some corps are so great, either where they were not until lately attached to any particular state, or where the state has been less provident, that the officers have solicited even to be supplied with the clothing destined for the common soldiery, coarse and unsuitable as it was. I had not power to comply with the request.

"The patience of men animated by a sense of duty and honour, will support them to a certain point, beyond which it will not go. I doubt not congress will be sensible of the danger of an extreme in this respect, and will pardon my anxiety to obviate it."

Before the troops destined for the grand expedition were put in motion, an enterprise of less extent was undertaken, which was completely successful. A plan for surprising the towns of the Onondagas, one of the nearest of the hostile tribes, having been formed by General Schuyler, and approved by the Commander-in-chief, Colonel Van Schaick, assisted by Lieutenant Colonel Willet, and Major Cochran, marched from fort Schuyler on the morning of the 19th of April, at the head of between five and six hundred men; and, on the third day, reached the point of destination. The whole settlement was destroyed, after which the detachment returned to fort Schuyler without the loss of a single man. For this handsome display of talents as a partisan, the thanks of congress were voted to Colonel Van Schaick, and the officers and soldiers under his command.

Colonel Van Schaick surprises and destroys one of the Indian settlements.

The cruelties exercised by the Indians in the course of the preceding year, had given a great degree of importance to the expedition now meditated against them; and the relative military strength and situation of the two parties, rendered it improbable that any other offensive operations could be carried on by the Americans in the course of the present campaign. The army under the command of Sir Henry Clinton, exclusive of the troops in the southern department, was computed at between sixteen and seventeen thousand men. The American army, the largest division of which lay at Middlebrook, under the immediate command of General Washington, was rather inferior to that of the British in real strength. The grand total, except those in the southern and western country, including officers of every description, amounted to about sixteen thousand. Three thousand of these were in New England under the command of General Gates; and the remaining thirteen

Expedition against the Indians meditated.

CHAP. V
1779

thousand were cantoned on both sides the North River. The bare statement of numbers, must show the incompetency of the American army to the expulsion of the British from either New York or Rhode Island. On their part, therefore, the plan of the campaign was, necessarily, defensive; and the hazards and difficulties attending the execution of even a defensive plan were considerable.

Independent of an extensive coast, at all places accessible to the invading army, the Hudson, penetrating deep into the country which was to be the theatre of action, gave great advantages in their military operations to those who commanded the water.

After the destruction of forts Clinton and Montgomery in 1777, it had been determined to construct the fortifications intended for the future defence of the North River, at West Point, a position which, being more completely embosomed in the hills, was deemed more defensible. The works had been prosecuted with unremitting industry, but were far from being completed.

Some miles below West Point, about the termination of the Highlands, is King's Ferry, where the great road, affording the most convenient communication between the middle and eastern states, crosses the North River. The ferry is completely commanded by the two opposite points of land. That on the west side, a rough and elevated piece of ground, is denominated Stony Point; and the other, on the east side, a flat neck of land projecting far into the water, is called Verplank's Point. The command of King's Ferry was an object worth the attention of either army; and Washington had comprehended the points which protect it within his plan of defence for the Highlands. A small but strong work, termed fort Fayette, was completed at Verplank's, and was garrisoned by a company commanded by Captain Armstrong. The works on Stony Point were unfinished. As the season for active operations approached, Sir Henry Clinton formed a plan for opening the campaign with a brilliant *coup de main* up the North River; and, towards the latter end of May, made preparations for the enterprise.

These preparations were immediately communicated to General Washington, who was confident that the British general meditated an attack on the forts in the highlands, or designed to take a position between those forts and Middlebrook, in order to interrupt the communication between the different parts of the American army, to prevent their reunion, and to beat them in detail. Measures were instantly taken to counteract either of these designs. The intelligence from New York was communicated to Generals Putnam and M'Dougal, who were ordered to hold themselves in readiness to march; and, on the 29th of May, the army

CHAP. V

1779

May.

moved by divisions from Middlebrook towards the highlands. On the 30th, the British army, commanded by Sir Henry Clinton in person, and convoyed by Sir George Collier, proceeded up the river; and General Vaughan, at the head of the largest division, landed next morning, about eight miles below Verplank's. The other division, under the particular command of General Patterson, but accompanied by Sir Henry Clinton, advancing farther up, landed on the west side within three miles of Stony Point.

June 1.

That place being immediately abandoned, General Patterson took possession of it on the same afternoon. He dragged some heavy cannon and mortars to the summit of the hill in the course of the night; and, at five next morning, opened a battery on fort Fayette, at the distance of about one thousand yards. During the following night, two galleys passed the fort, and, anchoring above it, prevented the escape of the garrison by water; while General Vaughan invested it closely by land. No means of defending the fort, or of saving themselves remaining, the garrison became prisoners of war. Immediate directions were given for completing the works at both posts, and for putting Stony Point, in particular, in a strong state of defence.

Fort Fayette surrendered to the British.

It is scarcely supposable that the views of Sir Henry Clinton in moving up the river, were limited to this single acquisition. The means employed were so disproportioned to the object, as to justify a belief that he contemplated farther and more important conquests. Whatever may have been his plans, the measures of precaution taken by Washington counteracted their execution; and before Clinton was in a situation to proceed against West Point, General M'Dougal was so strengthened, and the American army took such a position on the strong grounds about the Hudson, that the enterprise became too hazardous to be farther prosecuted.

After completing the fortifications on both sides the river, at King's Ferry, Sir Henry Clinton placed a strong garrison in each fort, and proceeded down the river to Philipsburg. The relative situation of the hostile armies presenting insuperable obstacles to any grand operation, they could be employed offensively only on detached expeditions. Connecticut from its contiguity to New York, and its extent of sea coast, was peculiarly exposed to invasion. The numerous small cruisers which plied in the Sound, to the great annoyance of British commerce, and the large supplies of provisions drawn from the adjacent country, for the use of the continental army, furnished great inducements to Sir Henry Clinton to direct his enterprises particularly against that state. He also hoped to draw General Washington from his impregnable position on the North River into the low country, and thus obtain an opportunity

CHAP. V

1779

July.

Invasion of Connecticut.

of striking at some part of his army, or of seizing the posts, which were the great object of the campaign. With these views, he planned an expedition against Connecticut, the command of which was given to Governor Tryon, who reached New Haven bay on the 5th of July, with about two thousand six hundred men.

General Washington was at the time on the lines, examining in person the condition of the works on Stony and Verplank's Points; in consequence of which, the intelligence which was transmitted to head quarters that the fleet had sailed, could not be immediately communicated to the governor of Connecticut, and the first intimation which that state received of its danger, was given by the appearance of the enemy. The militia assembled in considerable numbers with alacrity; but the British effected a landing, and took possession of the town. After destroying the military and naval stores found in the place, they re-embarked, and proceeded westward to Fairfield, which was reduced to ashes. The good countenance shown by the militia at this place is attested by the apology made by General Tryon for the wanton destruction of private property, which disgraced his conduct. "The village was burnt," he says, "to resent the fire of the rebels from their houses, and to mask our retreat."

July.

From Fairfield the fleet crossed the Sound to Huntingdon bay, where it remained until the eleventh, when it recrossed that water, after which the troops were landed in the night on the low pasture, a peninsula on the east side of the bay of Norwalk. About the same time, a much larger detachment from the British army directed its course towards Horse Neck, and made demonstrations of a design to penetrate into the country in that direction.

On the first intelligence that Connecticut was invaded, General Parsons, a native of that state, had been directed by General Washington to hasten to the scene of action. Placing himself at the head of about one hundred and fifty continental troops, who were supported by considerable bodies of militia, he attacked the British in the morning of the twelfth, as soon as they were in motion, and kept up an irregular distant fire throughout the day. But being too weak to prevent the destruction of any particular town on the coast, Norwalk was reduced to ashes; after which the British re-embarked, and returned to Huntingdon bay, there to wait for reinforcements. At this place, however, Tryon received orders to return to the White Stone; where, in a conference between Sir Henry Clinton and Sir George Collier, it was determined to proceed against New London with an increased force.

July.

On the invasion of Connecticut, the Commander-in-chief was prompt in his exertions to send continental troops from the nearest en-

CHAP. V 1779

campments to its aid; but, before they could afford any real service, Sir Henry Clinton found it necessary to recall Tryon to the Hudson.

General Washington had planned an enterprise against the posts at King's Ferry, comprehending a double attack, to be made at the same time, on both. But the difficulty of a perfect co-operation of detachments, incapable of communicating with each other, determined him to postpone the attack on Verplank's, and to make that part of the plan dependent on the success of the first. His whole attention therefore was turned to Stony Point; and the troops destined for this critical service, proceeded on it as against a single object.

The execution of the plan was entrusted to General Wayne, who commanded the light infantry of the army. Secrecy was deemed so much more essential to success than numbers, that no addition was made to the force already on the lines. One brigade was ordered to commence its march, so as to reach the scene of action in time to cover the troops engaged in the attack, should any unlooked-for disaster befall them; and Major Lee of the light dragoons, who had been eminently useful in obtaining the intelligence which led to the enterprise, was associated with General Wayne, as far as cavalry could be employed in such a service. The night

July.

of the fifteenth, and the hour of twelve, were chosen for the assault.

Stony Point is a commanding hill, projecting far into the Hudson, which washes three-fourths of its base. The remaining fourth is, in a great measure, covered by a deep marsh, commencing near the river on the upper side, and continuing into it below. Over this marsh there is only one crossing place; but at its junction with the river, is a sandy beach, passable at low tide. On the summit of this hill stood the fort, which was furnished with heavy ordnance. Several breast-works and strong batteries were advanced in front of the main work; and, about half way down the hill, were two rows of abattis. The batteries were calculated to command the beach and the crossing place of the marsh, and to rake and enfilade any column which might be advancing from either of those points towards the fort. In addition to these defences, several vessels of war were stationed in the river, and commanded the ground at the foot of the hill. The garrison consisted of about six hundred men, commanded by Colonel Johnson.

General Wayne arrived about eight in the afternoon at Spring Steel's, one and a half miles from the fort; and made his dispositions for the assault.

It was intended to attack the works on the right and left flanks at the same instant. The regiments of Febiger and of Meigs, with Major Hull's detachment, formed the right column; and Butler's regiment, with two companies un-

CHAP. V

1779

der Major Murfree, former the left. One hundred and fifty volunteers, led by Lieutenant Colonel Fleury and Major Posey, constituted the van of the right; and one hundred volunteers under Major Stewart, composed the van of the left. At half past eleven the two columns moved to the assault, the van of each with unloaded muskets, and fixed bayonets. They were each preceded by a forlorn hope of twenty men, the one commanded by Lieutenant Gibbon, and the other by Lieutenant Knox. They reached the marsh undiscovered; and, at twenty minutes after twelve, commenced the assault.

General Wayne surprises and takes Stony Point.

Both columns rushed forward under a tremendous fire. Surmounting every obstacle, they entered the works at the point of the bayonet; and, without discharging a single musket, obtained possession of the fort.

The humanity displayed by the conquerors was not less conspicuous, nor less honourable than their courage. Not an individual suffered after resistance had ceased.

All the troops engaged in this perilous service manifested a degree of ardour and impetuosity, which proved them to be capable of the most difficult enterprises; and all distinguished themselves, whose situation enabled them to do so. Colonel Fleury was the first to enter the fort and strike the British standard. Major Posey mounted the works almost at the same instant, and was the first to give the watch word—"The fort's our own."—Lieutenants Gibbon and Knox performed the service allotted to them with a degree of intrepidity which could not be surpassed. Of twenty men who constituted the party of the former, seventeen were killed or wounded.

Sixty three of the garrison were killed, including two officers. The prisoners amounted to five hundred and forty-three, among whom were one lieutenant colonel, four captains, and twenty subaltern officers. The military stores taken in the fort were considerable.*

The loss sustained by the assailants was not proportioned to the apparent danger of the enterprise. The killed and wounded did not exceed one hundred men; General Wayne, who marched with Febiger's regiment in the right column, received a slight wound in the head which stunned him for a time, but did not compel him to leave the column. Being supported by his aids, he entered the fort with a regiment. Lieutenant Colonel Hay was also among the wounded.

Although the design upon fort Fayette had yielded to the desire of securing the success of the attack on Stony Point, it had not been abandoned. Two brigades under General M'Dougal had been ordered to approach the works on Verplank's, in which Colonel Webster commanded,

* The author was in the covering party, visited the fort next day, and conversed with the officers who had been engaged in storming the works.

CHAP. V 1779

and be in readiness to attack them the instant General Wayne should obtain possession of Stony Point. That this detachment might not permit the favourable moment to pass unimproved, Wayne had been requested to direct the messenger who should convey the intelligence of his success to the Commander-in-chief, to pass through M'Dougal's camp, and give him advice of that event. He was also requested to turn the cannon of the fort against Verplank's, and the vessels in the river. The last orders were executed, and a heavy cannonade was opened on fort Fayette, and on the vessels, which compelled them to fall down the river. Through some misconception, never explained, the messenger despatched by General Wayne did not call on M'Dougal, but proceeded directly to head quarters. Thus, every advantage expected from the first impression made by the capture of Stony Point was lost; and the garrison had full leisure to recover from the surprise occasioned by that event, and to prepare for an attack. This change of circumstances made it necessary to change the plan of operation. General Howe was directed to take the command of M'Dougal's detachment, to which some pieces of heavy artillery were to be annexed. He was ordered, after effecting a breach in the walls, to make the dispositions for an assault, and to demand a surrender; but not to attempt a storm until it should be dark. To these orders, ex-

The Ruins of Stony Point—On the Hudson

Here, on the night of July 16, 1779, Brigadier-General (Mad Anththony) Wayne led his troops up the hill in darkness, surprised the British garrison and captured this British stronghold at the point of the bayonet. Not a shot was fired by the Americans, who lost fifteen killed and eighty-three wounded; the British sixty-three killed and 533 prisoners. The fortifications were destroyed and the place, being untenable, was abandoned shortly afterwards by the Americans.

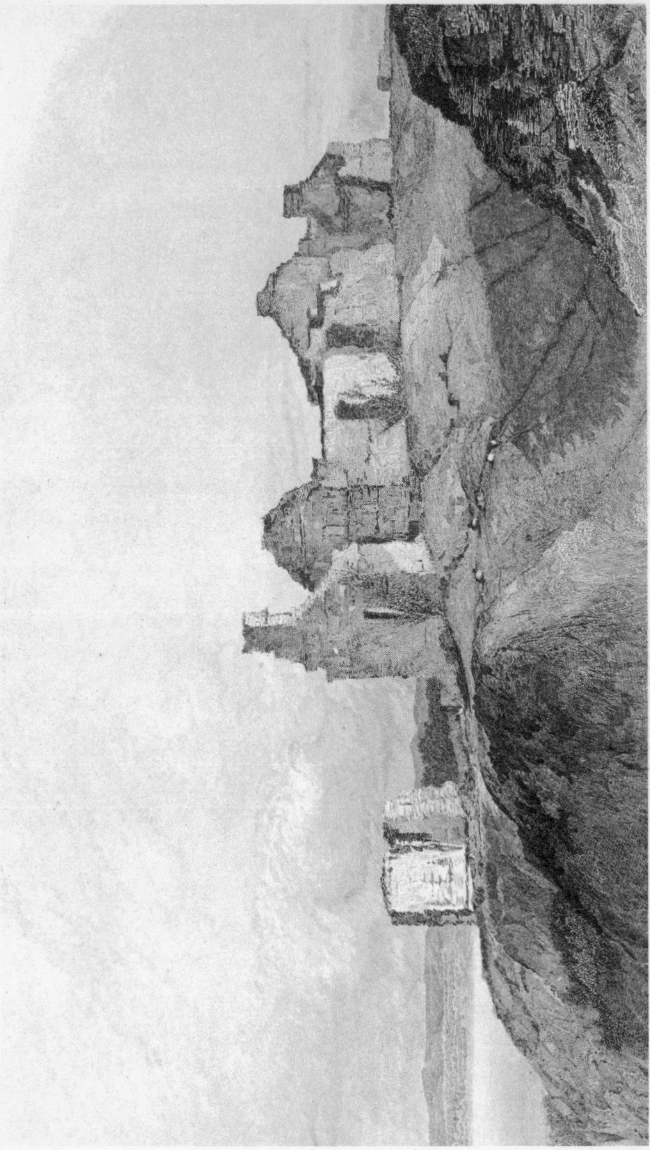

plicit instructions were added not to hazard his party by remaining before Verplank's, after the British should cross Croton River in force.

Through some unaccountable negligence in the persons charged with the execution of these orders, the battering artillery was not accompanied with suitable ammunition; and the necessary intrenching tools were not brought. These omissions were supplied the next day; but it was then too late to proceed against Verplank's.

On receiving intelligence of the loss of Stony Point, and of the danger to which the garrison of fort Fayette was exposed, Sir Henry Clinton relinquished his views on Connecticut, and made a forced march to Dobbs' Ferry. Some troops were immediately embarked to pass up the river, and a light corps was pushed forward to the Croton. This movement relieved fort Fayette.

The failure of the attempt to obtain possession of Verplank's Point leaving that road of communication still closed, diminished the advantages which had been expected to result from the enterprise so much, that it was deemed unadviseable to maintain Stony Point. On reconnoitring the ground, General Washington believed that the place could not be rendered secure with a garrison of less than fifteen hundred men; a number which could not be spared from the army without weakening it too much for farther operations. He determined there-

CHAP. V
1779

fore to evacuate Stony Point, and retire to the Highlands. As soon as this resolution was executed, Sir Henry Clinton repossessed himself of that post, repaired the fortifications, and placed a stronger garrison in it; after which he resumed his former situation at Philipsburg.

The two armies watched each other for some time. At length, Sir Henry Clinton, finding himself unable to attack Washington in the strong position he had taken, or to draw him from it, and being desirous of transferring the theatre of active war to the south, withdrew into York Island, and was understood to be strengthening the fortifications erected for its defence, as preparatory to the large detachments he intended making to reinforce the southern army.

Although this movement was made principally with a view to southern operations, it was in some degree hastened by the opinion, that New York required immediate additional protection during the absence of the fleet, which was about to sail for the relief of Penobscot.

Expedition against Penobscot.

Early in June, Colonel M'Clean, with six hundred and fifty men, had penetrated from Nova Scotia into the eastern parts of Maine, and taken possession of a strong piece of ground on the Penobscot, which he had begun to fortify.

The state of Massachusetts, alarmed at an invasion which threatened a serious diminution of territory, determined to dislodge him. A respectable fleet, commanded by Commodore Saltonstal, and an army of near four thousand men, under General Lovell, were prepared with so much celerity, that the whole armament appeared in the Penobscot as early as the 25th of July. July 25.

M'Clean had taken possession of a peninsula on the eastern side of Penobscot, and had intrenched the isthmus connecting it with the continent. The part towards the river was steep and difficult of access; and was also defended by his frigates and batteries, the principal of which was constructed about the centre of the peninsula.

After being repulsed in his first attempt, General Lovell effected a landing on the western part of the peninsula, where he ascended a precipice of two hundred feet; and, with the loss of only fifty men killed and wounded, drove the party which defended it from the ground. A battery was erected within seven hundred and fifty yards of the main work of the besieged, and a warm cannonade was kept up for several days on both sides.

Perceiving the difficulty of carrying the place with a militia impatient to return to their homes, General Lovell represented his situation to the government of Massachusetts, who applied to General Gates, then commanding at Providence, for a reinforcement of four hundred continental troops. This request was readily granted, and Jackson's regiment was ordered to Penobscot.

CHAP. V

1779

In the mean time an ineffectual cannonade was continued, and preparations were made to storm the works on the arrival of the expected reinforcements.

Such was the posture of affairs on the 13th of August, when Lovell received information that Sir George Collier had entered the river with a superior naval force. He re-embarked his whole army the following night, and drew up his flotilla in a crescent across the river, as if determined to maintain its position. This show of resistance was made in the hope of stopping Sir George Collier until the land forces on board the transports could be conveyed up the river, and disembarked on the western shore. But the British general was too confident in his strength to permit this stratagem to succeed; and, as he approached, the Americans sought for safety in flight. A general chase and unresisted destruction ensued. The ships of war were blown up, and the transports fled in the utmost confusion up the river. Being pursued by the British squadron, the troops landed in a wild uncultivated country; and were obliged to explore their way, without provisions, through a pathless wilderness, for more than a hundred miles. Exhausted with famine and fatigue, they at length gained the settled parts of the country, after having lost several men who perished in the woods.

While Sir Henry Clinton continued encamped just above Haerlem, with his upper posts at Kingsbridge, and the American army preserved its station in the Highlands, a bold plan was formed for surprising a British post at Powles Hook, which was executed with great address by Major Lee.

This officer was employed on the west side of the river with directions to observe the situation of the British in Stony Point, but, principally, to watch the motions of their main army. While his parties scoured the country, he obtained intelligence which suggested the idea of surprising and carrying off the garrison at Powles Hook, a point of land on the west side of the Hudson, immediately opposite the town of New York, penetrating deep into the river. On the point nearest New York, some works had been constructed, which were garrisoned by four or five hundred men.

A deep ditch, into which the water of the river flowed, having over it a drawbridge connected with a barred gate, had been cut across the isthmus, so as to make the Hook, in reality, an island. This ditch could be passed only at low water. Thirty paces within it was a row of abattis running into the river; and some distance in front of it, is a creek fordable only in two places.

This difficulty of access, added to the remoteness of the nearest corps of the American

CHAP. V 1779

army, impressed the garrison with the opinion that they were perfectly secure; and this opinion produced an unmilitary remissness in the commanding officer, which did not escape the vigilance of Lee.

On receiving his communications, General Washington was inclined to favour the enterprise they suggested; but withheld his full assent, until he was satisfied that the assailants would be able to make good their retreat.

The Hackensack, which communicates with the waters of the Hudson below New York, runs almost parallel with that river quite to its source, and is separated from it only a few miles. This neck is still farther narrowed by a deep creek which divides it, and empties into the Hackensack below fort Lee. West of that river runs the Passaick, which unites with it near Newark, and forms another long and narrow neck of land. From Powles Hook to the new bridge, the first place where the Hackensack could be crossed without boats, the distance is fourteen miles; and from the North River to the road leading from the one place to the other, there are three points of interception, the nearest of which is less than two miles, and the farthest not more than three. The British were encamped in full force along the North River, opposite to these points of interception. To diminish the danger of the retreat, it was intended to occupy the roads leading through the mountains of the Hudson to the Hackensack with a select body of troops.

Every preparatory arrangement being made, the night of the eighteenth of August was fixed on for the enterprise. A detachment from the division of Lord Stirling, including three hundred men designed for the expedition, was ordered down as a foraging party. As there was nothing unusual in this movement, it excited no suspicion. Lord Stirling followed with five hundred men, and encamped at the new bridge.

The British post at Powles Hook surprised by Major Lee and the garrison made prisoners.

Major Lee, at the head of three hundred men, took the road through the mountains which ran parallel to the North River; and, having secured all the passes into York Island, reached the creek which surrounds the Hook between two and three in the morning. He passed first the creek, and then the ditch undiscovered; and, about three in the morning, entered the main work, and with the loss of only two killed and three wounded, made one hundred and fifty-nine prisoners, including three officers. Very few of the British were killed. Major Sutherland, who commanded the garrison, threw himself with forty or fifty Hessians into a strong redoubt, which it was thought unadviseable to attack, because the time occupied in carrying it might endanger the retreat. Wasting no time in destroying what could easily be replaced, Major Lee hastened to bring off his prisoners and his detachment.

CHAP. V

1779

To avoid the danger of retreating up the narrow neck of land which has already been described, some boats had been brought in the course of the night to Dow's Ferry on the Hackensack, not far from Powles Hook. The officer who guarded them was directed to remain until the arrival of the troops engaged in the expedition, which, it was understood, would happen before day. The light having made its appearance without any intelligence from Major Lee, the officer having charge of the boats conjectured that the attack had been postponed; and, to avoid discovery, retired with them to Newark. The head of the retreating column soon afterwards reached the ferry; and, fatigued as they were by the toilsome march of the preceding night, were compelled to pass as rapidly as possible up the narrow neck of land between the two rivers to the new bridge. A horseman was despatched with this information to Lord Stirling, and the line of march was resumed.

About nine in the preceding evening, Major Buskirk had been detached up the North River with a considerable part of the garrison of Powles Hook, and some other troops, for the purpose of falling in with the American party supposed to be foraging about the English neighbourhood.

On receiving intelligence of the disappointment respecting the boats, Lord Stirling took the precaution to detach Colonel Ball with two hundred fresh men to meet Lee, and cover his retreat. Just after Ball had passed, Buskirk entered the main road, and fired on his rear. Taking it for granted that this was only the advanced corps of a large detachment sent to intercept the party retreating from Powles Hook, Ball made a circuit to avoid the enemy; and Buskirk, finding a detachment he had not expected, took the same measure to secure his own retreat. The two parties, narrowly missing each other, returned to their respective points of departure; and Lee reached the new bridge without interruption.*

This critical enterprise reflected much honour on the partisan with whom it originated, and by whom it was conducted. General Washington announced it to the army in his orders with much approbation; and congress bestowed upon it a degree of applause more adapted to the talent displayed in performing the service than to its magnitude.

Arrival of Admiral Arbuthnot.

A few days after the surprise of Powles Hook, the long expected fleet from Europe, under the command of Admiral Arbuthnot, having on board a reinforcement for the British army, arrived at New York. This reinforcement however did not enable Sir Henry Clinton to enter immediately on that active course of offensive

* The author states these facts from his own observation, and conversations with other officers of the detachment.

CHAP. V

1779

operations which he had meditated. It was soon followed by the Count D'Estaing, who arrived on the southern coast of America with a powerful fleet; after which the British general deemed it necessary to turn all his attention to his own security. Rhode Island, and the posts up the North River were evacuated, and the whole army was collected in New York, the fortifications of which were carried on with unremitting industry.

St. Lucia taken by the British. St. Vincents and Grenada by the French.

The Count D'Estaing and Admiral Byron, having sailed about the same time from the coast of North America, met in the West Indies, where the war was carried on with various success. St. Lucia surrendered to the British, in compensation for which the French took St. Vincents and Grenada. About the time of the capture of the latter island, D'Estaing received reinforcements which gave him a decided naval superiority; after which a battle was fought between the two hostile fleets, in which the Count claimed the victory, and in which so many of the British ships were disabled that the Admiral was compelled to retire into port in order to refit.

The earnest representations made on the part of the United States had prevailed on the cabinet of Versailles to instruct the Count D'Estaing to afford them all the aid in his power; and the present moment seemed a fit one for carrying these orders into execution. Letters from General Lincoln, from the executive of South Carolina, and from the French consul at Charleston, urged him to pay a visit to the southern states; and represented the situation of the British in Georgia to be such that his appearance would insure the destruction of the army in that quarter, and the recovery of the state.

Count D'Estaing with his fleet arrives on the southern coast of America.

Yielding to these solicitations, the Count sailed with twenty-two ships of the line, and eleven frigates, having on board six thousand soldiers, and arrived so suddenly on the southern coast of America, that the Experiment of fifty guns, and three frigates, fell into his hands. A vessel was sent to Charleston with information of his arrival, and a plan was concerted for the siege of Savannah. D'Estaing was to land three thousand men at Beaulieu on the 11th of September, and Lincoln was to cross the Savannah on the same day with one thousand Americans, and effect a junction with him.

The town of Savannah was, at that time, the head quarters of General Prevost. Apprehending no immediate danger, he had weakened the garrison by establishing several out-posts in Georgia; and by leaving Colonel Maitland with a strong detachment in the island of Port Royal, in South Carolina.

On the appearance of the French fleet, expresses were despatched to Colonel Maitland and to all the out-posts, directing the troops to re-

CHAP. V

1779

pair without loss of time to Savannah. These orders were promptly obeyed; and, on the 10th of September, the several detachments in Georgia had all arrived in safety, except the sick and convalescents of the garrison of Sunbury, who were intercepted.

September.

Siege of Savannah by the combined armies.

On the 11th, General Lincoln reached Zubly's Ferry, and, on the 15th, was assured that the French had disembarked in force. A junction of the two armies was formed the next day before the town of Savannah.

On the night of the 12th, the Count D'Estaing had landed about three thousand men at Beaulieu; and the next day, before the arrival of General Lincoln, had summoned the garrison to surrender to the arms of the King of France. Being desirous of gaining time, General Prevost answered the summons in such a manner as to encourage the opinion that he designed to capitulate; in the expectation of which a suspension of hostilities for twenty-four hours was granted. In that important interval, Colonel Maitland arrived from Beaufort, with the troops which had been stationed at that place.

As the French were in possession of the main channel by which the Savannah communicates with the sea, Colonel Maitland entered the town by a route which had been deemed impracticable. He came round by Dawfuskie, an island north of the mouth of the river, and landing in a deep marsh, drew his boats through it into the

Savannah, above the place where the ships lay at anchor, and thence made his way by small parties into the town.

On receiving this reinforcement, the resolution was taken to defend the place to the last extremity; and, the next day, this determination was communicated to the Count D'Estaing.

September.

After bringing up the heavy ordnance and stores from the fleet, the besieging army broke ground; and, by the first of October, had pushed their sap within three hundred yards of the abattis on the left of the British lines. Several batteries were opened on the besieged which played almost incessantly upon their works, but made no impression on them.

The situation of D'Estaing was becoming critical. More time had already been consumed on the coast of Georgia than he had supposed would be necessary for the destruction of the British force in that state. He became uneasy for the possessions of France in the West Indies, and apprehensive for the safety of the ships under his command. The naval officers remonstrated strenuously against longer exposing his fleet on an insecure coast, at a tempestuous season of the year, and urged the danger of being overtaken by a British squadron, when broken and scattered by a storm, with a degree of persevering earnestness which the Count found himself incapable of resisting.

CHAP. V

1779

In a few days the lines of the besiegers might have been carried by regular approaches, into the works of the besieged, which would have rendered the capture of the town and garrison inevitable. But D'Estaing declared that he could devote no more time to this object; and it only remained to raise the siege, or to attempt the works by storm. The latter part of the alternative was adopted.

On the left of the allied army, was a swampy hollow way which afforded a cover for troops advancing on the right flank of the besieged, to a point within fifty yards of their principal work. It was determined to march to the main attack along this hollow; and, at the same time, to direct feints against other parts of the lines.

Unsuccessful attempt to storm it.

On the morning of the 9th of October, before day, a heavy cannonade and bombardment were commenced from all the batteries, as preliminary to the assault. About three thousand five hundred French, and one thousand Americans, of whom between six and seven hundred were regulars, and the residue militia of Charleston, advanced in three columns, led by D'Estaing and Lincoln, aided by the principal officers of both nations, and made a furious assault on the British lines. Their reception was warmer than had been expected. The fire from the batteries of the besieged reached every part of the columns of the assailants which had emerged from the swamp, and did great execution. Yet the allied troops advanced with unabated ardour, passed through the abattis, crossed the ditch, and mounted the parapet. Both the French and Americans planted their standards on the walls, and were killed in great numbers, while endeavouring to force their way into the works. For about fifty minutes, the contest was extremely obstinate. At length, the columns of the assailants began to relax, and a pause was manifested in the assault.

In this critical moment, Major Glaziers, at the head of a body of grenadiers and marines, rushing suddenly from the lines, threw himself on those who had made their way into the redoubts, and drove them over the ditch and abattis into the hollow which they had marched to the attack. It became apparent that farther perseverance could produce no advantage, and a retreat was ordered.

In this unsuccessful attempt, the French lost in killed and wounded, about seven hundred men. Among the latter, were the Count D'Estaing himself, Major General De Fontanges, and several other officers of distinction. The continental troops lost two hundred and thirty-four men, and the Charleston militia, who, though associated with them in danger, were more fortunate, had one captain killed, and six privates wounded.

The loss of the garrison was astonishingly small. In killed and wounded, it amounted only

CHAP. V

1779

to fifty-five. So great was the advantage of the cover afforded by their works.

After this repulse, the Count D'Estaing announced to General Lincoln, his determination to raise the siege. The remonstrances of that officer were ineffectual; and the removal of the heavy ordnance and stores was commenced. This being accomplished, both armies moved from their ground on the evening of the 18th of October. The Americans, recrossing the Savannah at Zubly's Ferry, again encamped in South Carolina, and the French re-embarked.

The siege raised.

October 18.

Although the issue of this enterprise was the source of severe chagrin and mortification, the prudence of General Lincoln suppressed every appearance of dissatisfaction, and the armies separated with manifestations of reciprocal esteem.

The hopes which had brought the militia into the field being disappointed, they dispersed; and the affairs of the southern states wore a more gloomy aspect than at any former period.

On receiving intelligence of the situation of Lincoln, congress passed a resolution requesting General Washington to order the North Carolina troops, and such others as could be spared from the northern army, to the aid of that in the south; and assuring the states of South Carolina and Georgia of the attention of government to their preservation; but requesting them, for their own defence, to comply with the recommendations formerly made respecting the completion of their continental regiments, and the government of their militia while in actual service.

During these transactions in the south, the long meditated expedition against the Indians was prosecuted with success.

The largest division of the western army was to assemble at Wyoming, on the main branch of the Susquehanna, and General Sullivan expected to leave that place in the month of June. Such, however, were the delays in procuring provisions and military stores, that it was the last of July * before he could move from the place of rendezvous.

Another body of troops, designed to compose a part of the western army, had passed the winter on the Mohawk. On the 22d of August, these two divisions united, and the whole army, amounting to five thousand men, marched up the Tyoga, which led into the heart of the Indian country.

August.

Such extensive and tedious preparations could not be made unobserved. The plan of opera-

* While Sullivan was preparing to invade their country, the savages were not inactive. At the head of a small party of whites and Indians, Joseph Brandt fell upon the frontiers of New York, murdered several of the inhabitants, carried others into captivity, and burnt several houses. He was pursued by about one hundred and fifty militia, whom he drew into an ambuscade, and entirely defeated. A few days afterwards, Captain M'Donald, at the head of a small party, of whom a third were British, took a fort on the west branch of the Susquehanna, and made the garrison, amounting to thirty men, prisoners of war. The women and children, contrary to the usage of Indians, were permitted to retire into the settled country.—*Gordon.*

CHAP. V 1779

tions contemplated by Sullivan seems to have been completely understood; and, notwithstanding the vast superiority of his force, the Indians determined to defend their country. They resolved to risk a general action for its preservation, and selected the ground for the conflict with judgment.

About a mile in front of Newtown, they collected their whole force, estimated by General Sullivan at fifteen hundred men, but by themselves at only eight hundred, commanded by the two Butlers, Grey, Johnson, M'Donald, and Brandt. Five companies of whites, calculated at two hundred men, were united with them. They had constructed a breast-work about half a mile in length, on a piece of rising ground. The right flank of this work was covered by the river, which, bending to the right, and winding round their rear, exposed only their front and left to an attack. On the left, was a high ridge nearly parallel to the general course of the river, terminating somewhat below the breast-work; and still farther to the left, was another ridge running in the same direction, and leading to the rear of the American army. The ground was covered with pine interspersed with low shrub-oaks, many of which, for the purpose of concealing their works, had been cut up and stuck in front of them, so as to exhibit the appearance of being still growing. The road, after crossing a deep brook at the foot of the hill, turned to the right, and ran nearly parallel to the breast-work, so as to expose the whole flank of the army to their fire, if it should advance without discovering their position.

Parties communicating with each other were stationed on both hills, so as to fall on the right flank and rear of Sullivan, as soon as the action should commence.

August.

About eleven in the morning of the 29th of August, this work was discovered by Major Par, who commanded the advance guard of the army; upon which, General Hand formed the light infantry in a wood, about four hundred yards distant from the enemy, and stood upon his ground until the main body should arrive. In the mean time, a continual skirmishing was kept up between Par's rifle corps, and small parties of Indians who sallied from their works, and suddenly retreated, apparently with the hope of being incautiously pursued.

Conjecturing that the hills on his right were occupied by the savages, Sullivan ordered General Poor to take possession of that which led into his rear, and, thence, to turn the left, and gain the rear, of the breast-work; while Hand, aided by the artillery, should attack in front. These orders were promptly executed. While the artillery played on the works, Poor pushed up the mountain, and a sharp conflict commenced, which was sustained for some time, with considerable spirit on both sides. Poor con-

CHAP. V

1779

tinued to advance rapidly, pressing the Indians before him at the point of the bayonet, and occasionally firing on them. They retreated from tree to tree, keeping up an irregular fire, until he gained the summit of the hill. Perceiving that their flank was completely uncovered by this movement, and that they were in danger of being surrounded, the savages abandoned their breast-work, and, crossing the river, fled with the utmost precipitation.

Victory of General Sullivan at Newtown.

This victory cost the Americans about thirty men. The ascertained loss of the Indians was also inconsiderable. But they were so intimidated, that every idea of farther resistance was abandoned. As Sullivan advanced, they continued to retreat before him without harassing his main body, or even skirmishing with his detachments, except in a single instance.

He penetrated far into the heart of their country, which his parties scoured, and laid waste in every direction. Houses, corn-fields, gardens, and fruit trees, shared one common fate; and Sullivan executed strictly the severe but necessary orders he had received, to render the country completely uninhabitable for the present, and thus to compel the hostile Indians, by want of food, to remove to a greater distance.

The objects of the expedition being accomplished, Sullivan returned to Easton in

Pennsylvania, having lost only forty men by sickness and the enemy.

The devastation of the country has been spoken of with some degree of disapprobation; but this sentiment is the result rather of an amiable disposition in the human mind to condemn whatever may have the appearance of tending to aggravate the miseries of war, than of reflection. Circumstances existed which reconciled to humanity this seeming departure from it. Great Britain possessed advantages which ensured a controlling influence over the Indians, and kept them in almost continual war with the United States. Their habitual ferocity seemed to have derived increased virulence from the malignity of the whites who had taken refuge among them; and there was real foundation for the opinion that an annual repetition of the horrors of Wyoming could be prevented only by disabling the savages from perpetrating them. No means in the power of the United States promised so certainly to effect this desirable object, as the removal of neighbours whose hostility could be diminished only by terror, and whose resentments were to be assuaged only by fear.

While Sullivan laid waste the country on the Susquehanna, another expedition under Colonel Brodhead, was carried on from Pittsburg up the Alleghany, against the Mingo, Munscy, and Seneca tribes. At the head of between six and

CHAP. V

1779

seven hundred men, he advanced two hundred miles up the river, and destroyed the villages and corn-fields on its head branches. Here too the Indians were unable to resist the invading army.

After one unsuccessful skirmish, they abandoned their villages to a destruction which was inevitable, and sought for personal safety in their woods.

On receiving the communications of General Sullivan, congress passed a vote approving his conduct, and that of his army. That approbation, however, seems not to have extended beyond his conduct in the Indian country. His demands for military stores for the expedition had been so high; in his conversations with his officers, he had so freely censured the government for its failure to comply with those demands; in general orders, he had so openly complained of inattention to the preparations necessary to secure the success of the enterprise; that considerable offence was given to several members of congress, and still more to the board of war. From the operation of these causes, when Sullivan, at the close of the campaign, complained of ill health, and offered, on that account, to resign his commission, the endeavours of his friends to obtain a vote requesting him to continue in the service, and permitting him to retire from actual duty until his health should be restored, were overruled; and his resignation was accepted. The resolution permitting him to resign was, however, accompanied with one thanking him for his past services. 1779

Although these great exertions to terminate Indian hostility did not afford complete security to the western frontiers, they were attended with considerable advantages. The savages, though not subdued, were intimidated; and their incursions became less formidable, as well as less frequent.

The summer of 1779 passed away without furnishing any circumstance in America which could be supposed to have a material influence on the issue of the war. In Europe, however, an event took place which had been long anxiously expected, and was believed to be of decisive importance. Spain at length determined to make one common cause with France against Great Britain. It was supposed that the two powers would be able to obtain a complete ascendency at sea; and that their combined fleets would maintain a superiority on the American coast, as well as in Europe.

From the first determination of France to take part in the war, it appears to have been the earnest wish of the cabinet of Versailles to engage Spain likewise in the contest.

Her resentments against England, her solicitude to diminish the naval strength of that nation, and her wish to recover Jamaica, Gibraltar,

CHAP. V

1779

and the Floridas, urged her to seize the fair occasion now offered of dismembering the British empire, and accomplishing these favourite objects. But her dread of the effect which the independence of the United States might produce on her own colonies, mingled with some apprehensions of danger from the contest she was about to provoke, had produced an appearance of irresolution, which rendered her future course, for a time, uncertain. In this conflict of opposite interests, the influence of the cabinet of Versailles, and the jealousy of the naval power of Britain, at length obtained the victory; and his Catholic Majesty determined to prevent the reannexation of the United States to their mother country; but to effect this object by negotiation rather than by the sword.

Spain offers her mediation to the belligerent powers.

In pursuance of this pacific system, he offered his mediation to the belligerent powers. This proposition was readily accepted by France; but the minister of his Britannic Majesty evaded any explicit arrangements on the subject, while he continued to make general verbal declarations of the willingness of his sovereign to give peace to Europe under the mediation of his Catholic Majesty. In consequence of these declarations, the Spanish minister proposed a truce for a term of years, and that a congress of deputies from the belligerent powers should assemble at Madrid to adjust the terms of a permanent treaty; into which deputies from the United

States were to be admitted, as the representatives of a sovereign nation. Although an explicit acknowledgment of their independence was not to be required, it was to be understood that they should be independent in fact, and should be completely separated from the British empire.

This negotiation was protracted to a considerable length; and in the mean time, all the address of the cabinet of London was used to detach either France or the United States from their alliance with each other. Notice of it was given to the American government by the minister of France at Philadelphia, as well as by Mr. Arthur Lee, one of their agents in Europe; and congress was repeatedly urged by the former, to furnish those who might be authorized to represent them in the conferences for a general treaty, with ample powers and instructions to conclude it. An extraordinary degree of solicitude was manifested to hasten the full powers, and to moderate the claims of the United States.

It seems to have been the policy of the cabinet of Versailles to exclude the American States from a share of the fisheries, and to limit their western boundary to the settlements then made. Either from a real apprehension that the war might be protracted should the United States insist on the acknowledgment of their independence as a preliminary to any treaty, or from an

CHAP. V

1779

opinion that such preliminary acknowledgment would leave the terms of the treaty less under the control of France, and the American plenipotentiaries more masters of their own conduct, Monsieur Girard laboured to persuade congress to recede from that demand. If they could be independent in fact, he thought the form not worth contending for.*

While congress was employed in debating the instructions to their ministers, the negotiation was brought to a close. As Spain became prepared for hostilities, the offered mediation was pressed in such terms as to produce the necessity of either accepting or rejecting it. This drew from the cabinet of London a declaration that the independence of the United States was inadmissible; upon which his Catholic Majesty determined to take part in the war.

War between Spain and England.

On the departure of his minister from London without taking leave, the British government issued letters of marque and reprisal against the vessels and subjects of the Spanish crown; and a powerful Spanish fleet, which had been preparing during the negotiation, was expedited, to co-operate with that of France. Yet the independence of the United States was not acknowledged, nor was their minister accredited. Despatches, giving notice of the hostilities medi-

* The author has seen notes taken by a member of congress, of communications made by Mr. Girard, when admitted to an audience, which avow these sentiments. The secret journals of congress sustain this statement.

tated by his Catholic Majesty, were forwarded to Don Galvez, the governor of Louisiana, who collected a considerable military force at New Orleans, and reduced the settlements held by the British crown on the Mississippi, which had not been apprised of the war.

Intelligence of this important event was given to congress while that body was deliberating on the instructions to their negotiators. It is not impossible that this information had some influence on those deliberations; and, rendering the American government less solicitous about the future conduct of Spain, diminished the motives for making territorial sacrifices to that power. Their ministers were ordered to make it a preliminary article to any negotiation, that Great Britain should agree to treat with the United States, as sovereign, free, and independent; and that their independence should be expressly assured and confirmed by the terms of the treaty itself.

That the United States might be enabled to avail themselves without further delays, of any occasion which might be presented for terminating the war, Mr. John Adams, who was already in Europe, was authorized to negotiate a treaty of peace, and a commercial treaty with Great Britain; and Mr. Jay, at that time president of congress, was appointed minister plenipotentiary to the court of Madrid, with instructions to insist on the free navigation of the Mississippi;—

CHAP. V

1779

a claim to which Spain objected, and which was discountenanced by France.

As the campaign drew to a close without affording any solid foundation for the hope that the war was about to terminate, General Washington repeated those efforts which he had made so often and so unsuccessfully, to induce early preparations for the ensuing year. He submitted to the view of his government a detailed report of the whole army, which exhibited the alarming fact, that by the last of the following June, the terms of service of nearly one-half the men under his command would expire.

It was not the least considerable of the inconveniences attending the complex system of government then prevailing in the United States, that measures essential to the safety of the nation were never taken in season. Thus, when the time for raising the quotas of the respective states by voluntary enlistment had passed away, and the necessity of resorting to coercive means had become absolute, those means were so delayed, and so irregularly put in execution, that the terms of service of different portions of the army expired almost every month in the year; and raw troops, ignorant of the first rudiments of military duty, were introduced in the most critical moments of a campaign. Had timely and correspondent measures been taken by the states to raise their respective quotas by a specified time in the depth of winter, the recruits would have received the advantage of a few months training before they were brought into actual service, and the General, that of a certain uninterrupted force for each campaign. This course of proceeding had been continually recommended, and the recommendation had been as continually neglected.

Letter from General Washington to Congress.

"In the more early stages of the contest," said the Commander-in-chief to congress, in a letter of the 8th of November, "when men might have been enlisted for the war, no man, as my whole conduct, and the uniform tenor of my letters will evince, was ever more opposed to short enlistments than I was; and while there remained a prospect of obtaining recruits on a permanent footing in the first instance, as far as duty and a regard to my station would permit, I urged my sentiments in favour of it. But the prospect of keeping up an army by voluntary enlistments being changed, or at least standing on too precarious and uncertain a footing to depend on for the exigency of our affairs, I took the liberty in February, 1778, in a particular manner, to lay before the committee of arrangement then with the army at Valley Forge, a plan for an annual draught, as the surest and most certain, if not the only means left us, of maintaining the army on a proper and respectable ground. And, more and more confirmed in the propriety of this opinion by the intervention of a variety of circumstances, unnecessary to detail, I again took

CHAP. V

1779

the freedom of urging the plan to the committee of conference in January last; and, having reviewed it in every point of light, and found it right, at least the best that has occurred to me, I hope I shall be excused by congress in offering it to them, and in time for carrying into execution for the next year; if they should conceive it necessary for the states to complete their quotas of troops.

"The plan I would propose is, that each state be informed by congress annually of the *real deficiency* of its troops, and called upon to make it up, or such less specific number as congress may think proper, by a draught. That the men draughted join the army by the first of January, and serve until the first of January in the succeeding year. That from the time the draughts join the army, the officers of the states from which they come, be authorized and directed to use their endeavours to enlist them for the war, under the bounties granted to the officers themselves, and to the recruits, by the act of the 23d of January, 1779, viz: ten dollars to the officer for each recruit, and two hundred to the recruits themselves. That all state, county, and town bounties to draughts, if practicable, be entirely abolished, on account of the uneasiness and disorders they create among the soldiery, the desertions they produce, and for other reasons which will readily occur. That on or before the first of October annually, an abstract, or return, similar to the present one, be transmitted to congress, to enable them to make their requisitions to each state with certainty and precision. This I would propose as a general plan to be pursued; and I am persuaded that this, or one nearly similar to it, will be found the best now in our power, as it will be attended with the least expense to the public, will place the service on the footing of order and certainty, and will be the only one that can advance the general interest to any great extent."

These representations on the part of the Commander-in-chief were not more successful than those which had before been made. Although the best dispositions existed in congress, the proceedings of that body were unavoidably slow; and the difficulty of effecting a concert of measures among thirteen sovereign states, was too great to be surmounted. In consequence of these radical defects in the system itself, the contributions of men made by the states continued to be irregular, uncertain, and out of season; and the army could never acquire that consistency and stability, which would have resulted from an exact observance of the plan so often recommended.

On receiving information of the disaster which had been sustained by the allied arms at Savannah, Sir Henry Clinton resumed his plan of active operations against the southern states. A large embarkation took place soon after that

CHAP. V

1779

event had been announced to him, which sailed from the Hook towards the end of December. The troops were commanded by himself in person, and the fleet by Admiral Arbuthnot. The defence of New York and its dependencies were entrusted to General Knyphausen.

The preparations made in New York for some distant enterprise were immediately communicated by his faithful intelligencers to General Washington, who conjectured its object, and hastened the march of the troops designed to reinforce General Lincoln.

The season for action in a northern climate being over, the General turned his attention to the distribution of his troops in winter quarters. Habit had familiarized the American army to the use of huts constructed by themselves; and both officers and men were content to pass the winter in a hutted camp. In disposing of the troops, therefore, until the time for action should return, wood and water, a healthy situation, convenience for supplies of provisions, stations which would enable them to cover the country, and to defend particular positions, were the objects taken into consideration, and were all to be consulted.

The American army goes into winter quarters.

With a view to these various circumstances, the army was thrown into two great divisions. The northern was to be commanded by General Heath; and its chief object was the security of West Point, and of the posts on the North

1779

River, as low as King's Ferry. Subordinate to this, was the protection of the country on the Sound, and down the Hudson to the neighbourhood of Kingsbridge. The other and principal division, under the immediate command of General Washington, was put under cover, late in December, in the neighbourhood of Morristown.

CHAPTER VI.

South Carolina invaded....The British fleet passes the bar, and gets possession of the harbour of Charleston....Opinion of General Washington on the propriety of defending that place....Sir Henry Clinton invests the town....Tarlton surprises an American corps at Monk's Corner....Fort Moultrie surrendered....Tarlton defeats Colonel White....General Lincoln capitulates....Buford defeated....Arrangements for the government of South Carolina and Georgia.... Sir Henry Clinton embarks for New York....General Gates takes command of the Southern army....Is defeated near Camden....Death of De Kalb....Success of General Sumpter....He is defeated.

1780 THE departure of the French fleet produced a sudden change in the prospects of the southern states. The sanguine hopes which had been entertained of the recovery of Georgia, gave place to gloomy and well founded apprehensions for South Carolina.

The facility with which General Prevost had passed through the state, and the assurances he had received of the indisposition of a large portion of the people to defend themselves, disclosed too certainly the true situation of the country, not to convince all discerning men that a real attempt at conquest would be made the ensuing year. General Lincoln perceived the approaching danger, without being able to provide against it. His power, as a military com-

CHAP. VI

1780

mander, was too limited, and his influence on the government of the state too weak, to draw forth even the means it possessed in time for its protection.

Though the preservation of its metropolis was of vast importance to the state, no preparations were making to put it in a condition to stand a siege. The forts on the islands were in ruins, and the works across the neck remained unfinished. The representations made on this subject to the governor by General Lincoln were not disregarded; but from some defect in the existing law, the executive found it impracticable to obtain labour for these interesting objects.

Admiral Arbuthnot arrived at Savannah on the 31st of January. One of his transports, which had been separated from the fleet in a storm, was brought into Charleston harbour on the 23d of that month; and the prisoners gave the first certain intelligence that the expedition from New York was destined against the capital of South Carolina.

January 23.

Before the middle of February, the fleet entered the harbour, or inlet, of North Edisto; and landed the troops without opposition on St. John's Island. A part of the fleet was sent round to blockade the harbour of Charleston, while the army proceeded slowly and cautiously from Stono Creek to Wappoo Cut, and through the islands of St. John and St. James.

Sir Henry Clinton invests Charleston.

CHAP. VI

1780

This delay, in the event so fatal, but then deemed so propitious to the American arms, was employed to the utmost advantage in improving the defence of Charleston. The legislature had enabled the executive to employ slaves to work on the fortifications; and had passed an act delegating great powers to the Governor and such of his council as he could conveniently consult. Under these acts, six hundred slaves were employed on the works, and vigorous, though not very successful measures were taken by the executive to assemble the militia of the country. The fallacious hope was entertained that, if the town could be rendered defensible, the garrison would be made sufficiently strong by reinforcements from the north, and by the militia of the state, to maintain the place and compel Sir Henry Clinton to raise the siege.

The American army being too weak to make any serious opposition to the progress of the British through the country, the cavalry, with a small corps of infantry, were directed to hover on their left flank; and the other troops, consisting of about fourteen hundred regulars fit for duty, aided by the militia, were drawn into the town, and employed on the works.

Understanding that great exertions were making to improve the fortifications, and that the garrison was gaining strength, Sir Henry Clinton ordered General Patterson to join him with the troops which could be spared from Georgia, and directed Lieutenant Colonel Tarlton, after supplying the horses which had been lost during a very stormy voyage from New York, to cover his march through South Carolina. In one of the excursions of that active officer to disperse the militia who assembled to oppose the progress of Patterson through the country, his cavalry encountered Lieutenant Colonel Washington, who commanded the remnant of Baylor's regiment, and were driven back with some loss; but the want of infantry disabled Washington from pressing his advantage.

Colonel Washington defeats Tarlton.

In defending Charleston, the command of the harbour is of great importance. To preserve this advantage, congress had ordered four frigates to South Carolina, which, with the marine force belonging to the state, and two French vessels, were placed under the command of Commodore Whipple.

General Washington was the more sanguine in the hope of defending the harbour, because it was understood that the bar was impassable by a ship of the line, and that even a large frigate could not be brought over it, without first taking out her guns, or careening her so much that the crew would be unable to work her.

On sounding within the bar it was discovered that the water was too shallow for the frigates to act with any effect, and that, in making the attempt, they would be exposed to the fire of the batteries which the assailants had erected.

CHAP. VI
1780

Under these circumstances, the officers of the navy were unanimously of opinion that no successful opposition could be made at the bar, and that the fleet might act more advantageously in concert with the fort on Sullivan's Island.

The intention of disputing the passage over the bar being abandoned, Commodore Whipple moored his squadron in a line with fort Moultrie, in a narrow passage between Sullivan's Island and the middle ground; and the British ships, without their guns, passed the bar, and anchored in five fathom hole.

It being now thought impossible to prevent the fleet from passing fort Moultrie, and taking such stations in Cooper River as would enable them to rake the batteries on shore, and to close that communication between the town and country, the plan of defence was once more changed, and the armed vessels were carried into the mouth of Cooper River, and sunk in a line from the town to Shute's folly.

This was the critical moment for evacuating the town. The loss of the harbour rendered the defence of the place, if not desperate, so improbable, that the hope to maintain it, could not have been rationally entertained by a person, who was not deceived by the expectation of aids much more considerable than were actually received.

When this state of things was communicated to General Washington, by Lieutenant Colonel

Laurens, he said in reply, "The impracticability of defending the bar, I fear, amounts to the loss of the town and garrison. At this distance it is impossible to judge for you. I have the greatest confidence in General Lincoln's prudence; but it really appears to me, that the propriety of attempting to defend the town, depended on the probability of defending the bar; and that when this ceased, the attempt ought to have been relinquished. In this, however, I suspend a definitive judgment, and wish you to consider what I say as confidential." Unfortunately, this letter did not arrive in time to influence the conduct of the besieged.

Opinion of General Washington on the subject of defending Charleston.

Having crossed Ashley River, Sir Henry Clinton moved down the neck, and, on the night of the first of April, broke ground within eight hundred yards of the American lines.

April 1.

The defences of Charleston had been constructed under the direction of a Mr. Laumay, a French gentleman in the American service; and, although not calculated to resist a regular siege, were far from being contemptible.

While the besiegers were employed on their first parallel, the garrison received a considerable reinforcement. General Woodford, who had marched from Morristown in December, entered the town with the old continental troops of the Virginia line, now reduced to seven hundred effectives. General Hogan, with the line of North Carolina, had arrived before him. The

CHAP. VI 1780 garrison consisted of rather more than two thousand regular troops, of about one thousand North Carolina militia, and of the citizens of Charleston. The exertions of the Governor to bring in the militia of South Carolina had not succeeded.

April 9. By the 9th of April, Sir Henry Clinton completed his first parallel extending across the neck, and mounted his guns in battery. His works formed an oblique line, from six to seven hundred yards distant from those of the besieged. About the same time, Admiral Arbuthnot passed Sullivan's Island, under a heavy and well directed fire from fort Moultrie, then commanded by Colonel Pinckney, and anchored under James' Island near fort Johnson, just out of gunshot of the batteries of the town.

Being now in complete possession of the harbour, the British General and Admiral sent a joint summons to General Lincoln, demanding the surrender of the town, to which he returned this firm and modest answer. "Sixty days have elapsed since it has been known that your intentions against this town were hostile, in which, time has been afforded to abandon it; but duty and inclination point to the propriety of supporting it to the last extremity."

On receiving this answer, the besiegers opened their batteries, but seemed to rely principally on proceeding by sap quite into the American lines.

About this time, the Governor with half the members of the council, went into the country, in the hope of collecting a respectable force in the rear, and on the left flank of the besieging army. The Lieutenant Governor, and the other members of the council remained in town.

Hitherto, Sir Henry Clinton had not extended his lines north of Charleston neck, and the communication of the garrison with the country north-east of Cooper remained open. The American cavalry, under the command of General Huger, had passed that river, and was stationed in the neighbourhood of Monk's corner, about thirty miles above Charleston. As an additional security to this, the only remaining communication, two posts of militia were established, one between the Cooper and the Santee rivers, to which the Governor repaired in person; and another at a ferry on the Santee, where boats were to be collected for the purpose of facilitating the passage of the American army over that river, should it be deemed adviseable to evacuate the town.

Such importance was attached to this object, that Lincoln, after Woodford had entered Charleston, detached a part of his regular troops, to throw up some works about nine miles above the town, on Wando, the eastern branch of Cooper, and on Lamprere's point. The militia, it was hoped, though unwilling to enter Charleston, might be drawn to these posts.

CHAP. VI

1780

April 14.

Tarlton surprises and defeats an American corps at Monk's corner.

After the fleet had entered the harbour, Sir Henry Clinton turned his attention to the country on the east of Cooper, to acquire the possession of which it was necessary to disable the American cavalry. This service was committed to Lieutenant Colonel Webster, who detached Tarlton with the horse and a corps of infantry to execute it. He succeeded completely. Conducted in the night through unfrequented paths to the American videttes, he entered the camp with them, killed and took about one hundred men, and dispersed the residue, who saved themselves on foot in a swamp. Near fifty wagons loaded with military stores, and about four hundred horses, fell into the hands of the victors.

This decisive blow gave Lieutenant Colonel Webster possession of the whole country between Cooper and Wando; and closed the only route by which the garrison could have retreated.

The besiegers had now commenced their second parallel, and it became every day more apparent that the town must ultimately yield to their regular approaches. An evacuation was proposed, and Lincoln is understood to have been in favour of that measure; but the remonstrances of the principal inhabitants, who entreated him not to abandon them to the fury of a disappointed enemy, added to the great difficulty which must attend such an attempt, especially when opposed by the civil government, deterred him from adopting the only course

1780

which afforded even a probability, by saving his army, of saving the southern states.

Soon after the affair at Monk's corner, Sir Henry Clinton received a reinforcement of three thousand men from New York. This addition to his strength enabled him to detach largely to the aid of Lieutenant Colonel Webster, after which Lord Cornwallis took command of the troops on that side of Cooper River.

April 20.

Upon this change of situation, Lincoln called another council of war. Notwithstanding the multiplied difficulties attending an evacuation of Charleston, he appears to have been still inclined to it. But a number of fortunate circumstances must have concurred to render a retreat possible; and the attempt was effectually prevented by the opposition of the civil government. The opinion seems to have prevailed, that the escape of the garrison would be followed by the destruction of the town, and the ruin of its inhabitants.

The council advised that a capitulation should be proposed, and that the town should be surrendered on condition that the garrison should be at liberty still to bear arms, and that the inhabitants should be secured in their persons and property. These propositions being rejected, hostilities recommenced.

The besiegers had completed their second parallel, and had begun the third, when Colonel Henderson made a vigorous sally on their right,

CHAP. VI

1780

which was attended with some success. That this was the only sortie made during the siege, is to be ascribed to the weakness of the garrison. General Lincoln deemed it necessary to reserve all his strength to man his lines in the event of an assault, or to force a retreat, should he determine to evacuate the city.

In this state of things, General Du Portail, who had been directed to join the southern army, was conducted by secret ways into the town. He perceived the impossibility of defending the place, and repeated the proposition for attempting a retreat. This proposition was again rejected; and it only remained to defer the surrender as long as possible, in the vain hope that some fortunate occurrence might bring relief.

Every day diminished this hope, and added to the difficulties of the besieged. The admiral took possession of Mount Pleasant, which induced the immediate evacuation of Lamprere's point; soon after which the garrison of fort Moultrie, amounting to about two hundred men,* surrendered themselves prisoners of war. On the same day, the cavalry which had escaped the disaster at Monk's corner, and had been reassembled under the command of Colonel White, of New Jersey, was again surprised and defeated by Lieutenant Colonel Tarlton at Lanneau's ferry.

The garrison of fort Moultrie surrender themselves prisoners of war.

* After the fleet passed the fort, Colonel Pinckney and a part of the garrison were withdrawn.

The investment of the town was now complete; the advances were rapid; and it became obvious that the place could be defended only a few days longer. The besiegers had finished their third parallel; and by a sap pushed to the dam that supplied the canal with water, had drained it in many places to the bottom. The garrison, fatigued and worn out with constant duty, was too weak to man the lines sufficiently; their guns were almost all dismounted; most of the embrasures demolished; their shot nearly expended; their provisions, with the exception of a few cows, entirely consumed; and the approaches of the besiegers so near, that their marksmen frequently picked off the men from the guns, and killed † any person who showed himself above the works.

In this state of things, the garrison was summoned, a second time, to surrender; on which a council was again called, which advised a capitulation. In pursuance of this advice, General Lincoln proposed terms which were refused, and hostilities recommenced.

The besiegers now advanced their works in front of their third parallel, crossed the canal, pushed a double sap to the inside of the abattis, and approached within twenty yards of the American works. Preparations for an assault by sea and land were making. With less than three

† Colonel Parker and Captain Peyton, two valuable officers from Virginia, fell in this manner.

CHAP. VI

1780

thousand men, many of whom were militia, lines three miles in extent were to be defended against the flower of the British army, assisted by a powerful maritime force. Convinced that success was not possible, the citizens prepared a petition to General Lincoln, entreating him to surrender the town on the terms which had been offered by the besiegers.

General Lincoln capitulates.

This proposition was made and accepted; and the capitulation was signed on the 12th of May.

May 12.

The town, and all public stores were surrendered. The garrison, as well the citizens who had borne arms as the continental troops, militia, and sailors, were to be prisoners of war. The garrison were to march out of town, and to deposite their arms in front of their works; but their drums were not to beat a British march, nor their colours to be reversed. The militia were to retire to their homes on parole, and their persons and property, as well as the persons and property of the inhabitants of the town, to be secure while they adhered to their paroles.

These terms being agreed on, the garrison laid down their arms, and General Leslie was appointed to take possession of the town.

The defence of Charleston was obstinate, but not bloody. The besiegers conducted their approaches with great caution; and the besieged, too weak to hazard repeated sorties, kept within their lines. The loss on both sides was nearly equal. That of the British was seventy-six killed and one hundred and eighty-nine wounded; and that of the Americans, excluding the inhabitants of the town not bearing arms, was ninety-two killed, and one hundred and forty-eight wounded.

From the official returns made to Sir Henry Clinton by his deputy adjutant general, the number of prisoners, exclusive of sailors, amounted to five thousand six hundred and eighteen men. This report, however, presents a very incorrect view of the real strength of the garrison. It includes every male adult inhabitant of the town. The precise number of privates in the continental regiments, according to the report made to congress by General Lincoln, was one thousand nine hundred and seventy-seven; of whom five hundred were in the hospital.

The unfortunate are generally condemned; and the loss of the garrison of Charleston so maimed the force, and palsied the operations of the American government in the south, that censure was unsparingly bestowed on the officer who had undertaken and persevered in the defence of that place. In his justificatory letter to the Commander-in-chief, General Lincoln detailed at large the motives of his conduct, and stated the testimony on which those delusive hopes of substantial assistance were founded, which tempted him to remain in town, until the un-

CHAP. VI
1780

expected arrival of the reinforcement from New York deprived him of the power to leave it.

The importance of that great mart of the southern states, which had become the depot for the country to a considerable extent around it; the magazines and military stores there collected, which, from the difficulty of obtaining wagons, could not be removed; the ships of war, which must be sacrificed should the town be evacuated; the intention of congress that the place should be defended; the assurances received that the garrison should be made up to ten thousand men, of whom nearly one half would be regular troops; the anxious solicitude of the government of South Carolina; all concurred to induce the adoption of a measure which, in its consequences, was extremely pernicious to the United States. In the opinion of those who were best enabled to judge of his conduct, General Lincoln appears to have been completely justified. The confidence of his government, and the esteem of the Commander-in-chief, sustained no diminution.

Sir Henry Clinton was aware of the impression his conquest had made, and of the value of the first moments succeeding it. Calculating on the advantages to be derived from showing an irresistible force in various parts of the country at the same time, he made three large detachments from his army;—the first and most considerable, towards the frontiers of North Carolina; the second to pass the Saluda to

Ninety-Six; and the third up the Savannah towards Augusta.

Lord Cornwallis, who commanded the northern detachment, received intelligence, soon after passing the Santee, that Colonel Buford, with about four hundred men, was retreating in perfect security towards North Carolina. He detached Lieutenant Colonel Tarlton with his legion, the infantry being mounted, in pursuit of this party. That officer, by making a movement of near one hundred miles in two days, overtook Buford, in a line of march, at the Waxhaws, and demanded a surrender on the terms which had been granted to the garrison of Charleston. This was refused. While the flags were passing, Tarlton continued to make his dispositions for the assault, and, the instant the truce was over, his cavalry made a furious charge on the Americans, who had received no orders to engage, and who seem to have been uncertain whether to defend themselves or not. In this state of dismay and confusion, some fired on the assailants, while others threw down their arms and begged for quarter. None was given. Colonel Buford escaped with a few cavalry; and about one hundred infantry, who were in advance, saved themselves by flight; but the regiment was almost demolished. Tarlton, in his official report, says that one hundred and thirteen were killed on the spot, one hundred and fifty so badly wounded as to be incapable of

Buford defeated.

CHAP. VI 1780

being moved, and fifty-three were brought away as prisoners. The loss of the British was five killed and fourteen wounded.

Tarlton gives a very different account of the circumstances which preceded this massacre. He says that the demand for a surrender was made long before Buford was overtaken, and was answered by a defiance; that, on overtaking him, the British vanguard made prisoners of a sergeant and four light dragoons, in the presence of the two commanders, who immediately prepared for action; that as he advanced to the charge, when within fifty paces, the American infantry presented, and were commanded by their officers to retain their fire until the British cavalry should be nearer.*

The American officers who survived the carnage of the day, generally assert that flags passed after being overtaken, that they had received no orders from Colonel Buford when the charge was made, and that the fire of their troops was retained until the enemy was upon them, because they did not think themselves authorized to give it. The facts that Buford's field pieces were not discharged, and that the loss was so very unequal, are not to be reconciled with the idea of deliberate preparation for

* Lieutenant Bowyer, an American officer who was in the engagement, near the person of Colonel Buford, in a letter which the author has lately seen, states this affair in a manner not much conflicting with the statement made of it by Colonel Tarlton.

1780

battle, and justify the belief that the statement made by the American officers is correct.

After the defeat of Buford, scarcely the semblance of opposition remained in South Carolina and Georgia. The military force employed by congress was nearly destroyed; the spirit of resistance seemed entirely broken; and a general disposition to submit to the victor displayed itself in almost every part of the country.

The two other detachments saw no appearance of an enemy. They received the submission of the inhabitants, who either became neutral by giving their paroles, not to bear arms against his Britannic Majesty, or took the oaths of allegiance, and resumed the character of British subjects.

To keep up this disposition, garrisons were posted in different stations, and a series of measures was pursued for the purpose of settling the civil affairs of the province, and of giving stability to the conquest which had been made.

Sir Henry Clinton takes measures for settling the government of South Carolina and Georgia.

June 3.

So entirely did the present aspect of affairs convince Sir Henry Clinton of the complete subjugation of the state, and of the favourable disposition of the people towards the British government, that he ventured to issue a proclamation, in which he discharged the militia who were prisoners from their paroles, with the exception of those who were taken in Charleston and fort Moultrie, and restored them to all the rights and duties of British subjects; declaring,

CHAP. VI
1780

at the same time, that such of them as should neglect to return to their allegiance, should be considered and treated as enemies and rebels.

This proclamation disclosed to the inhabitants their real situation. It proved that a state of neutrality was not within their reach; that the evils of war were unavoidable; that they must arrange themselves on the one side or the other; and that the only alternative presented to them was, to drive the enemy out of their country, or take up arms against their countrymen.

June 5.

With the most sanguine hopes that the southern states would be reunited to the British empire, Sir Henry Clinton embarked for New York, leaving about four thousand British troops in South Carolina, under the command of Lord Cornwallis.

His lordship found it necessary to suspend the expedition he had meditated against North Carolina. The impossibility of supporting an army in that state before harvest, as well as the intense heat of the season, required this delay. His first care was to distribute his troops through South Carolina and the upper parts of Georgia, so as to promote the great and immediate objects of enlisting the young men who were willing to join his standard, of arranging the plan of a militia, and of collecting magazines at convenient places.

In the mean time, he despatched emissaries to his friends in North Carolina, to inform them of the necessary delay of his expedition into their country, and to request them to attend to their harvest, collect provisions, and remain quiet until late in August or early in September, when the King's troops would be ready to enter the province.

The impatience of the royalists, stimulated by the triumph of their friends in a neighbouring state, and by the necessary severities of a vigilant government, could not be restrained by this salutary counsel. Anticipating the immediate superiority of their party, they could not brook the authority exercised over them, and broke out into premature and ill concerted insurrections, which were vigorously encountered, and generally suppressed. One body of them, however, amounting to about eight hundred men, led by Colonel Bryan, marched down the east side of the Yadkin to a British post at the Cheraws, whence they proceeded to Camden.

Having made his dispositions, and fixed on Camden as the place for his principal magazines, Cornwallis left the command of the frontiers to Lord Rawdon, and retired to Charleston for the purpose of making those farther arrangements of a civil nature, which the state of affairs and the interest of his sovereign might require.

His lordship, as well as Sir Henry Clinton, seems to have supposed the state of South Carolina to be as completely subdued in sentiment

CHAP. VI 1780

as in appearance. Impatient to derive active aids from the new conquest, his measures were calculated to admit of no neutrality. For some time these measures seemed to succeed, and professions of loyalty were made in every quarter. But under this imposing exterior, lurked a mass of concealed discontent, to which every day furnished new aliment, and which waited only for a proper occasion to show itself.

The people of the lower parts of South Carolina, though far from being united, were generally attached to the revolution, and had entered into the war with zeal. They were conducted by a high spirited and intelligent gentry, who ardently sought independence as a real and permanent good.

Several causes had combined to suspend the operation of this sentiment. Many of their leaders were prisoners; and the brilliant successes of the British arms had filled numbers with despair. Others were sensible of the inutility of present resistance; and a still greater number, fatigued and harassed with militia duty, were willing to withdraw from the conflict, and, as spectators, to await its issue. To compel these men to share the burdens of the war, was to restore them to their former friends.

Late in March, General Washington had obtained the consent of congress to reinforce the southern army with the troops of Maryland and Delaware, and with the first regiment of artillery. This detachment was to be commanded by the Baron De Kalb, a German veteran who had engaged early in the service of the United States.

Such, however, was the deranged state of American finances, and such the depression of public credit, that these troops could not be put immediately in motion. They were at length embarked at the Head of Elk, and conveyed by water to Petersburg, in Virginia, whence they marched towards South Carolina. Their progress was delayed by that difficulty of obtaining subsistence which had induced Lord Cornwallis to suspend the invasion of North Carolina until harvest should be gathered. No preparations having been made for them, they were reduced to the necessity of spreading themselves over the country in small detachments, to collect corn, and grind it for their daily food. In this manner they proceeded through the upper parts of North Carolina to Deep River, and encamped near Buffalo Ford in July. At this place the Baron halted for a few days, in some uncertainty respecting his future course.*

The militia of North Carolina, commanded by General Caswell, were beyond the Pedee, on the road to Camden, and had nearly consumed the scanty supplies which could be gleaned from a country that was far from being productive. The Baron was premeditating on a plan for leaving the direct road and moving up the coun-

* Journal of Colonel Williams.

CHAP. VI

1780

try to the fertile banks of the Yadkin, when the approach of Major General Gates was announced by the arrival of his aid-de-camp, Major Armstrong.*

Aware of the danger to which the loss of Charleston had exposed that part of the confederacy, congress deemed it of the utmost importance to select a general for that department, in whom great military talents should be combined with that weight of character which might enable him to draw out the resources of the country. They turned their eyes on Gates; † and sanguine hopes were entertained that the conqueror of Burgoyne would prove the saviour of the southern states. On the 13th of June, he was called to the command in the southern department, and was directed to repair immediately to the army. He entered, without loss of time, on the duties of his station; and, on the 25th of July, reached the camp, where he was received by the Baron De Kalb with the utmost cordiality and respect.

General Gates appointed to the command of the southern army.

July.

The approach of this army, and the information that great exertions were making in Virginia to augment it, revived the hopes of South Carolina, and brought again into action a spirit supposed to be extinguished. The British troops having occupied the north-western parts of the

* Journal of Colonel Williams.

† This appointment was made without consulting the Commander-in-chief. He had determined, if consulted, to recommend General Greene.

state, the most active friends of the revolution in that quarter had fled from their homes, and sought an asylum in North Carolina and Virginia. As the discontents of their countrymen increased, and the prospect of being supported by regular troops brightened, a small body of these exiles, amounting to less than two hundred, assembled together, and choosing Colonel Sumpter, an old continental officer, for their chief, entered South Carolina. They skirmished with the royal militia and small corps of regulars on the frontiers, sometimes successfully, and always with the active courage of men fighting for the recovery of their property. The followers of Sumpter were soon augmented to six hundred men; and a disposition once more to take up arms showed itself in various parts of the state. Some corps of militia, which had been embodied under the authority of Lord Cornwallis, deserted his standard, and joined their countrymen. Perceiving this change of temper, the British general thought it necessary to draw in his out-posts, and to collect his troops into larger bodies.

On taking command of the southern army, General Gates directed the troops to hold themselves in readiness to march at a moment's warning; and, on the morning of the 27th, put the whole in motion. Disregarding the judicious remonstrances which were made to him against pursuing the direct road, he determined on tak-

CHAP. VI 1780 ing the nearest route to the advanced post of the British on Lynch's Creek, a few miles from Camden. The motives assigned by himself for passing through this barren country were, the necessity of uniting with Caswell, who had evaded the orders repeatedly given him to join the army, the danger of dispiriting the troops, and intimidating the people of the country, by pursuing a route not leading directly towards the enemy, and the assurances he had received that supplies would overtake him, and would be prepared for him on the road.

These assurances were not fulfilled; and, the country being still more barren than had been anticipated, the distress of the army was extreme. The soldiers subsisted on a few lean cattle found in the woods, and a very scanty supply of green corn and peaches. Encouraged by the example of their officers, who shared all their sufferings, and checked occasional murmurs, they struggled through these difficulties, and, after effecting a junction with General Caswell and with Lieutenant Colonel Porterfield,* the army reached Clermont, sometimes called

August 13. Rugely's mills, on the 13th of August. Possession was taken of this place without any oppo-

* This valuable officer was pressing forward to Charleston when that place surrendered. Continuing to advance, he was within one day's march of Colonel Buford, when that officer was defeated. Colonel Porterfield still remained on the frontiers of the Carolinas; and had the address not only to avoid the fate of every other corps sent to the relief of Charleston, but to subsist his men; and keep up the semblance of holding that part of South Carolina.

sition from Lord Rawdon, who, on the approach of the American army, drew in his out-posts, and assembled all his forces at Camden.*

The day after the arrival of Gates at Clermont, he was joined by seven hundred militia from Virginia, commanded by Brigadier General Stevens, an officer of considerable merit, who, during the campaigns of 1777 and 1778, had commanded a continental regiment. On the same day, an express arrived from Colonel Sumpter, with information that an escort of clothing, ammunition, and other stores for the garrison at Camden, was on the way from Ninety-Six, and must pass the Wateree at a ferry about a mile from Camden, which was covered by a small redoubt on the opposite side of the river. One hundred regular infantry with two brass field-pieces, were immediately detached to join Colonel Sumpter, who was ordered to reduce the redoubt, and to intercept the convoy.*

To attract the attention of the garrison in Camden, and thus co-operate with the expedition under Sumpter, it was determined in a council of general officers to put the army in motion that evening, and to take a post about seven miles from Camden with a deep creek in front.

The sick, the heavy baggage, and the military stores were ordered under a guard to Waxhaws,† and the army was directed to be in readiness to

* Journal of Colonel Williams.
† Colonel Williams says these orders were not executed.

CHAP. VI 1780

march precisely at ten in the evening in the following order.

Colonel Armand's legion composed the van. Porterfield's light infantry, reinforced by a company of picked men from Stevens's brigade, covered the right flank of the legion; while Major Armstrong's light infantry of North Carolina militia, reinforced in like manner from Caswell's division, covered the left. The Maryland division, followed by the North Carolina and Virginia militia, with the artillery, composed the main body and rear guard; and the volunteer cavalry were equally distributed on the flanks of the baggage.

In the event of an attack in front by the British cavalry, the infantry on the flanks were directed to march up, and to continue their fire on the assailants. It was supposed they would enable Colonel Armand to resist the shock; and his orders were positive to maintain his ground against the cavalry, whatever their numbers might be.‡

At the time of communicating these orders to Colonel Otho H. Williams, the Deputy Adjutant General, Gates, showed him a rough estimate of the army, making it upwards of seven thousand. Convinced that this estimate was exaggerated, Colonel Williams availed himself of his means of information to make an abstract of the whole, which he presented to the general,

‡ Journal of Colonel Williams.

and which exhibited exactly three thousand and fifty-two in the column of present fit for duty, of whom more than two-thirds were militia. Gates expressed some surprise at the numbers, but said, "there are enough for our purpose," and directed the orders to be issued to the army. About ten at night, the line of march was taken up, and the army had advanced about half way to Camden, when a firing commenced in front.*

Intelligence of the approach of the American army, and of the defection of the country between Pedee and the Black River, had been communicated to Lord Cornwallis, and had induced him to hasten in person to Camden, which place he reached the day Gates arrived at Clermont.

The British army did not much exceed two thousand men, of whom about nineteen hundred were regulars; but, as the whole country was rising, Lord Cornwallis apprehended that every day would strengthen his enemy, and therefore determined to attack him in his camp; hoping, by a prompt execution of this resolution, to surprise him. By one of those caprices of fortune on which great events often depend, he marched from Camden to attack Gates in Clermont, at the very hour that Gates moved from that place towards Camden.*

August 16.

About half past two in the morning, the advanced parties of the hostile armies, to their mutual surprise, met in the woods, and began to

* Journal of Colonel Williams.

CHAP. VI
1780

skirmish with each other. Some of Armand's cavalry being wounded by the first fire, threw the others into disorder, and the whole recoiled so suddenly that the first Maryland regiment, composing the front of the column was broken, and the whole line thrown into consternation. From this first impression, the raw troops never recovered. The light infantry, however, particularly Porterfield's corps, behaved so well as to check the advance of the British. Unfortunately, their gallant commander received a mortal wound, which compelled him to leave his regiment. Yet a part of it kept its ground; and, with the aid of the legion infantry, stopped the British van; upon which order was restored to the American army.

The officers were immediately employed in forming a line of battle in front. The Maryland division, including the troops of Delaware, were on the right, the North Carolina militia in the centre, and the Virginia militia on the left.

In this rencounter some prisoners were made, from one of whom Colonel Williams drew the information that the British army, consisting of near three thousand men, commanded by Lord Cornwallis in person, was in full march five or six hundred yards in front. This intelligence was immediately communicated to General Gates, who had supposed Lord Cornwallis to be still in Charleston. The general officers were assembled in the rear of the line, and this information submitted to them. After a short silence, Stevens said, "Gentlemen, is it not too late to do any thing but fight?" No other advice being given, General Gates, who seems to have been himself disposed to risk a battle, directed the officers to repair to their respective commands.

The ground on which the army was drawn up was so narrowed by a marsh on each flank, as to admit of removing the first Maryland brigade, so as to form a second line about two hundred yards in rear of the first. The artillery was placed in the centre of the first line, and Armstrong's light infantry was ordered to cover a small interval between the flank of the left wing and the marsh.

Frequent skirmishes occurred during the night between the advanced parties, with scarcely any other effect than to discover the situation of the armies, evince the intention of the generals, and serve as a prelude to the events of the succeeding morning.

At dawn of day the British appeared in front, advancing in column. Lieutenant Colonel Webster commanded on the right, and Lord Rawdon on the left. The seventy-first regiment composed the reserve. Four field pieces were attached to the left, and one to the corps de reserve.

Captain Singleton opened some field pieces on the front of the column, at the distance of about

CHAP. VI
1780

two hundred yards, soon after which the American left was ordered to commence the action. It was then perceived that the British right was advancing in line; and as Stevens led on his brigade in good order, Colonel Williams advanced in front with a few volunteers, intending by a partial fire to extort that of the enemy at some distance, and thereby diminish its effect on the militia. The experiment did not succeed. The British rushed forward with great impetuosity, firing and huzzaing at the same time; and the terrified militia, disregarding the exertions of Stevens, who, in the firm tone of courage, endeavoured to inspire them with confidence in the bayonets they had just received, threw down their loaded muskets, fled from the field with the utmost precipitation, and were followed by the light infantry of Armstrong. The whole North Carolina division, except one regiment commanded by Colonel Dixon, an old continental officer, which was posted nearest the continental troops, followed the shameful example. Other parts of the same brigade, which was commanded by Gregory, paused for an instant; but the terror of their brethren was soon communicated to them, and they also threw away their arms, and sought for safety in flight. Their general, while endeavouring to rally them, was dangerously wounded.

Tarlton's legion charged them as they broke, and pursued them in their flight. Gates, in person, assisted by their generals, made several efforts to rally the militia; but the alarm in their rear still continuing, they poured on like a torrent, and bore him with them. He hastened with General Caswell to Clermont, in the hope of stopping a sufficient number of them at their old encampment, to cover the retreat of the continental troops; but this hope was entirely disappointed. Believing the continental troops also to be dispersed, he gave up all as lost, and retreated with a few friends to Charlotte, about eighty miles from the field of battle, where he left General Caswell to assemble the neighbouring militia, and proceeded himself to Hillsborough, in order to concert some plan of farther defence with the government.

Entirely deserted by the militia who composed the whole centre and left wing of the army, the continental troops, with the Baron De Kalb at their head, were left without orders, under circumstances which might have justified a retreat. But taking counsel from their courage, and seeing only the path of duty, they preferred the honourable and dangerous part of maintaining their position. They were charged by Lord Rawdon about the time the militia on their left were broken by Webster; but the charge was received with unexpected firmness. The bayonet was occasionally resorted to by both parties, and the conflict was maintained for near three quarters of an hour with equal obsti-

CHAP. VI 1780 nacy. During this time, the regiment on the left of the second Maryland brigade being covered by the reserve, so that it could be only engaged in front, gained ground and made prisoners.

The reserve, having its left entirely exposed, was flanked by the British right wing under Webster; who, after detaching a part of his cavalry and light infantry in pursuit of the flying militia, wheeled on that brigade, and attacking it in front and round the left flank, threw it into some disorder. The soldiers were, however, quickly rallied, and renewed the action with unimpaired spirit. Overpowered by numbers, they were again broken, and by the exertion of their officers were again formed, so as still to maintain the combat, and still to cover the flank of their brethren of the second brigade, who were in a manner blended with the enemy, and who kept up a desperate conflict in the hope of yet obtaining the victory.

The fire of the whole British army was now directed against these two devoted brigades. They had not lost an inch of ground when Lord Cornwallis, perceiving that they were without cavalry, pushed his dragoons upon them, and at the same instant, charged them with the bayonet. These gallant troops were no longer able to keep the field. They were at length broken; and, as they did not give way until intermingled with the enemy, they dispersed and fled in confusion. Before they were reduced to this last extremity, the Baron De Kalb, who fought on foot with the second Maryland brigade, fell under eleven wounds. His aid-de-camp, Lieutenant Colonel Du Buysson, received him in his arms, announced his rank and nation to the surrounding foe, and begged that they would spare his life. While thus generously exposing himself to save his friend, he received several wounds, and, with his general, was taken prisoner. The Baron expired in a few hours, and spent his last breath in dictating a letter, expressing the warmest affection for the officers and men of his division, and the most exalted admiration of their courage and good conduct.*

Death of De Kalb.

Never was a victory more complete. Every corps was broken and dispersed in the woods. The general officers were divided from their men; and, except Rutherford of the North Carolina militia who was made a prisoner, reached Charlotte at different times. Colonel Williams, who witnessed the whole battle, and bore a conspicuous part in it, concludes his very animated description of it, with the observation, that "if in this affair the militia fled too soon, the regulars may be thought almost as blameable for remaining too long on the field; especially after all hope of victory must have been despaired of." He censures freely the conduct of the brigadiers, who gave, he says, no orders whatever to their brigades.

* Journal of Colonel Williams.

CHAP. VI 1780

About two hundred wagons, with a great part of the baggage, military stores, small arms, and all the artillery, fell into the hands of the conqueror. The loss of men could never be accurately ascertained, as no returns were received from the militia. Of the North Carolina division, between three and four hundred were made prisoners, and between sixty and one hundred were wounded. Of the Virginia militia, three were wounded on the field; and, as they were the first to fly, not many were taken.

For the numbers engaged, the loss sustained by the regulars was considerable. It amounted to between three and four hundred men, of whom a large portion were officers. The British accounts state the loss of the American army at eight or nine hundred killed, and about one thousand prisoners; while their own is said to be only three hundred and twenty-five, of whom two hundred and forty-five were wounded. Although many of the militia were killed during the flight, this account is probably exaggerated. It would seem too, that while the continental troops kept the field, the loss on both sides, in that part of the action, must have been nearly equal.

On his retreat, the day of the battle, General Gates received information of the complete success of Sumpter. That officer had, on the evening that Lord Cornwallis marched from Camden, reduced the redoubt on the Wateree, captured the guard, and intercepted the escort with the stores.

This gleam of light cheered the dark gloom which enveloped his affairs but for a moment. He was soon informed that this corps also was defeated, and entirely dispersed.

On hearing of the disaster which had befallen Gates, Sumpter began to retreat up the south side of the Wateree. Believing himself out of danger, he had halted on the twenty-eighth, during the heat of the day, near the Catawba Ford, to give his harassed troops some repose. At that place he was overtaken by Tarlton, who had been detached in pursuit of him on the morning of the 17th, and who, advancing with his accustomed celerity, entered the American camp so suddenly, as in a great measure to cut off the men from their arms. Some slight resistance made from behind the wagons was soon overcome, and the Americans fled precipitately to the river and woods. Between three and four hundred of them were killed and wounded; their baggage, artillery, arms, and ammunition were lost; and the prisoners and stores they had taken, were recovered. This advantage was gained with the loss of only nine men killed and six wounded.

August 18.

Two videttes had been placed by Sumpter, on the road along which Tarlton had advanced, who fired upon his van and killed one of his dragoons, upon which they were both sabred.

CHAP. VI

1780

We are informed by Colonel Tarlton that the inquiries made by Sumpter respecting the two shots, were answered by an assurance from an officer, just returned from the advanced sentries, that the militia were firing at cattle.

August 19.

Intelligence of this disaster reached Charlotte next day. Generals Smallwood and Gist were then arrived at that place, and about one hundred and fifty straggling, dispirited, half famished officers and soldiers had also dropped in. It was thought adviseable to retreat immediately to Salisbury. From that place, General Gates directed the remnant of the troops to march to Hillsborough, where he was endeavouring to assemble another army, which might enable him yet to contend for the southern states.

CHAPTER VII.

Distress in the American camp....Expedition against Staten Island....Requisitions on the states....New scheme of finance....Committee of congress deputed to camp....Resolution to make up depreciation of pay....Mutiny in the line of Connecticut....General Knyphausen enters Jersey....Sir Henry Clinton returns to New York....Skirmish at Springfield....Exertions to strengthen the army....Bank established in Philadelphia....Contributions of the ladies....Farther proceedings of the states....Arrival of a French armament in Rhode Island....Changes in the quartermaster's department....Enterprise against New York abandoned ....Naval superiority of the British.

WHILE disasters thus crowded on each other in the southern states, the Commander-in-chief found himself surrounded with difficulties, which required his utmost exertions to avoid calamities equally distressing. His urgent requisitions for men to supply the places of those who were leaving the service, were not complied with, and the soldiers who remained, could scarcely be preserved from either perishing with cold and hunger, or dispersing and living on plunder. 1780

General Greene and Colonel Wadsworth, who had, for the preceding year, been at the head of the quartermaster and commissary departments, possessed distinguished merit, and had employed assistants of unquestionable ability and integrity. Yet, for a great part of the campaign,

CHAP. VII

1780

the rations were frequently reduced, and the army was rarely supplied with provisions for more than a few days in advance. Soon after coming into winter quarters, the magazines were exhausted, and afforded neither meat nor flour to be delivered to the men.

This state of things had been long foreseen; and all the means in the power of the Commander-in-chief had been used to prevent it. Repeated representations of the actual famine with which the army was threatened, had been made to congress, and to the state governments; but no adequate relief was afforded; and such was the condition of the finances, so embarrassing the state of affairs, that it was perhaps attainable only by measures which the governments could not venture to adopt.

The rapid depreciation of the continental currency, had long been viewed with apprehensive anxiety by the enlightened friends of the revolution, and various unsuccessful expedients had been essayed for the purpose of checking its progress. All perceived that the great quantity in circulation was the principal cause of the diminution of its value; and congress had resolved not to exceed two hundred millions of dollars in their emissions. In the mean time, the utmost endeavours were used to defer an evil so justly dreaded, and among the expedients employed, was that of withholding from the public agents, the money which was necessary for public purposes. This unwise experiment, while it defeated its own object, threatened the dissolution of the American army.

The difference between the value of the article at the times of contract and of payment was soon perceived, and, of course, influenced its price. But this was the least mischievous consequence of this mistaken policy. The public agents contracted enormous debts which they were unable to discharge. Repeated disappointments destroyed their credit; and, towards the close of the year 1779, they found it impracticable to obtain supplies for the subsistence of the army.

From these causes, the contracts entered into could not be co-extensive with the public wants; and many of those which were made were not complied with.

In this critical state of things, an entire revolution was made in the commissary department. Such was the prejudice against the system adopted by Great Britain, for supplying by contract, that it had been usual to allow, as a compensation to the commissary, a stipulated commission on all the monies expended on public account. After some time, this allowance was supposed to be an inducement to purchase at high prices; and an arrangement was made on the first of January, by which the commissary general was to receive a fixed nominal salary in the paper currency, and was permitted to appoint assistants whose compensations were also fixed, and who were to defray, out of those compensations, all the expenses attending the transactions of the business. The practice of allowing them rations and forage was discontinued.

This new system was unfortunately so modified as to increase the embarrassments of the department. It was found difficult to obtain assistants and agents for the compensation allowed; and those who were willing to be employed, were unequal to the duties assigned them.

For several days, the soldiers were reduced to half allowance, and sometimes to less. At length, affairs came to the crisis which had long been threatened; and, early in January, a letter was received from Colonel Wadsworth, informing the general that it was absolutely out of his power to supply the army longer with meat, as he was without money, and had totally exhausted his credit. About the same time, the assistant commissary, residing in camp, gave notice that his stock of provisions was on the point of being expended, and that he had no immediate prospect of a farther supply.

This state of things compelled the Commander-in-chief to adopt efficacious measures, to relieve the immediate and pressing wants of his soldiers. He required from each county in the state of Jersey, a quantity of meat and flour proportioned to its resources, to be raised and forwarded to the army within a limited time, not exceeding six days. In a circular letter addressed to the magistrates, he stated the pressing wants of the army, and the necessity of resorting to coercion should his requisition fail.

To the honour of the magistrates and people of New Jersey, although their country was much exhausted, the supplies required were instantly furnished, and a temporary relief obtained.

The patient and uncomplaining fortitude with which the soldiers bore their sufferings, was strong evidence of their patriotism, and could not fail to make a deep impression on their general. But while their virtues excited his sensibilities, he expressed his fears very freely to congress, that they might be too severely tried.

The unusual severity of the winter, seemed to furnish an opportunity for active enterprise, which the Commander-in-chief observed, without being able to improve. The garrison of New York and its immediate dependencies, was supposed to be reduced to ten or eleven thousand effectives; and the security heretofore derived from its insular situation no longer existed. The ice was so strong that the whole army, with its train of wagons and artillery, might pass over without danger. This circumstance afforded a glorious occasion for striking a blow, which, if

CHAP. VII

1780

successful, would most probably terminate the war. The effort would seem not to have exceeded the strength of America, could that strength have been exerted in proper season; but the government possessed neither sufficient energy nor concentration of power to call it forth; and this opportunity passed away, as many which present themselves in the course of human affairs, must pass away, if those who should take advantage of them, only begin to deliberate about making preparations in the season for action.

The force under the immediate command of General Washington, was decidedly inferior to that in New York; and so far was he from having reason to expect immediate reinforcements, that congress had not agreed on making a requisition for them. In addition to this feebleness in point of numbers, the soldiers were not half clothed; provisions for immediate use could be obtained only by contributions from the people; the quartermaster's department was unable to put an army in motion; and the military chest did not contain a dollar.

Under the pressure of this combination of discouraging circumstances, the active mind of Washington still looked forward to the possibility of deriving some advantage from the exposed situation of his adversary.

The troops on Staten Island were computed at one thousand or twelve hundred men; and the firm bridge of ice now uniting that island to the Jersey shore, seemed to furnish an opportunity for bearing off this corps. General Washington determined to make the attempt with two thousand five hundred men, to be commanded by Major General Lord Stirling. The more distant troops moved down on sleds; and, to favour a surprise, the opinion was inculcated that they only constituted a relief for the detachment already on the lines.

January.

On the night of the 14th of January, Lord Stirling moved over from De Hart's point; and, detaching Lieutenant Colonel Willet to Decker's house, where Buskirk's regiment was stationed, proceeded himself to the watering place, where the main body was posted. Notwithstanding the precautions which had been taken, the alarm had been given at each post, and the troops had saved themselves in their works; so that only a few prisoners were made. Contrary to the intelligence previously received, the communication with New York was still open; and the works appeared too strong to justify the hazard of attempting to carry them by assault.

January 17.

The object of the expedition being unattainable, Lord Stirling commenced his retreat, which was effected with inconsiderable loss. A body of cavalry, which charged his rear, was repulsed; but, from the intenseness of the cold, and the defectiveness of his means to protect his

CHAP. VII 1780

men from it, some of them were frost bitten, and a few stragglers were made prisoners.

The excessive cold continuing, the rivers were soon afterwards completely blocked up. Even arms of the sea were passable on the ice; and the islands about the mouth of the Hudson, presented the appearance of one whole and unbroken continent. This state of things produced a great degree of suffering among all classes in New York. The supplies usually received by water failed totally, and a great scarcity of provisions and of fuel was the consequence. To increase this scarcity, the American troops on the lines were so disposed as to interrupt the communication between the country and the town; and these arrangements produced a partisan war, in which the advantage was rather on the side of the British.

In one of the most important of these skirmishes, Captain Roberts, of Massachusetts, with fourteen of his men, were killed on the spot; seventeen were wounded, of whom three died in a few days; and Lieutenant Colonel Thompson, of Massachusetts, who commanded the party, two captains, four subalterns, and ninety non-commissioned officers and privates were made prisoners.

The emission of the full sum of two hundred millions of dollars in continental bills of credit, which congress had solemnly resolved not to exceed, had been completed in November, 1779, and the money was expended. The requisitions on the states to replenish the treasury by taxes were not fully complied with; and, had they even been strictly observed, would not have produced a sum equal to the public expenditure. It was therefore necessary to devise other measures for the prosecution of the war. During the distresses which brought the army to the brink of dissolution, these measures were under consideration. So early as December, 1779, congress had determined to change the mode of supplying the army from purchases to requisitions of specific articles on the several states. As preliminary to this system, commissioners were appointed to make the estimates, and to introduce every practicable reform in the expenditures. This subject was under deliberation until the 25th of February, when sundry resolutions were passed, apportioning on the states their respective quotas of provisions, spirits, and forage, for the ensuing campaign. The value of the several articles was estimated in specie; and assurances were given that accounts between the states should be regularly kept, and finally settled in Spanish milled dollars.

For the purpose of inducing and facilitating a compliance with these requisitions, congress also resolved, "that any state which shall have taken the necessary measures for furnishing its quota, and have given notice thereof to congress, shall be authorized to prohibit any continental quar-

CHAP. VII
1780

termaster or commissary from purchasing within its limits."

These resolutions, constituting the basis of a new system on which the future subsistence of the army was essentially to depend, were too deeply interesting not to receive the anxious attention of the Commander-in-chief. With regret, he communicated to congress the radical defects he perceived in their arrangements, with his apprehensions that this untried scheme would fail in practice.

His judgment, and the judgment of all men engaged in high and responsible situations, was decidedly in favour of conducting the war on a national rather than on a state system. But, independent of this radical objection, economy had been so much more consulted than the probable necessities of the army, that, in almost every article, the estimate had fallen far short of the demand to be reasonably expected.

The total omission to provide means for supplying occasional deficiencies from the surplus resources of any particular state, was an error of still greater magnitude. It was obvious that the demand in any state which should become the theatre of war, would be much greater than its quota; and experience had shown that the carriage of specific articles from distant places was always difficult and expensive, and sometimes impracticable. Yet no means were adopted to supply such extraordinary demand, whatever might be the resources of the country. A still more radical objection to the system was the principle, enabling any state which should take means to comply with the requisition, and should notify those means to the government of the United States, to prohibit the continental agents from making any purchases within its territory. Among the states which adopted the proposition of congress was New Jersey, in which the largest division of the army was stationed. Its legislature passed an act prohibiting the purchase of provisions within its jurisdiction by the staff of the continental line, under severe penalties; and refused to authorize its own agents to provide for any emergency however pressing. It was an additional objection to these requisitions, that they specified no periods of the year within which certain portions of the articles demanded should be raised, and consequently might be complied with, although the army should be left destitute of every necessary for a considerable part of the campaign.

These suggestions, however, with others less material to the military operations, did not receive the attention which was due to their importance. A disposition in the members of congress, growing inevitably out of the organization of the government, to consult the will of their respective states, and to prefer that will to any other object, had discovered itself at an

CHAP. VII

1780

early period, and had gained strength with time. The state of the national treasury was calculated to promote this disposition. It was empty, and could be replenished only by taxes, which congress had not the power to impose; or by new emissions of bills of credit, which the government had pledged the public faith not to make, and which would rest for their redemption only on that faith, which would be violated in the very act of their emission. Under these circumstances, it required a degree of energy seldom found, to struggle with surrounding difficulties for the preservation of a general system, and to resist the temptation to throw the nation at the feet of the states, in whom the vital principle of power, the right to levy taxes, was exclusively vested. While the continental currency preserved its value, this essential defect of the constitution was, in some measure, concealed. The facility with which money was obtained from the press, was a temporary substitute for the command of the resources of the country. But when this expedient failed, it was scarcely possible to advance a single step, but under the guidance of the respective states.

Whatever might be the future effect of this system, it was impracticable to bring it into immediate operation. The legislatures of the several states, by whom it was to be adopted, and carried into execution, were, many of them, not then in session; and were to meet at different times through the ensuing spring. It was consequently to be expected that great part of the summer would pass away before the supplies to be raised by the measure, could be brought into use. In the mean time, and until a new scheme of finance, which accompanied the requisition of specific articles, should be tried, there was no regular provision for the army. Bills to the amount of £100,000 sterling, payable at six months' sight, were drawn on Mr. Jay, and others to the same amount, on Mr. Laurens, who were empowered to negotiate loans in Europe. These bills were sold in small sums on pressing occasions; and the loan offices remained open for the purpose of borrowing from individuals.

Financial regulations.

This new scheme of finance was a second essay to substitute credit unsupported by solid funds, and resting solely on the public faith, for money.

The vast quantity of bills unavoidably emitted before the establishment of regular governments possessing sufficient energy to enforce the collection of taxes, or to provide for their redemption, and before the governments of Europe were sufficiently confident of their stability to afford them aid or credit, was assigned by congress as the principal cause of that depreciation which had taken place in the continental currency. The United States were now, they said, under different circumstances.

CHAP. VII

1780

Their independence was secure; their civil governments were established and vigorous; and the spirit of their citizens ardent for exertion. The government being thus rendered competent to the object, it was necessary to reduce the quantity of paper in circulation, and to appropriate funds that should ensure the punctual redemption of the bills.

For these purposes, the several states were required to continue to bring into the continental treasury, monthly, from February to April inclusive, their full quotas of fifteen millions of dollars. In complying with this requisition, one Spanish milled dollar was to be received in lieu of forty dollars of the paper currency.

The bills so brought in were not to be reissued, but destroyed; and other bills, not to exceed one dollar for every twenty received in discharge of taxes, were to be emitted.

These bills were to be redeemable within six years, and were to bear an interest of five *per centum per annum*, to be paid at the time of their redemption in specie, or, at the election of the holder, annually, in bills of exchange drawn by the United States on their commissioners in Europe, at four shillings and six pence sterling for each dollar. They were to be issued in ascertained proportions on the funds of the several states, with a collateral security on the part of the government, to pay the quota of any particular state, which the events of the war might render incapable of complying with its own engagements. The bills were to be deposited in the continental loan-offices of the several states, and were to be signed only as the money then in circulation should be brought in by taxes or otherwise. After being signed, six-tenths of them were to be delivered to the states on whose funds they were to be issued, and the remaining four-tenths to be retained for the use of the continent.

The operation of this scheme of finance was necessarily suspended by the same causes which suspended that for requiring specific articles. It depended on the sanction and co-operation of the several state legislatures, many of which were yet to convene.

As it would be impracticable to maintain the value of the money about to be emitted, should the states continue to issue bills of credit, they were earnestly requested to suspend future emissions, and to call the current paper out of circulation. But the time for this measure was not yet arrived, and many of the states continued the use of the press till late in the following year.

The establishment of the army for the ensuing campaign was fixed at thirty-five thousand two hundred and eleven men, and the measures for recruiting it were founded on the state system, which was become entirely predominant.

CHAP. VII
1780

The few intelligent statesmen who could combine practical good sense with patriotism, perceived the dangerous inefficacy of a system which openly abandoned the national character, and proceeded on the principle that the American confederacy was no more than an alliance of independent nations.

That great delays would be experienced, that the different parts of the plan would be acted on too unequally and too uncertainly to furnish a solid basis for military calculations, that the system would be totally deranged in its execution, were mischiefs foreseen and lamented by many, as resulting inevitably from a course of measures to which the government of the Union was under the painful necessity of submitting.

"Certain I am," said the Commander-in-chief, in a confidential letter to a member of the national legislature, "that unless congress speaks in a more decisive tone; unless they are vested with powers by the several states, competent to the great purposes of the war, or assume them as matter of right, and they and the states respectively act with more energy than they hitherto have done, our cause is lost. We can no longer drudge on in the old way. By ill-timing the adoption of measures; by delays in the execution of them, or by unwarrantable jealousies; we incur enormous expenses, and derive no benefit from them. One state will comply with a requisition from congress; another neglects to do it; a third executes it by halves; and all differ in the manner, the matter, or so much in point of time, that we are all working up hill; and, while such a system as the present one, or rather want of one, prevails, we ever shall be unable to apply our strength or resources to any advantage.

"This, my dear sir, is plain language to a member of congress; but it is the language of truth and friendship. It is the result of long thinking, close application, and strict observation. I see one head gradually changing into thirteen; I see one army branching into thirteen; and, instead of looking up to congress as the supreme controlling power of the United States, consider themselves as dependent on their respective states. In a word, I see the power of congress declining too fast for the respect which is due to them as the great representative body of America, and am fearful of the consequences."

But whatever might be his objections to the proposed system, General Washington was unremitting in his endeavours to render the plan perfect in detail, and to give to its execution all the aid which his situation and influence enabled him to afford.

The distresses of the army for food, which had found temporary relief in the particular exertions of the magistrates and people of New Jersey, soon returned; and it became once more

CHAP. VII
1780

necessary, even after the magazines had been in some degree replenished, to recur to the same persons for assistance. The supplies of forage had failed, and a great proportion of the horses had perished, or been rendered unfit for use. Neither funds nor credit were possessed for the purchase of others, and the quarter-master-general found himself unable to transport provisions from remote magazines into camp. This circumstance reduced the Commander-in-chief to the painful necessity of calling on the patriotism of private citizens, under the penalty of a military impressment, should a voluntary contribution be refused, for those means of conveyance which the government could not supply.

The want of food was not the only difficulty to be surmounted. Others of a serious nature presented themselves. The pay of an officer was reduced by the depreciation of the currency, to such a miserable pittance as to be unequal to the supply of the most moderate demands. The pay of a major general would no longer hire an express rider, and that of a captain would not purchase the shoes in which he marched. The American officers were not rich; and many of them had expended their *little all* in the service. If they had exhausted their private funds, or if they possessed none, they could rely only on the state to which they belonged for such clothing as the state might be willing or able to furnish. These supplies were so insufficient and unequal, as to produce extreme dissatisfaction. In the lines of some of the states, the officers gave notice in a body, of their determination to resign on a given day, if some decent and certain provision should not be made for them. The remonstrances of the Commander-in-chief produced an offer to serve as volunteers until their successors should be appointed; and, on the rejection of this proposition, they were with difficulty induced to remain in service.

Under these complicated embarrassments, it required all that enthusiastic patriotism which pre-eminently distinguishes the soldier of principle; all that ardent attachment to the cause of their country which originally brought them into the field, and which their sufferings could not diminish; all the influence of the Commander-in-chief, whom they almost adored; to retain in the service men who felt themselves neglected, and who believed themselves to be the objects of the jealousy of their country, rather than of its gratitude.

Among the privates, causes of disgust grew out of the very composition of the army, which increased the dissatisfaction produced by their multiplied wants.

The first effort made to enlist troops for the war had, in some degree, succeeded. While these men found themselves obliged to continue in service without compensation, and often without the common necessaries of life, they per-

CHAP. VII
1780

ceived the vacant ranks in their regiments filled up by men who were to continue only for a few months, and who received bounties for that short service, from individuals or from the states, which were of great real value, and which appeared to soldiers not acquainted with the actual state of depreciation, to be immense. They could not fail to compare situations, and to repine at engagements which deprived them of advantages which they saw in possession of others. Many were induced to contest those engagements; * many to desert a service in which they experienced such irritating inequalities; and all felt with the more poignant indignation, those distressing failures in the commissary department, which so frequently recurred.

Committee of Congress deputed to camp.

In consequence of the strong representations made to congress on these various causes of disquiet, a committee of three members repaired to camp for the purpose of consulting with the Commander-in-chief on such arrangements as the means in possession of the government would enable it to make, and the present state of the army might require. In representing the condition of the troops, they said, "That the army was unpaid for five months; that it seldom had more than six days' provisions in advance, and was on several occasions, for several successive days,

* In some instances, the civil power of the state in which such soldiers happened to be, attempted to interfere and to discharge even those belonging to the lines of other states, who asserted their right to be discharged. It was with some difficulty the general could arrest this dangerous interposition.

without meat; that the army was destitute of forage; that the medical department had neither tea, chocolate, wine, nor spirituous liquors of any kind; that every department of the army was without money, and had not even the shadow of credit left; that the patience of the soldiers, borne down by the pressure of complicated sufferings, was on the point of being exhausted."

To relieve this gloomy state of things by transfusing into it a ray of hope for the future, a resolution was passed, declaring that congress would make good to the line of the army, and to the independent corps thereof, the deficiency of their original pay, which had been occasioned by the depreciation of the continental currency; and that the money or other articles heretofore received, should be considered as advanced on account, to be comprehended in the settlement to be finally made. The benefits of this resolution were confined to those who were then in actual service, or should thereafter come into it, and who were engaged for the war or for three years.

This resolution was published in general orders, and had considerable influence on the army, but not sufficient to remove the various causes of dissatisfaction which existed, and were continually multiplying. The engagement to make good the depreciation of their pay, was an act of justice too long withheld; and no promise for the future, could supply the place of present comfortable subsistence. No hope was given

CHAP. VII 1780 that their condition, in this respect, would be improved. For a considerable time, the troops received only from one-half to one-eighth of a ration of meat; and, at length, were several days without a single pound of that necessary article.

This long course of suffering had unavoidably produced some relaxation of discipline, and had gradually soured the minds of the soldiers to such a degree, that their discontents broke out into actual mutiny.

May 25. On the 25th of May, two regiments belonging to Connecticut paraded under arms with a declared resolution to return home, or to obtain subsistence at the point of the bayonet. The soldiers of the other regiments, though not actually joining the mutineers, showed no disposition to suppress the mutiny. By great exertions on the part of the officers, aided by the appearance of a neighbouring brigade of Pennsylvania, then commanded by Colonel Stewart, the leaders were secured, and the two regiments brought back to their duty. Some sentiments, however, were disclosed by the soldiers, in answer to the remonstrances of their officers, of a serious and alarming nature. Their pay was now five months in arrear, and the depreciation of the money, they said, was such, that it would be worth nothing when received. When reminded of the late resolution of congress for making good the loss sustained by depreciation, of the reputation acquired by their past good conduct,

1780

and of the value of the object for which they were contending; they answered that their sufferings were too great to be longer supported; that they wanted present relief; and must have some present substantial recompense for their services. A paper was found in the brigade, which appeared to have been brought by some emissary from New York, stimulating the troops to the abandonment of the cause in which they were engaged.

The discontents of the army, and the complaints excited in the country by the frequent requisitions on the people of New Jersey, had been communicated, with such exaggeration, to the officer commanding in New York, as to induce the opinion that the American soldiers were ready to desert their standards; and the people of New Jersey to change their government. To countenance these dispositions, General Knyphausen embarked at Staten Island, and landed in the night with about five thousand men at Elizabethtown Point, in New Jersey. Early next morning he marched towards Springfield, by the way of Connecticut Farms, but soon perceived that the real temper, both of the country and the army, had been misunderstood.

June 6.

General Knyphausen enters Jersey.

On the appearance of the enemy, the militia assembled with alacrity, and aided the small patrolling parties of continental troops in harassing him on his march from Elizabethtown to the Connecticut Farms, a distance of five or

CHAP. VII
1780

six miles, where a halt was made. In a spirit of revenge, unworthy the general of an army, more in the character of Tryon who was present, than of Knyphausen who commanded, this settlement was reduced to ashes.*

From the Farms, Knyphausen proceeded to Springfield. The Jersey brigade, commanded by General Maxwell, and the militia of the adjacent country, took an advantageous position at that place, and seemed determined to defend it. Knyphausen halted in its neighbourhood, and remained on his ground until night.

Having received intelligence of this movement, General Washington put his army in motion early in the same morning that Knyphausen marched from Elizabethtown Point, and advanced to the Short Hills, in the rear of Springfield, while the British were in the neighbourhood of that place. Dispositions were made for an engagement the next morning, but Knyphausen retired in the night to the place of his disembarkation.

---

* This circumstance would scarcely have deserved notice had it not been accompanied by one of those melancholy events, which even war does not authorize, and which made, at the time, a very deep impression.

Mrs. Caldwell, the wife of the clergyman of the village, had been induced to remain in her house, under the persuasion that her presence might protect it from pillage, and that her person could not be endangered, as Colonel Dayton who commanded the militia determined not to stop in the settlement. While sitting in the midst of her children, with a sucking infant in her arms, a soldier came up to the window and discharged his musket at her. She received the ball in her bosom, and instantly expired.

General Washington continued on the hills near Springfield, too weak to hazard an engagement, but on ground chosen by himself. His continental troops did not exceed three thousand men. A return of the whole army under his immediate command, made on the 3d of June, exhibited in the column, of present, fit for duty, only three thousand seven hundred and sixty, rank and file. So reduced was that force on which America relied for independence. "You but too well know," said General Washington in a letter to a friend, giving an account of this incursion, "and will regret with me the cause which justifies this insulting manœuvre on the part of the enemy. It deeply affects the honour of the states, a vindication of which could not be attempted in our present circumstances, without most intimately hazarding their security; at least so far as it may depend on the preservation of the army. Their character, their interest, their all that is dear, call upon them in the most pressing manner, to place the army immediately on a respectable footing."

The long continuance of Knyphausen at Elizabethtown, strengthened a suspicion that Sir Henry Clinton was about to return from South Carolina, and intended, without disembarking his troops, to proceed up the Hudson to West Point; and that the movement into Jersey was a feint designed to cover the real object.

CHAP. VII

1780

The letters of the Commander-in-chief, addressed about this period, to those who might be supposed to possess influence in the government of the Union, or in those of the states, exhibit his conjectures respecting the designs of his adversary, as well as his apprehensions from the condition of his own army. To the committee of congress, in camp, he observed, "General Knyphausen still continues in the Jerseys with all the force which can be spared from New York, a force greatly superior to ours. Should Sir Henry join him, their superiority will be decided, and equal to almost any thing they may think proper to attempt. The enemy, it is true, are at this time inactive; but their continuance in their present position proves that they have some project of importance in contemplation. Perhaps they are only waiting until the militia grow tired and return home, (which they are doing every hour,) to prosecute their designs with the less opposition. This would be a critical moment for us. Perhaps they are waiting the arrival of Sir Henry Clinton, either to push up the North River against the Highland posts, or to bend their whole force against this army. In either case, the most disastrous consequences are to be apprehended. You, who are well acquainted with our situation, need no arguments to evince the danger.

"The militia of this state have run to arms, and behaved with an ardour and spirit of which

CHAP. VII

1780

there are few examples. But perseverance, in enduring the rigours of military service, is not to be expected from those who are not by profession obliged to it. The reverse of this opinion has been a great misfortune in our affairs, and it is high time we should recover from an error of so pernicious a nature. We must absolutely have a force of a different composition, or we must relinquish the contest. In a few days, we may expect to rely almost entirely on our continental force, and this, from your own observation, is totally inadequate to our safety. The exigency calls loudly on the states to carry all the recommendations of the committee into the most vigorous and immediate execution; but more particularly that for completing our batteries by a draught with all possible expedition."

June 18.

Sir Henry Clinton returns to New York.

In this precise state of things, he received intelligence of the return of Sir Henry Clinton from the conquest of South Carolina.

The regular force in New York and its dependencies was now estimated at twelve thousand men, great part of whom might be drawn into the field for any particular purpose, because Sir Henry Clinton could command about four thousand militia and refugees for garrison duty.

In communicating to congress the appearance of the British fleet off the Hook, General Washington observed, "a very alarming scene may shortly open, and it will be happy for us if we

CHAP. VII 1780

shall be able to steer clear of some serious misfortune in this quarter. I hope the period has not yet arrived, which will convince the different states by fatal experience, that some of them have mistaken the true situation of this country. I flatter myself, however, that we may still retrieve our affairs if we have but a just sense of them, and are actuated by a spirit of liberal policy and exertion equal to the emergency. Could we once see this spirit generally prevailing, I should not despair of a prosperous issue of the campaign. But there is no time to be lost. The danger is imminent and pressing; the obstacles to be surmounted are great and numerous; and our efforts must be instant, unreserved, and universal."

On the arrival of Sir Henry Clinton, the design of acting offensively in the Jerseys was resumed; but, to divide the American army, demonstrations were made of an intention to seize West Point. To be in readiness for either object, General Greene was left at Springfield with two brigades of continental troops, and with the Jersey militia; while, with the greater part of his army, General Washington proceeded slowly towards Pompton, watching attentively the movements of the British, and apparently unwilling to separate himself too far from Greene. He had not marched farther than Rockaway, eleven miles beyond Morristown, when the British army advanced from

1780

Elizabethtown towards Springfield in great force. General Washington detached a brigade to hang on their right flank, and returned with the residue of his army five or six miles, in order to be in a situation to support Greene.

June.

Early in the morning of the 23d, the British army moved in two columns, with great rapidity, towards Springfield. Major Lee was advanced on the Vauxhall road, which was taken by the right column; and Colonel Dayton on the direct road, which was taken by the left. Both these corps made every possible exertion to check the advancing enemy, while General Greene concentrated his little army at Springfield. Scarcely had he made his dispositions, when the British front appeared, and a cannonade commenced between their van and the American artillery which defended a bridge over Rahway, a small river running east of the town, which was guarded by Colonel Angel with less than two hundred men. Colonel Shreve was posted at a second bridge, also over a branch of the Rahway, in order to cover the retreat of Angel from the first. Major Lee with his dragoons and the piquets under Captain Walker, supported by Colonel Ogden, was directed to defend a bridge on the Vauxhall road. The residue of the continental troops were drawn up on high ground, in the rear of the town, with the militia on their flanks.

Skirmish at Springfield.

CHAP. VII
1780

The right column of the British advanced on Lee, who disputed the passage of the bridge until a considerable body of the enemy forded the river above him, and gained the point of a hill which endangered his position. At this instant, their left attacked Colonel Angel, who defended himself with persevering gallantry. The conflict was sharp, and was maintained for about half an hour, when, compelled by superior numbers to give way, he retired in good order, and brought off his wounded. His retreat was covered by Colonel Shreve, who, after Angel had passed him, was ordered by General Greene to join his brigade. The English then took possession of the town and reduced it to ashes.

The obstinate resistance which had been encountered; the gallantry and discipline displayed by the continental troops who had been engaged; the strength of Greene's position; the firm countenance maintained by his troops, small detachments of whom kept up a continual skirmishing with a view to save a part of the town; all contributed to deter Sir Henry Clinton from a farther prosecution of his original plan. He withdrew that afternoon to Elizabethtown; and, in the following night, passed over to Staten Island. It is probable that the caution manifested during this expedition is to be ascribed to the intelligence that a formidable fleet and army from France was daily expected on the coast.

When the Marquis de Lafayette obtained permission to visit his native country, he retained, with his rank in the American army, that zeal for the interests of the United States, which the affectionate attentions he had received, and the enthusiasm of a soldier in the cause of those for whom he had made his first campaigns, were calculated to inspire in a young and generous mind, in favour of an infant people, struggling for liberty and self-government with the hereditary rival of his nation.

He was received at the court of Versailles with every mark of favour and distinction;* and all his influence was employed in impressing on the cabinet, the importance and policy of granting succours to the United States.

Lafayette brings intelligence of aid from France.

Having succeeded in this favourite object, and finding no probability of active employment on the continent of Europe, he obtained permission to return to America. He arrived late in April at Boston, and hastened to head quarters; whence he proceeded to the seat of Government with the information that his most Christian Majesty had consented to employ a considerable land and naval armament in the United States, for the ensuing campaign. This

* After he had visited the ministers, an arrest of eight days, during which he resided with his relation the Marshal de Noailles, was imposed on him for the sake of form and in honour of the royal authority, which he had disregarded by proceeding to America. After the expiration of this term he presented himself to the King, who graciously said he pardoned his disobedience, in consideration of his good conduct and of his services.—*Letter from Gen. Lafayette.*

CHAP. VII

1780

Exertions of Congress and of the Commander-in-chief to strengthen the army.

intelligence gave a new impulse both to congress and the state legislatures. The states from New Hampshire to Virginia inclusive were required to pay, within thirty days, ten millions of dollars, part of their quotas which became due on the first of March; and specie bills to the amount of fifty thousand dollars were drawn on Messieurs Franklin and Jay. These sums were sacredly appropriated to the objects of bringing the army into the field, and forwarding their supplies.

The defects in the requisition system, which had been suggested by General Washington, were corrected; and the committee in camp, at the head of which was the late General Schuyler, was empowered, at the request of the Commander-in-chief, to take such measures as were in the power of congress, for drawing out the resources of the nation.

To give effect to these resolutions, the several state legislatures from New Hampshire to Virginia inclusive, were requested to invest the Executives, or some other persons, with powers sufficiently ample to comply with such applications as might be made to them by the committee in camp, and a circular letter was addressed to the state governments, urging them to second the efforts of Congress.

Letters equally stimulating were written by the committee from camp; and the well earned influence of the Commander-in-chief was also employed to induce an exertion proportioned to the crisis. In addition to those incentives which might operate on ardent minds, he endeavoured, by a temperate review of the situation and resources of the belligerent powers, to convince the judgment that America would have real cause to fear the issue of the contest, should she neglect to improve the advantage to be afforded by the succours expected from France.*

Under the impressions produced by these representations, the state legislatures, generally, passed the laws which were required; but the energy displayed in their passage was not maintained in their execution. In general, the assemblies followed the example of congress, and apportioned on the several counties or towns within the state, the quota to be furnished by each. This division of the state was again to be subdivided into classes, each of which was to furnish a man by contributions or taxes imposed upon itself.

Tardy proceedings of the states.

These operations were slow and unproductive.

It was not on the state sovereignties only that beneficial effects were produced by a candid statement of public affairs, several patriotic individuals contributed largely from their private funds to the aid of the public. The merchants, and other citizens of Philadelphia, with a zeal guided by that sound discretion which turns expenditure to the best account, established a bank,

* See note No. III. at the end of the volume.

CHAP. VII
1780

for the support of which they subscribed £315,000, Pennsylvania money, to be paid, if required, in specie, the principal object of which was to supply the army with provisions and rum. By the plan of this bank, its members were to derive no emolument whatever from the institution. For advancing their credit and their money, they required only that congress should pledge the faith of the Union to reimburse the costs and charges of the transaction in a reasonable time, and should give such assistance to its execution as might be in their power.

The ladies of Philadelphia too gave a splendid example of patriotism, by large donations for the immediate relief of the suffering army. This example was extensively followed; * but it is not by the contributions of the generous that a war can or ought to be maintained. The purse of the nation alone can supply the expenditures

* This instance of patriotism on the part of our fair and amiable countrywomen, is far from being single. Their conduct throughout the war was uniform. They shared with cheerfulness and gaiety, the privations and sufferings to which the distress of the times exposed their country. In every stage of this severe trial, they displayed virtues which have not been always attributed to their sex, but which it is believed they will, on every occasion calculated to unfold them, be found to possess. With a ready acquiescence, with a firmness always cheerful, and a constancy never lamenting the sacrifices which were made, they not only yielded up all the elegancies, delicacies, and even conveniences to be furnished by wealth and commerce, relying on their farms and on domestic industry for every article of food and raiment, but, consenting to share the produce of their own labour, they gave up without regret, a considerable portion of the covering designed for their own families, to supply the wants of the distressed soldiers; and heroically suppressed the involuntary sigh which the departure of their brothers, their sons, and their husbands, for the camp, rended from their bosoms.

of a nation; and, when all are interested in a contest, all ought to contribute to its support. Taxes, and taxes only, can furnish for the prosecution of a national war, means which are just in themselves, or competent to the object. Notwithstanding these donations, the distresses of the army, for clothing especially, still continued; and were the more severely felt when a co-operation with French troops was expected. So late as the 20th of June, General Washington informed congress, that he still laboured under the painful and humiliating embarrassment of having no shirts for the soldiers, many of whom were destitute of that necessary article. "For the troops to be without clothing at any time," he added, "is highly injurious to the service, and distressing to our feelings; but the want will be more peculiarly mortifying when they come to act with those of our allies. If it be possible, I have no doubt, immediate measures will be taken to relieve their distress.

"It is also most sincerely wished, that there could be some supplies of clothing furnished to the officers. There are a great many whose condition is still miserable. This is, in some instances, the case with the whole lines of the states. It would be well for their own sakes, and for the public good, if they could be furnished. They will not be able, when our friends come to co-operate with us, to go on a common routine

CHAP. VII
1780

of duty; and if they should, they must, from their appearance, be held in low estimation."

This picture presents in strong colours, the real patriotism of the American army. One heroic effort, though it may dazzle the mind with its splendour, is an exertion most men are capable of making; but continued patient suffering and unremitting perseverance, in a service promising no personal emolument, and exposing the officer unceasingly, not only to wants of every kind, but to those circumstances of humiliation which seem to degrade him in the eyes of others, demonstrate a fortitude of mind, a strength of virtue, and a firmness of principle, which ought never to be forgotten.

As the several legislative acts for bringing the army into the field, did not pass until the months of June and July, General Washington remained uninformed of the force on which he might rely, and was consequently unable to form any certain plan of operations.

This suspense was the more cruelly embarrassing, as, in the event of an attempt upon New York, it was of the utmost importance that the French fleet should, on its arrival, take possession of the harbour, which was then weakly defended. But, should this measure be followed by a failure to furnish the requisite support, it would not only be ineffectual; but, in a very possible state of things, might sacrifice the fleet itself.

Should it be ascertained that the states were either unable or unwilling to make the exertions necessary for the siege of New York, other objects presented themselves against which the allied arms might be turned to advantage. To avoid the disgrace and danger of attempting what could not be effected, and the reproach of neglecting any attainable object, were equally desirable, and equally required a correct knowledge of the measures which would be taken by the states.

In a letter to congress communicating his anxiety on this interesting subject, and his total want of information respecting it, General Washington observed, "The season is come when we have every reason to expect the arrival of the fleet, and yet, for want of this point of primary consequence, it is impossible for me to form a system of co-operation. I have no basis to act upon; and, of course, were this generous succour of our ally now to arrive, I should find myself in the most awkward, embarrassing, and painful situation. The general and the admiral, from the relation in which I stand, as soon as they approach our coast, will require of me a plan of the measures to be pursued, and there ought of right to be one prepared; but circumstanced as I am, I can not even give them conjectures. From these considerations, I have suggested to the committee, by a letter I had the honour of addressing them yesterday, the

CHAP. VII indispensable necessity of their writing again 1780 to the states, urging them to give immediate and precise information of the measures they have taken and of the result. The interest of the states, the honour and reputation of our councils, the justice and gratitude due to our allies, all require that I should, without delay, be enabled to ascertain and inform them, what we can or can not undertake. There is a point which ought now to be determined, on the success of which all our future operations may depend, on which, for want of knowing our prospects, I can make no decision. For fear of involving the fleet and army of our allies in circumstances which would expose them, if not seconded by us, to material inconvenience and hazard, I shall be compelled to suspend it, and the delay may be fatal to our hopes."

The tardy proceedings of the states were not less perplexing to congress than to the Commander-in-chief. To the minister of his most Christian Majesty, who had in the preceding January communicated the probability of receiving succour from France, that body, without calculating accurately the means of complying with its engagements, had pledged itself unequivocally for effectual co-operation. The minister was assured, that the United States had expectations on which they could rely with confidence, of bringing into the field, for the next campaign, an army of twenty-five thousand men; and that such numbers of militia might be added to this continental force, as would render it competent to any enterprise against the posts occupied by the British within the United States.

Assurances were also given that ample supplies of provisions for the combined armies should be laid up in magazines under the direction of congress. The French minister addressed congress on this subject about the time that General Washington expressed so strongly, the necessity of knowing with certainty, on what reinforcements he was to calculate.

Thus pressed by their general and their ally, congress renewed their urgent requisitions on the states, and desired the several governments to correspond weekly with the committee at head quarters, on the progress made in complying with them.

In the mean time, General Washington meditated unceasingly on the course to be pursued in the various contingencies which might happen; and endeavoured to prepare for any plan of operations which circumstances might render adviseable. The arrival of Sir Henry Clinton diminished the variety of aspects in which the relative situation of the two armies was to be contemplated, and rendered the success of an attempt on New York more doubtful. It was now thought adviseable that the armament from France, instead of sailing directly to

CHAP. VII

1780

the Hook, should proceed in the first instance to Rhode Island; where, after disembarking the troops, and providing for the sick, it might wait until a definitive plan of operations should be concerted.

July 13.

On the 13th of July, while the result of the measures adopted by the several states remained uncertain, the French fleet entered the harbour of Newport, and letters were soon afterwards received from the Count de Rochambeau and the Chevalier Tunay, the officers commanding the land and naval forces, transmitting to General Washington an account of their arrival, of their strength, their expectations, and their orders.

Arrival of a French armament in Rhode Island.

The troops designed to serve in the United States had assembled, early in the year, at Brest; but the transports at that place having been chiefly employed for an armament destined for the West Indies; and the ports from which it had been intended to draw others, being blockaded, only the first division, consisting of five thousand men, had arrived at Newport; but letters from France contained assurances that the second division of the army might soon be expected.

To obviate those difficulties which had occurred on former occasions respecting rank, the orders given to Lieutenant General Count de Rochambeau, which were inclosed in his first letter, placed him entirely under the command of General Washington. The French troops were to be considered as auxiliaries, and were, according to the usages of war, to cede the post of honour to the Americans.*

Convinced that cordial harmony between the allied forces was essential to their success, both generals cultivated carefully the friendly dispositions felt by the troops towards each other. Warm professions of reciprocal respect, esteem, and confidence, were interchanged between them; and each endeavoured to impress on the other, and on all the military and civil departments, the conviction that the two nations, and two armies, were united by the ties of interest and affection. On this occasion, General Washington recommended to his officers, as a symbol of friendship and affection for their allies, to engraft on the American cockade, which was black, a white relief, that being the colour of the French cockade.

Late as was the arrival of the French troops, they found the Americans unprepared for active and offensive operations. Not even at that time were the numbers ascertained which would be furnished by the states. Yet it was necessary for General Washington to communicate a plan of the campaign to the Count de Rochambeau.

The season was already so far advanced that preparations for the operations contemplated eventually, on the arrival of the second division

* These orders were given at the instance of General Lafayette.—*Correspondence with General Lafayette.*

CHAP. VII
1780

of the French fleet, must be immediately made, or there would not be time, though every circumstance should prove favourable, to execute the design against New York. Such a state of things so ill comported with the engagements of congress, and with the interests of the nation, that, trusting to his being enabled, by the measures already taken by the states, to comply with what was incumbent on him to perform, he determined to hazard much rather than forego the advantages to be derived from the aids afforded by France. In communicating this resolution to congress, he said—"Pressed on all sides by a choice of difficulties in a moment which required decision, I have adopted that line of conduct which comported with the dignity and faith of congress, the reputation of these states, and the honour of our arms. I have sent on definitive proposals of co-operation to the French general and admiral. Neither the period of the season, nor a regard to decency, would permit delay. The die is cast, and it remains with the states either to fulfil their engagements, preserve their credit, and support their independence, or to involve us in disgrace and defeat. Notwithstanding the failures pointed out by the committee, I shall proceed on the supposition that they will, ultimately, consult their own interest and honour and not suffer us to fail for the want of means which it is evidently in their power to afford. What has been done, and is doing, by

Beverly Robinson Mansion at West Point

Benedict Arnold made this house his headquarters while in command of the fort and garrison there. It was here that Washington came to breakfast with Arnold, one September morning in 1780 and made the discovery that his host had turned traitor and was conspiring to surrender West Point to the British.

some of the states, confirms the opinion I have entertained of sufficient resources in the country. Of the disposition of the people to submit to any arrangement for bringing them forth, I see no reasonable ground to doubt. If we fail for want of proper exertions in any of the governments, I trust the responsibility will fall where it ought; and that I shall stand justified to congress, my country, and the world."

A decisive naval superiority, however, was considered as the basis of any enterprise to be undertaken by the allied arms. This naval superiority being assumed, the outlines of the plan were drawn, and the 5th of August was named as the day on which the French troops should re-embark, and the American army assemble at Morrissania.

This plan was committed to Major General the Marquis de la Fayette, who was authorized to explain the situation of the American army, and the views of the General, to the Count de Rochambeau. It was to be considered as preliminary to any operation—that the fleet and army of France should continue their aid until the enterprise should succeed, or be abandoned by mutual consent.

The Chevalier de Tunay did not long maintain his superiority at sea. Three days after he reached Newport, Admiral Greaves arrived with six ships of the line, and transferred it to the British. On his appearance off the Hook, Ar-

CHAP. VII 1780

buthnot passed the bar with four ships of the line; and hearing that De Tunay had reached Rhode Island, proceeded thither, and cruised off the harbour. The Count de Rochambeau had been put into possession of all the forts and batteries about Newport, and the fleet had been moved in a line so as to co-operate with the land forces. This position appearing too formidable to be attempted by the fleet alone, Arbuthnot continued to cruise off Block Island.

As the commanders of the allied forces still cherished the hope of acquiring a superiority at sea, the design on New York was only suspended. This hope was strengthened by intelligence that the Count de Guichen had been joined in the West Indies by a powerful Spanish armament. The Chevalier de Tunay had despatched a packet to inform him that he was blocked up by a superior force, and to solicit such reinforcements as the situation of the Count might enable him to spare. Relying on the success of this application, and on the arrival of the second division of the squadron from Brest, the American general impatiently expected the moment when De Tunay would be enabled to act offensively.

In this crisis of affairs, a derangement took place in a most important department, which threatened to disconcert the whole plan of operations, though every other circumstance should prove favourable.

The immense expenditure of the quartermaster's department—the inadequacy of the funds with which it was supplied—the reciprocal disgusts and complaints produced by these causes, had determined congress to make still another radical change in the system. This subject had been taken up early in the winter; but such were the delays inseparable from the proceedings of the government, that the report of the committee was not made until the month of March, nor finally decided on until the middle of July.

This subject was too interesting to the army, and to the important operations meditated for the campaign, not to engage the anxious attention of the Commander-in-chief. At his request, the quartermaster general, while the army lay in winter quarters, repaired to Philadelphia for the purpose of giving congress all the information he possessed. He proposed to withdraw the management of the department almost entirely from the civil government, and to place it under the control of the person who should be at its head, subject only to the direction of the Commander-in-chief.

The views of congress were entirely different. While the subject remained suspended before that body, it was taken up by the committee of co-operation at head quarters, where the combined experience and talents of Generals Washington, Schuyler, and Greene, were employed in digesting a system adapted to the actual situa-

CHAP. VII
1780

tion of the United States, which was recommended to congress. To give the more weight to his opinion by showing its disinterestedness, General Greene offered to continue in the discharge of the duties assigned to him, without any other extra emolument than his family expenses. This plan, whatever might have been its details, was, in its general outlines, unacceptable to congress. A system was, at length, completed by that body, which General Greene believed to be incapable of execution. Resolving not to take upon himself the responsibility of measures the issue of which must be calamitous and disgraceful, he determined to withdraw from a station in which he despaired of being useful.

Apprehending the worst consequences from his resignation in so critical a moment, General Washington pressed him to suspend this decisive step, until the effect of an application from himself and from the committee of co-operation should be known. Their representations produced no effect. The resolution to make this bold experiment was unalterable. General Greene's resignation was accepted; and the letter conveying it excited so much irritation, that a design was intimated of suspending his command in the line of the army. But these impressions soon wore off, and the resentment of the moment subsided. Colonel Pickering, who succeeded General Greene, possessed, in an eminent degree, those qualities which fitted him to combat and subdue the difficulties of his department. To great energy of mind and body, he added a long experience in the affairs of the continent, with an ardent zeal for its interests; and General Greene himself, with several of the former officers, at the request of the Commander-in-chief, continued for some time after their resignation, to render all the services in their power; but there was a defect of means, for which neither talents nor exertion could compensate.

In the commissary department the same distress was experienced. General Washington was driven to the necessity of emptying the magazines at West Point, and of foraging on a people whose means of subsisting themselves were already nearly exhausted by the armies on both sides. The inadequate supplies drawn from these sources afforded but a short relief; and, once more, at a time when the public imagination was contemplating brilliant plans, the execution of which required steady courage with persevering labour, and consequently ample magazines, the army was frequently reduced to the last extremity by the want of food.

So great were the embarrassments produced by the difficulty of procuring subsistence that, although the second division of the fleet from Brest was daily expected, General Washington found it necessary to countermand the orders under which the militia were marching to camp.

CHAP. VII

1780

Such was the state of preparation for the campaign, when intelligence was brought by the Alliance frigate that the port of Brest was blockaded. In the hope, however, that the combined fleets of France and Spain would be able to raise the blockade, General Washington adhered steadily to his purpose respecting New York, and continued his exertions to provide the means for its execution. The details of the plan of co-operation continued to be the subject of a correspondence with the Count de Rochambeau, and the Chevalier de Tunay; and, at length, a personal interview was agreed upon, to take place on the 21st of September, at Hartford, in Connecticut.

In this interview, ulterior eventual measures, as well as an explicit and detailed arrangement for acting against New York, were the subjects of consideration. No one of the plans, however, then concerted for the present campaign, was carried into execution. All, except an invasion of Canada, depended on a superiority at sea, which was soon rendered almost hopeless by certain information that the Count de Guichen had sailed for Europe.

Enterprise against New York relinquished.

Not long after receiving this information, Admiral Rodney arrived at New York with eleven ships of the line and four frigates. This reinforcement not only disconcerted all the plans of the allies, but put it in the power of the Brit-

Naval superiority of the British.

1780

ish to prosecute in security their designs in the south.

Plans for the campaign abandoned.

It may well be supposed that the Commander-in-chief did not relinquish, without infinite chagrin, the sanguine expectations he had formed of rendering this summer decisive of the war. Never before had he indulged so strongly the hope of happily terminating the contest. In a letter to an intimate friend, this chagrin was thus expressed. "We are now drawing to a close an inactive campaign, the beginning of which appeared pregnant with events of a very favourable complexion. I hoped, but I hoped in vain, that a prospect was opening which would enable me to fix a period to my military pursuits, and restore me to domestic life. The favourable disposition of Spain, the promised succour from France, the combined force in the West Indies, the declaration of Russia, (acceded to by other powers of Europe, humiliating the naval pride and power of Great Britain) the superiority of France and Spain by sea in Europe, the Irish claims and English disturbances, formed in the aggregate an opinion in my breast, (which is not very susceptible of peaceful dreams) that the hour of deliverance was not far distant; for that, however unwilling Great Britain might be to yield the point, it would not be in her power to continue the contest. But alas! these prospects, flattering as they were, have proved delusive; and I see nothing before us but accumulating dis-

CHAP. VII 1780

tress. We have been half of our time without provisions, and are likely to continue so. We have no magazines, nor money to form them. We have lived upon expedients until we can live no longer. In a word, the history of the war is a history of false hopes and temporary devices, instead of system and economy. It is in vain, however, to look back, nor is it our business to do so. Our case is not desperate, if virtue exists in the people, and there is wisdom among our rulers. But to suppose that this great revolution can be accomplished by a temporary army; that this army will be subsisted by state supplies; and that taxation alone is adequate to our wants, is in my opinion absurd, and as unreasonable as to expect an inversion of the order of nature to accommodate itself to our views. If it were necessary, it could be easily proved to any person of a moderate understanding, that an annual army, or any army raised on the spur of the occasion, besides being unqualified for the end designed, is, in various ways that could be enumerated, ten times more expensive than a permanent body of men under good organization and military discipline; which never was, nor will be the case with raw troops. A thousand arguments, resulting from experience and the nature of things, might also be adduced to prove that the army, if it is to depend upon state supplies, must disband or starve, and that taxation alone (especially at this late hour) can not furnish the means to carry on the war. Is it not time to retract from error, and benefit by experience? Or do we want farther proof of the ruinous system we have pertinaciously adhered to."

CHAPTER VIII.

Treason and escape of Arnold....Trial and execution of Major André....Precautions for the security of West Point....Letter of General Washington on American affairs....Proceedings of congress respecting the army ....Major Talmadge destroys the British stores at Coram....The army retires into winter quarters....Irruption of Major Carlton into New York....European transactions.

1780 WHILE the public mind was anticipating great events from the combined arms of France and America, treason lay concealed in the American camp, and was plotting the ruin of the American cause.

The great services and military talents of General Arnold, his courage in battle, and patient fortitude under excessive hardships, had secured to him a high place in the opinion of the army and of his country.

Not having sufficiently recovered from the wounds received before Quebec and at Saratoga to be fit for active service, and having large accounts to settle with the government which required leisure, he was, on the evacuation of Philadelphia in 1778, appointed to the command in that place.

Unfortunately, that strength of principle and correctness of judgment, which might enable him to resist the various seductions to which his fame and rank exposed him in the metropolis of the

Union, were not associated with the firmness which he had displayed in the field, and in the most adverse circumstances. Yielding to the temptations of a false pride, and forgetting that he did not possess the resources of private fortune, he indulged in the pleasures of a sumptuous table and expensive equipage, and soon swelled his debts to an amount which it was impossible to discharge. Unmindful of his military character, he engaged in speculations which were unfortunate; and with the hope of immense profit, took shares in privateers which were unsuccessful. His claims against the United States were great, and he looked to them for the means of extricating himself from the embarrassments in which his indiscretions had involved him; but the commissioners to whom his accounts were referred for settlement, had reduced them considerably; and, on his appeal from their decision to congress, a committee reported that the sum allowed by the commissioners was more than he was entitled to receive.

He was charged with various acts of extortion on the citizens of Philadelphia, and with peculating on the funds of the continent. Not the less soured by these multiplied causes of irritation, from the reflection that they were attributable to his own follies and vices, he gave full scope to his resentments, and indulged himself in expressions of angry reproach against, what he termed, the ingratitude of his country, which pro-

CHAP. VIII 1780

voked those around him, and gave great offence to congress. Having become peculiarly odious to the government of Pennsylvania, the Executive of that state exhibited formal charges against him to congress, who directed that he should be arrested and brought before a court martial. His trial was concluded late in January, 1779, and he was sentenced to be reprimanded by the Commander-in-chief. This sentence was approved by congress and carried into execution.

From the time the sentence against him was approved, if not sooner, his proud unprincipled spirit revolted from the cause of his country, and determined him to seek an occasion to make the objects of his resentment, the victims of his vengeance. Turning his eyes on West Point as an acquisition which would give value to treason, and inflict a mortal wound on his former friends, he sought the command of that fortress for the purpose of gratifying both his avarice and his hate. *

To New York, the safety of West Point was peculiarly interesting; and, in that state, the reputation of Arnold was particularly high. To its delegation he addressed himself; and one of

* The author is informed by General Lafayette that Arnold, while commanding at West Point, endeavoured to obtain from General Washington the names of his secret emissaries in New York, and his means of communicating with them. He pressed Lafayette, who had also his private intelligencers, for the same information. His applications were of course unsuccessful. It cannot be doubted that his object was to commit the additional crime of betraying them to Sir Henry Clinton.

its members had written a letter to General Washington, suggesting doubts respecting the military character of Howe, to whom its defence was then entrusted, and recommending Arnold for that service. This request was not forgotten. Some short time afterwards, General Schuyler mentioned to the Commander-in-chief a letter he had received from Arnold intimating his wish to join the army, but stating his inability, in consequence of his wounds, to perform the active duties of the field. General Washington observed that, as there was a prospect of a vigorous campaign, he should be gratified with the aid of General Arnold. That so soon as the operations against New York should commence, he designed to draw his whole force into the field, leaving even West Point to the care of invalids and a small garrison of militia. Recollecting however the former application of a member of congress respecting this post, he added, that "if, with this previous information, that situation would be more agreeable to him than a command in the field, his wishes should certainly be indulged."

This conversation being communicated to Arnold, he caught eagerly at the proposition, though without openly discovering any solicitude on the subject; and, in the beginning of August, repaired to camp, where he renewed the solicitations which had before been made indirectly.

CHAP. VIII

1780

At this juncture, Sir Henry Clinton embarked on an expedition he meditated against Rhode Island, and General Washington was advancing on New York. He offered Arnold the left wing of the army, which that officer declined under the pretexts mentioned in his letter to General Schuyler.

Incapable of suspecting a man who had given such distinguished proofs of courage and patriotism, the Commander-in-chief was neither alarmed at his refusal to embrace so splendid an opportunity of recovering the favour of his countrymen, nor at the embarrassment accompanying that refusal. Pressing the subject no farther, he assented to the request which had been made, and invested Arnold with the command of West Point. Previous to his soliciting this station, he had, in a letter to Colonel Robinson, signified his change of principles, and his wish to restore himself to the favour of his Prince by some signal proof of his repentance. This letter opened the way to a correspondence with Sir Henry Clinton, the immediate object of which, after obtaining the appointment he had solicited, was to concert the means of delivering the important post he commanded to the British general.

Major John André, an aid-de-camp of Sir Henry Clinton, and adjutant general of the British army, was selected as the person to whom the maturing of Arnold's treason, and the ar-

1780

rangements for its execution should be entrusted. A correspondence was carried on between them under a mercantile disguise, in the feigned names of Gustavus and Anderson; and, at length, to facilitate their communications, the Vulture sloop of war moved up the North River, and took a station convenient for the purpose, but not so near as to excite suspicion.

Treason and escape of Arnold.

The time when General Washington met the Count de Rochambeau at Hartford was selected for the final adjustment of the plan; and, as a personal interview was deemed necessary, Major André came up the river, and went on board the Vulture. The house of a Mr. Smith, without the American posts, was appointed for the interview; and to that place both parties repaired in the night—André being brought under a pass for John Anderson, in a boat despatched from the shore. While the conference was yet unfinished, day light approached; and, to avoid discovery, Arnold proposed that André should remain concealed until the succeeding night. He is understood to have refused peremptorily to be carried within the American posts; but the promise to respect this objection was not observed. They continued together the succeeding day; and when, in the following night, his return to the Vulture was proposed, the boatmen refused to carry him because she had shifted her station during the day, in consequence of a gun which was moved to the shore without the knowledge

CHAP. VIII 1780

of Arnold, and brought to bear upon her. This embarrassing circumstance reduced him to the necessity of endeavouring to reach New York by land. To accomplish this purpose, he reluctantly yielded to the urgent representations of Arnold; and, laying aside his regimentals, which he had hitherto worn under a surtout, put on a plain suit of clothes, and received a pass from General Arnold, authorizing him, under the name of John Anderson, to proceed on the public service to the White Plains, or lower if he thought proper.

With this permit, he had passed all the guards and posts on the road unsuspected, and was proceeding to New York in perfect security, when one of three militia men who were employed between the lines of the two armies, springing suddenly from his covert into the road, seized the reins of his bridle, and stopped his horse. Losing his accustomed self-possession, Major André, instead of producing the pass * from General Arnold, asked the man hastily where he belonged? He replied "to below;" a term implying that he was from New York. "And so," said André, not suspecting deception, "am I." He then declared himself to be a British officer on urgent business, and begged that he might not be detained. The ap-

* Mr. Johnson says he did produce it; but that, on being surprised, he had thrust a paper containing a plan of the route in his boot, which, having been perceived, was demanded, and led to his discovery.

Where Washington Stayed During André's Trial

In this brick house at Tappan, Rockland County, New York, the American Commander-in-Chief, during September, 1780, awaited the result of the trial of Major John André, who conspired with Benedict Arnold for the betrayal of West Point to the British. Fourteen American officers sat in judgment on André and ordered his execution on October 2, 1780. In Tappan also is still standing the old Tavern where André was imprisoned.

pearance of the other militia men disclosed his mistake, too late to correct it. He offered a purse of gold, and a valuable watch, with tempting promises of ample reward from his government, if they would permit him to escape; but his offers were rejected, and his captors proceeded to search him. They found concealed in his boots, in Arnold's hand writing, papers containing all the information which could be important respecting West Point. When carried before Lieutenant Colonel Jameson, the officer commanding the scouting parties on the lines, he still maintained his assumed character, and requested Jameson to inform his commanding officer that Anderson was taken. Jameson despatched an express with this communication. On receiving it, Arnold comprehended the full extent of his danger, and, flying from well merited punishment, took refuge on board the Vulture.

When sufficient time for the escape of Arnold was supposed to have elapsed, André, no longer affecting concealment, acknowledged himself to be the adjutant general of the British army. Jameson, seeking to correct the mischief of his indiscreet communication to Arnold, immediately despatched a packet to the Commander-in-chief containing the papers which had been discovered, with a letter from André, relating the manner of his capture, and accounting for the disguise he had assumed.

CHAP. VIII

1780

The express was directed to meet the Commander-in-chief, who was then on his return from Hartford; but, taking different roads, * they missed each other, and a delay attended the delivery of the papers, which insured the escape of Arnold.

Precautions for the security of West Point.

Every precaution was immediately taken for the security of West Point; after which, the attention of the Commander-in-chief was turned to André. A board of general officers, of which Major General Greene was president, and the two foreign generals, Lafayette and Steuben, were members, was called, to report a precise state of his case, and to determine the character in which he was to be considered, and the punishment to which he was liable.

The frankness and magnanimity with which André had conducted himself from the time of

* General Lafayette adds some circumstances which are not found among the manuscript papers of General Washington. The Commander-in-chief with Generals Lafayette and Knox had turned from the direct route in order to visit a redoubt. Colonels Hamilton and M'Henry, the aids-de-camp of Generals Washington and Lafayette, went forward to request Mrs. Arnold not to wait breakfast. Arnold received André's billet in their presence. He turned pale, left them suddenly, called his wife, communicated the intelligence to her and left her in a swoon, without the knowledge of Hamilton and M'Henry. Mounting the horse of his aid-de-camp, which was ready saddled, and directing him to inform General Washington on his arrival that Arnold was gone to receive him at West Point, he gained the river shore, and was conveyed in a canoe to the Vulture.

The Commander-in-chief, on his arrival, was informed that Arnold awaited him at West Point. Taking it for granted that this step had been taken to prepare for his reception, he proceeded thither without entering the house, and was surprised to find that Arnold was not arrived. On returning to the quarters of that officer he received Jameson's despatch, which disclosed the whole mystery.

his appearance in his real character, had made a very favourable impression on all those with whom he had held any intercourse. From this cause he experienced every mark of indulgent attention which was compatible with his situation; and, from a sense of justice as well as of delicacy, was informed, on the opening of the examination, that he was at liberty not to answer any interrogatory which might embarrass his own feelings. But, as if only desirous to rescue his character from imputations which he dreaded more than death, he confessed every thing material to his own condemnation, but would divulge nothing which might involve others.

Trial and execution of Major André.

The board reported the essential facts which had appeared, with their opinion that Major André was a spy, and ought to suffer death. The execution of this sentence was ordered to take place on the day succeeding that on which it was pronounced.

Superior to the terrors of death, but dreading disgrace, André was deeply affected by the mode of execution which the laws of war decree to persons in his situation. He wished to die like a soldier, not as a criminal. To obtain a mitigation of his sentence in this respect, he addressed a letter * to General Washington, replete with the feelings of a man of sentiment and honour. But the occasion required that the example should make its full impression, and this request

* See note No. IV. at the end of the volume.

CHAP. VIII
1780

could not be granted. He encountered his fate with composure and dignity; and his whole conduct interested the feelings of all who witnessed it.

The general officers lamented the sentence which the usages of war compelled them to pronounce; and never perhaps did the Commander-in-chief obey with more reluctance the stern mandates of duty and policy. The sympathy excited among the American officers by his fate, was as universal as it is unusual on such occasions; and proclaims alike the merit of him who suffered, and the humanity of those who inflicted the punishment.

Great exertions were made by Sir Henry Clinton, to whom André was particularly dear, first, to have him considered as protected by a flag of truce, and afterwards, as a prisoner of war.

Even Arnold had the hardihood to interpose. After giving a certificate of facts tending, as he supposed, to exculpate the prisoner, exhausting his powers of reasoning on the case, and appealing to the humanity of the American general, he sought to intimidate that officer, by stating the situation of many of the most distinguished individuals of South Carolina, who had forfeited their lives, but had hitherto been spared through the clemency of the British general. This clemency, he said, could no longer be extended to them should Major André suffer.

It may well be supposed that the interposition of Arnold could have no influence on Washington. He conveyed Mrs. Arnold to her husband in New York, † and also transmitted his clothes and baggage, for which he had written; but, in every other respect, his letters, which were unanswered, were also unnoticed.

The mingled sentiments of admiration and compassion excited in every bosom for the unfortunate André, seemed to increase the detestation in which Arnold was held. "André," said General Washington in a private letter, "has met his fate with that fortitude which was to be expected from an accomplished man and a gallant officer; but I am mistaken if *at this time* Arnold is undergoing the torments of a mental hell. He wants feeling. From some traits * of

† General Lafayette mentions a circumstance not previously known to the author, which serves to illustrate the character of Washington, and to mark the delicacy of his feelings towards even the offending part of that sex which is entitled to all the consŏlation and protection man can afford it.

The night after Arnold's escape, when his letter respecting André was received, the general directed one of his aids to wait on Mrs. Arnold, who was convulsed with grief, and inform her that he had done every thing which depended on him to arrest her husband, but that, not having succeeded, it gave him pleasure to inform her that her husband was safe. It is also honourable to the American character, that during the effervescence of the moment, Mrs. Arnold was permitted to go to Philadelphia, to take possession of her effects, and to proceed to New York under the protection of a flag, without receiving the slightest insult.

* This allusion is thus explained in a private letter from Colonel Hamilton—"This man (Arnold) is in every sense despicable. In addition to the scene of knavery and prostitution during his command in Philadelphia, which the late seizure of his papers has unfolded, the history of his command at West Point is a history of little as well as great villanies. He practised every dirty act of peculation, and even stooped to connexions with the suttlers to defraud the public."

his character which have lately come to my knowledge, he seems to have been so hardened in crime, so lost to all sense of honour and shame, that, while his faculties still enable him to continue his sordid pursuits, there will be no time for remorse."

From motives of policy, or of respect for his engagements, Sir Henry Clinton conferred on Arnold the commission of a brigadier general in the British service, which he preserved throughout the war. Yet it is impossible that rank could have rescued him from the contempt and detestation in which the generous, the honourable, and the brave, could not cease to hold him. It was impossible for men of this description to bury the recollection of his being a traitor, a sordid traitor, first the slave of his rage, then purchased with gold, and finally secured at the expense of the blood of one of the most accomplished officers in the British army.

His representations of the discontent of the country and of the army concurring with reports from other quarters, had excited the hope that the loyalists and the dissatisfied, allured by British gold, and the prospect of rank in the British service, would flock to his standard, and form a corps at whose head he might again display his accustomed intrepidity. With this hope he published an address to the inhabitants of America, in which he laboured to palliate his own guilt, and to increase their dissatisfaction with the existing state of things. CHAP. VIII 1780

This appeal to the public was followed by a proclamation addressed "To the officers and soldiers of the continental army, who have the real interests of their country at heart, and who are determined to be no longer the tools and dupes of congress or of France."

The object of this proclamation was to induce the officers and soldiers to desert the cause they had embraced from principle, by holding up to them the very flattering offers of the British general, and contrasting the substantial emoluments of the British service with their present deplorable condition. He attempted to cover this dishonourable proposition with a decent garb, by representing the base step he invited them to take, as the only measure which could restore peace, real liberty, and happiness, to their country.

These inducements did not produce their intended effect. Although the temper of the army might be irritated by real suffering, and by the supposed neglect of government, no diminution of patriotism had been produced. Through all the hardships, irritations, and vicissitudes of the war, Arnold remains the solitary instance of an American officer who abandoned the side first embraced in this civil contest, and turned his sword upon his former companions in arms.

CHAP. VIII

1780

When the probable consequences of this plot, had it been successful, were considered, and the combination of apparent accidents by which it was discovered and defeated, was recollected, all were filled with awful astonishment; and the devout perceived in the transaction, the hand of Providence guiding America to independence.

The thanks of congress were voted to the three militia men * who had rendered this invaluable service; and a silver medal, with an inscription expressive of their fidelity and patriotism, was directed to be presented to each of them. In addition to this flattering testimonial of their worth, and as a farther evidence of national gratitude, a resolution was passed granting to each, two hundred dollars per annum during life, to be paid in specie or an equivalent in current money.

The efforts of General Washington to obtain a permanent military force, or its best substitute, a regular system for filling the vacant ranks with draughts who should join the army on the first day of January in each year, were still continued. Notwithstanding the embarrassments with which congress was surrounded, it is not easy to find adequate reasons for the neglect of representations so interesting, and of recommendations apparently so essential to the safety of the United States.

---

* Their names were John Paulding, David Williams, and Isaac Vanwert.

CHAP. VIII

1780

Parties in Congress.

Private letters disclose the fact that two parties still agitated congress. One entered fully into the views of the Commander-in-chief. The other, jealous of the army, and apprehensive of its hostility to liberty when peace should be restored, remained unwilling to give stability to its constitution by increasing the numbers who were to serve during the war. They seemed to dread the danger from the enemy to which its fluctuations would expose them, less than the danger which might be apprehended for the civil authority from its permanent character. They caught with avidity at every intelligence which encouraged the flattering hope of a speedy peace, * but entered reluctantly into measures founded on the supposition that the war might be of long duration. Perfectly acquainted with the extent of the jealousies entertained on this subject, although, to use his own expressions to a friend, "Heaven knows how unjustly," Gen-

* The following extract from a private letter of General Washington to a member of congress, shows how sensible he was of the mischief produced by this temper. "The satisfaction I have in any successes that attend us, even in the alleviation of misfortunes, is always allayed by the fear that it will lull us into security. Supineness, and a disposition to flatter ourselves, seem to make parts of our national character. When we receive a check and are not quite undone, we are apt to fancy we have gained a victory; and when we do gain any little advantage, we imagine it decisive, and expect the war immediately to end. The history of the war is a history of false hopes and temporary expedients. Would to God they were to end here! This winter, if I am not mistaken, will open a still more embarrassing scene than we have yet experienced, to the southward. I have little doubt, should we not gain a naval superiority, that Sir Henry Clinton will detach to the southward to extend his conquests. I am far from being satisfied that we shall be prepared to repel his attempts."

CHAP. VIII eral Washington had foreborne to press the

1780 necessity of regular and timely reinforcements to his army so constantly and so earnestly as his own judgment directed. But the experience of every campaign furnished such strong additional evidences of the impolicy and danger of continuing to rely on temporary expedients, and the uncertainty of collecting a force to co-operate with the auxiliaries from France was so peculiarly embarrassing, that he at length resolved to conquer the delicacy by which he had been in some degree restrained, and to open himself fully on the subject which he deemed more essential than any other to the success of the war.

August.

In August, while looking anxiously for such a reinforcement to the Chevalier de Tunay as would give him the command of the American seas, and while uncertain whether the campaign might not pass away without giving a single advantage promised at its opening, he transmitted a letter to congress, fully and freely imparting his sentiments on the state of things.

Letter of General Washington on American affairs.

As this letter contains an exact statement of American affairs, according to the view taken of them by General Washington, and a faithful picture of the consequences of the ruinous policy which had been pursued, drawn by the man best acquainted with them, copious extracts from it will, at least, be excused.

After examining the sources of supplies for the campaign, he proceeds to say—"But while we are meditating offensive operations which may not be undertaken at all, or, being undertaken, may fail, I am persuaded congress are not inattentive to the present state of the army, and will view in the same light with me the necessity of providing in time against a period (the first of January) when one half of our present force will dissolve. The shadow of an army that will remain, will have every motive, except mere patriotism, to abandon the service, without the hope which has hitherto supported them, of a change for the better. This is almost extinguished now, and certainly will not outlive the campaign, unless it finds something more substantial to rest upon. This is a truth of which every spectator of the distresses of the army can not help being convinced. Those at a distance may speculate differently; but on the spot an opinion to the contrary, judging human nature on the usual scale, would be chimerical.

"The honourable the committee of congress, who have seen and heard for themselves, will add their testimony to mine; and the wisdom and justice of congress can not fail to give it the most serious attention. To me it will appear miraculous, if our affairs can maintain themselves much longer in their present train. If either the temper or the resources of the country will not admit of an alteration, we may expect soon to be reduced to the humiliating condition of seeing the cause of America, in America, up-

CHAP. VIII
1780

held by foreign arms. The generosity of our allies has a claim to all our confidence, and all our gratitude; but it is neither for the honour of America, nor for the interest of the common cause, to leave the work entirely to them."

He then reviewed the resources of Great Britain; and, after showing her ability still to prosecute the war, added—"The inference from these reflections is, that we can not count upon a speedy end of the war; and that it is the true policy of America not to content herself with temporary expedients, but to endeavour, if possible, to give consistency and solidity to her measures. An essential step to this will be immediately to devise a plan and put it in execution, for providing men in time to replace those who will leave us at the end of the year; and for subsisting and for making a reasonable allowance to the officers and soldiers.

"The plan for this purpose ought to be of general operation, and such as will execute itself. Experience has shown that a peremptory draught will be the only effectual one. If a draught for the war or for three years can be effected, it ought to be made on every account; a shorter period than a year is inadmissible.

"To one who has been witness to the evils brought upon us by short enlistments, the system appears to have been pernicious beyond description; and a crowd of motives present themselves to dictate a change. It may easily be shown that all the misfortunes we have met with in the military line, are to be attributed to this cause.

"Had we formed a permanent army in the beginning, which, by the continuance of the same men in service, had been capable of discipline, we never should have to retreat with a handful of men across the Delaware in 1776, trembling for the fate of America, which nothing but the infatuation of the enemy could have saved; we should not have remained all the succeeding winter at their mercy, with sometimes scarcely a sufficient body of men to mount the ordinary guards, liable at every moment to be dissipated, if they had only thought proper to march against us; we should not have been under the necessity of fighting at Brandywine with an unequal number of raw troops, and afterwards of seeing Philadelphia fall a prey to a victorious army; we should not have been at Valley Forge with less than half the force of the enemy, destitute of every thing in a situation neither to resist nor to retire; we should not have seen New York left with a handful of men, yet an overmatch for the main army of these states, while the principal part of their force was detached for the reduction of two of them; we should not have found ourselves this spring so weak as to be insulted by five thousand men, unable to protect our baggage and magazines, their security depending on a good countenance, and a want

CHAP. VIII 1780

of enterprise in the enemy; we should not have been, the greatest part of the war, inferior to the enemy, indebted for our safety to their inactivity, enduring frequently the mortification of seeing inviting opportunities to ruin them, pass unimproved for want of a force which the country was completely able to afford; to see the country ravaged, our towns burnt, the inhabitants plundered, abused, murdered, with impunity from the same cause."

After presenting in detail the embarrassments under which the civil departments of the army also had laboured, in consequence of the expensiveness and waste inseparable from its temporary character, he proceeded to observe—"There is every reason to believe, that the war has been protracted on this account. Our opposition being less, made the successes of the enemy greater. The fluctuation of the army kept alive their hopes; and at every period of a dissolution of a considerable part of it, they have flattered themselves with some decisive advantages. Had we kept a permanent army on foot, the enemy could have had nothing to hope for, and would in all probability have listened to terms long since. If the army is left in its present situation, it must continue an encouragement to the efforts of the enemy; if it is put in a respectable one, it must have a contrary effect; and nothing I believe will tend more to give us peace the ensuing winter. Many circumstances will contribute to a negotiation. An army on foot, not only for another campaign, but for several campaigns, would determine the enemy to pacific measures, and enable us to insist upon favourable terms in forcible language. An army insignificant in numbers, dissatisfied, crumbling to pieces, would be the strongest temptation they could have to try the experiment a little longer. It is an old maxim that the surest way to make a good peace is to be well prepared for war.

"I can not forbear returning in this place to the necessity of a more ample and equal provision for the army. The discontents on this head have been gradually matured to a dangerous extremity. There are many symptoms that alarm and distress me. Endeavours are using to unite both officers and men in a general refusal of the money, and some corps now actually decline receiving it. Every method has been taken to counteract it, because such a combination in the army would be a severe blow to our declining currency. The most moderate insist that the accounts of depreciation ought to be liquidated at stated periods, and certificates given by government for the sums due. They will not be satisfied with a general declaration that it shall be made good.

"I have often said, and I beg leave to repeat it, the half pay provision is in my opinion the most politic and effectual that can be adopted. On the whole, if something satisfactory be not

CHAP. VIII

1780

done, the army (already so much reduced in officers by daily resignations as not to have a sufficiency to do the common duties of it) must either cease to exist at the end of the campaign, or will exhibit an example of more virtue, fortitude, self-denial, and perseverance, than has perhaps ever yet been paralleled in the history of human enthusiasm.

"The dissolution of the army is an event that can not be regarded with indifference. It would bring accumulated distress upon us; it would throw the people of America into a general consternation; it would discredit our cause throughout the world; it would shock our allies. To think of replacing the officers with others is visionary. The loss of the veteran soldiers could not be replaced. To attempt to carry on the war with militia against disciplined troops, will be to attempt what the common sense and common experience of mankind will pronounce to be impracticable. But I should fail in respect to congress, to dwell on observations of this kind in a letter to them."

Proceedings of Congress respecting the army.

At length the committee presented their report, reorganizing the regiments, reducing their number, and apportioning on the several states their respective numbers to complete the establishment. This report, being approved by congress, was transmitted to the Commander-in-chief for his consideration. By this arrangement, the states were required to recruit their quotas for the war, and to bring them into the field by the first of January; but, if in any state, it should be found impracticable to raise the men for the war by the first day of December, it was recommended to such state to supply the deficiency with men engaged to serve for not less than one year.

In compliance with the request of congress, General Washington submitted his objections to the plan, in a long and respectful letter.

He recommended that legionary corps should be substituted in the place of regiments entirely of cavalry. He thought it more adviseable that the infantry attached to the cavalry should compose a part of the corps permanently, than that it should be drawn occasionally from the regiments of foot.

The reduction in the number of regiments appeared to him a subject of great delicacy. The last reduction, he said, had occasioned many to quit the service, independent of those who were discontinued; and had left durable seeds of discontent among those who remained. The general topic of declamation was, that it was as hard as dishonourable, for men who had made every sacrifice to the service, to be turned out of it, at the pleasure of those in power, without an adequate compensation. In the maturity to which their uneasiness had now risen from a continuance of misery, they would be still more impatient under an attempt of a similar nature.

CHAP. VIII

1780

It was not, he said, the intention of his remarks to discourage a reform, but to show the necessity of guarding against the ill effects which might otherwise attend it, by making an ample provision both for the officers who should remain in the service, and for those who should be reduced. This should be the basis of the plan; and without it, the most mischievous consequences were to be apprehended. He was aware of the difficulty of making a present provision sufficiently ample to give satisfaction; but this only proved the expediency of making one for the future, and brought him to that which he had so frequently recommended as the most economical, the most politic, and the most effectual, that could be devised; this was half pay for life. Supported by the prospect of a permanent provision, the officers would be tied to the service, and would submit to many momentary privations, and to those inconveniences, which the situation of public affairs rendered unavoidable. If the objection drawn from the principle that the measure was incompatible with the genius of the government should be thought insurmountable, he would propose a substitute, less eligible in his opinion, but which would answer the purpose. It was to make the present half pay for seven years, whole pay for the same period. He also recommended that depreciation on the pay received, should be made up to the officers who should be reduced.

No objection occurred to the measure now recommended, but the expense it would occasion. In his judgment, whatever would give consistency to the military establishment, would be ultimately favourable to economy. It was not easy to be conceived, except by those who had witnessed it, what an additional waste and increased consumption of every thing, and consequently what an increase of expense, resulted from laxness of discipline in an army; and where officers thought they did a favour by holding their commissions, and the men were continually fluctuating, to maintain discipline was impossible. Nothing could be more obvious to him than that a sound military establishment and real economy were the same. That the purposes of war would be greatly promoted by it was too clear to admit of argument. He objected also to the mode of effecting the reduction. This was by leaving it to the several states to select the officers who should remain in service. He regretted that congress had not thought proper to retain the reduction and incorporation of the regiments under their own discretion. He regretted that it should be left to the states, not only because it was an adherence to the state system, which in the arrangements of the army, he disapproved; but because also he feared it would introduce much confusion and discontent in a business which ought to be conducted with the greatest circumspection. He feared also that professing

CHAP. VIII 1780

to *select* the officers to be retained in service would give disgust both to those who should be discontinued, and to those who should remain. The former would be sent away under the public stigma of inferior merit, and the latter would feel no pleasure in a present preference, when they reflected that, at some future period, they might experience a similar fate.

He wished with much sincerity that congress had been pleased to make no alteration in the term of service, but had confined their requisition to men who should serve for the war, to be raised by enlistment, draught, or assessment, as might be found necessary. As it now stood, there would be very few men for the war, and all the evils of temporary engagements would still be felt. In the present temper of the states, he entertained the most flattering hopes that they would enter on vigorous measures to raise an army for the war, if congress appeared decided respecting it; but if they held up a different idea as admissible, it would be again concluded that they did not think an army for the war essential. This would encourage the opposition of men of narrow, interested, and feeble tempers, and enable them to defeat the primary object of the revolution.

This letter was taken into consideration; and the measures it recommended were pursued in almost every particular. Even the two great principles which were viewed with most jealousy,

—an army for the war, and half pay for life,—were adopted. It would have greatly abridged the calamities of America, could these resolutions have been carried into execution. Every effort for the purpose was made by the Commander-in-chief.

To place the officers of the army in a situation which would render their commissions valuable, and hold out to them the prospect of a comfortable old age, in a country saved by their blood, their sufferings, and the labours of their best years, was an object which had always been dear to the heart of General Washington, and he had seized every opportunity to press it on congress. That body had approached it slowly, taking step after step with apparent reluctance, as the necessity of the measure became more and more obvious.

The first resolution on the subject, passed in May, 1778, allowed to all military officers who should continue in service during the war, and not hold any office of profit under the United States or any of them, half pay for seven years, if they lived so long. At the same time the sum of eighty dollars, in addition to his pay, was granted to every non-commissioned officer and soldier who should serve to the end of the war. In 1779 this subject was resumed. After much debate, its farther consideration was postponed; and the officers and soldiers were recommended to the attention of their several states, with a

CHAP. VIII 1780

declaration that their patriotism, valour, and perseverance, in defence of the rights and liberties of their country, had entitled them to the gratitude, as well as the approbation of their fellow citizens.

In 1780, a memorial from the general officers, depicting in strong terms the situation of the army, and requiring present support, and some future provision, was answered by a reference to what had been already done, and by a declaration "That patience, self-denial, fortitude and perseverance, and the cheerful sacrifice of time and health, are necessary virtues which both the citizen and soldier are called to exercise, while struggling for the liberties of their country; and that moderation, frugality, and temperance, must be among the chief supports, as well as the brightest ornaments of that kind of civil government which is wisely instituted by the several states in this Union."

This philosophic lecture on the virtues of temperance to men who were often without food, and always scantily supplied, was still calculated to assuage irritations fomented by the neglect which was believed to have been sustained. In a few days afterwards, the subject was brought again before congress, and a more conciliating temper was manifested. The odious restriction, limiting the half pay for seven years to those who should hold no post of profit under the United States or any of them, was removed; and the bounty allowed the men was extended to the widows and orphans of those who had died or should die in the service; at length, the vote passed which has been stated, allowing half pay for life to all officers who should serve in the armies of the United States to the end of the war.

Resolutions were also passed, recommending it to the several states to make up the depreciation on the pay which had been received by the army; and it was determined that their future services should be compensated in the money of the new emission, the value of which, it was supposed, might be kept up by taxes and by loans.

While the government of the Union was thus employed in maturing measures for the preservation of its military establishment, the time for action passed away without furnishing any material event. The hostile armies continued to watch each other until the season of the year forced them out of the field.

Just before retiring into winter quarters, a handsome enterprise was executed by Major Talmadge, of Colonel Sheldon's regiment of light dragoons. That gentleman had been generally stationed on the lines, on the east side of the North River, and had been distinguished for the accuracy of his intelligence.

He was informed that a large magazine of forage had been collected at Coram, on Long

CHAP. VIII

1780

Island, which was protected by the militia of the country, the cruisers in the Sound, and a small garrison in its neighbourhood.

Major Talmadge destroys the British stores at Coram.

At the head of a detachment of eighty dismounted dragoons, under the command of Captain Edgar, and of eight or ten who were mounted, he passed the Sound where it was twenty miles wide, marched across the island in the night, and so completely surprised the fort, that his troops entered the works on three different sides before the garrison was prepared to resist them. The British took refuge in two houses connected with the fortifications, and commenced a fire from the doors and windows. These were instantly forced open; and the whole party, amounting to fifty-four, among whom were a lieutenant colonel, captain, and subaltern, were killed or taken. Stores to a considerable amount were destroyed, the fort was demolished, and the magazines were consumed by fire. The objects of the expedition being accomplished, Major Talmadge recrossed the Sound without having lost a man. On the recommendation of General Washington, congress passed a resolution, expressing a high sense of the merit of those engaged in the expedition.

Nov. 21.

December.

The army retires into winter quarters.

No objects for enterprise presenting themselves, the troops were placed in winter quarters early in December. The Pennsylvania line was stationed near Morristown; the Jersey line about Pompton, on the confines of New York and New

Jersey; and the troops belonging to the New England states, at West Point, and in its vicinity, on both sides the North River. The line of the state of New York remained at Albany, to which place it had been detached for the purpose of opposing an invasion from Canada.

Irruption of Major Carlton into New York.

Major Carlton, at the head of one thousand men, composed of Europeans, Indians, and Tories, had made a sudden irruption into the northern parts of New York, and taken forts Ann and George, with their garrisons. At the same time, Sir John Johnson, at the head of a corps composed of the same materials, appeared on the Mohawk. Several sharp skirmishes were fought in that quarter with the continental troops, and a regiment of new levies, aided by the militia of the country. General Clinton's brigade was ordered to their assistance; but before he could reach the scene of action, the invading armies had retired, after laying waste the whole country through which they passed.

While the disorder of the American finances, the exhausted state of the country, and the debility of the government, determined Great Britain to persevere in offensive war against the United States, by keeping alive her hopes of conquest, Europe assumed an aspect not less formidable to the permanent grandeur of that nation, than hostile to its present views. In the summer of 1780, Russia, Sweden, and Denmark, entered into the celebrated compact, which has

CHAP. VIII

1780

European transactions.

been generally denominated "THE ARMED NEUTRALITY." Holland had also declared a determination to accede to the same confederacy; and it is not improbable that this measure contributed to the declaration of war which was made by Great Britain against that power towards the close of the present year.

The long friendship which had existed between the two nations was visibly weakened from the commencement of the American war. Holland was peculiarly desirous of participating in that commerce which the independence of the United States would open to the world: and, from the commencement of hostilities, her merchants, especially those of Amsterdam, watched the progress of the war with anxiety, and engaged in speculations which were profitable to themselves and beneficial to the United States. The remonstrances made by the British minister at the Hague against this conduct, were answered in the most amicable manner by the government, but the practice of individuals continued the same.

When the war broke out between France and England, a number of Dutch vessels trading with France, laden with materials for shipbuilding, were seized, and carried into the ports of Great Britain, although the existing treaties between the two nations were understood to exclude those articles from the list of contraband of war. The British cabinet justified these acts of violence, and persisted in refusing to permit naval stores to be carried to her enemy in neutral bottoms. This refusal, however, was accompanied with friendly professions, with an offer to pay for the vessels and cargoes already seized, and with proposals to form new stipulations for the future regulation of that commerce.

The States General refused to enter into any negotiations for the modification of subsisting treaties; and the merchants of all the great trading towns, especially those of Amsterdam, expressed the utmost indignation at the injuries they had sustained. In consequence of this conduct, the British government required those succours which were stipulated in ancient treaties, and insisted that the *casus fœderis* had now occurred. Advantage was taken of the refusal of the States General to comply with this demand, to declare the treaties between the two nations at an end.

The temper produced by this state of things, inclined Holland to enter into the treaty for an armed neutrality; and, in November, the Dutch government acceded to it. Some unknown causes prevented the actual signature of the treaty on the part of the States General, until a circumstance occurred which was used for the purpose of placing them in a situation not to avail themselves of the aid stipulated by that confederacy to its members.

CHAP. VIII

1780

While Mr. Lee, one of the ministers of the United States, was on a mission to the courts of Vienna and Berlin, he fell in company with a Mr. John de Neufwille, a merchant of Amsterdam, with whom he held several conversations on the subject of a commercial intercourse between the two nations, the result of which was, that the plan of an eventual commercial treaty was sketched out, as one which might thereafter be concluded between them. This paper had received the approbation of the Pensionary Van Berkel, and of the city of Amsterdam, but not of the States General.

Mr. Henry Laurens, late president of congress, was deputed to the States General with this plan of a treaty, for the double purpose of endeavouring to complete it, and of negotiating a loan for the use of his government. On the voyage he was captured by a British frigate; and his papers, which he had thrown overboard, were rescued from the waves by a British sailor. Among them was found the plan of a treaty which has been mentioned, and which was immediately transmitted to Sir Joseph Yorke, the British minister at the Hague, to be laid before the government.

The explanations of this transaction not being deemed satisfactory by the court of London, Sir Joseph Yorke received orders to withdraw from the Hague, soon after which war was proclaimed against Holland.

This bold measure, which added one of the first maritime powers in Europe to the formidable list of enemies with whom Britain was already encompassed, was perhaps, not less prudent than courageous.

There are situations, to which only high minded nations are equal, in which a daring policy will conduct those who adopt it, safely through the very dangers it appears to invite; dangers which a system suggested by a timid caution might multiply instead of avoiding. The present was, probably, one of those situations. Holland was about to become a member of the armed neutrality, after which her immense navigation would be employed, unmolested, in transporting the property of the enemies of Britain, and in supplying them with all the materials for shipbuilding, or the whole confederacy must be encountered.

America, however, received with delight the intelligence that Holland also was engaged in the war; and founded additional hopes of its speedy termination on that event.

CHAPTER IX.

Transactions in South Carolina and Georgia....Defeat of Ferguson....Lord Cornwallis enters North Carolina....Retreats out of that state....Major Wemyss defeated by Sumpter....Tarlton repulsed....Greene appointed to the command of the Southern army....Arrives in camp....Detaches Morgan over the Catawba ....Battle of the Cowpens....Lord Cornwallis drives Greene through North Carolina into Virginia....He retires to Hillsborough....Greene recrosses the Dan.... Loyalists under Colonel Pyle cut to pieces....Battle of Guilford....Lord Cornwallis retires to Ramsay's mills....To Wilmington....Greene advances to Ramsay's mills....Determines to enter South Carolina.... Lord Cornwallis resolves to march to Virginia.

1780

Transactions in South Carolina and Georgia.

IN the South, Lord Cornwallis, after having nearly demolished the American army at Camden, found himself under the necessity of suspending, for a few weeks, the new career of conquest on which he had intended to enter. His army was enfeebled by sickness as well as by action; the weather was intensely hot, and the stores necessary for an expedition into North Carolina had not been brought from Charleston. In addition, a temper so hostile to the British interests had lately appeared in South Carolina as to make it unsafe to withdraw any considerable part of his force from that state, until he should subdue the spirit of insurrection against his authority. Exertions were made in other parts of the state, not inferior to those of Sumpter in the north-west. Colonel Marion, who had been compelled by the wounds he received in Charleston to retire into the country, had been promoted by Governor Rutledge to the rank of a brigadier general. As the army of Gates approached South Carolina, he had entered the north-eastern parts of that state with only sixteen men; had penetrated into the country as far as the Santee; and was successfully rousing the well-affected inhabitants to arms, when the defeat of the 16th of August chilled the growing spirit of resistance which he had contributed to increase.

With the force he had collected, he rescued about one hundred and fifty continental troops who had been captured at Camden, and were on their way to Charleston. Though compelled, for a short time, to leave the state, he soon returned to it, and at the head of a few spirited men, made repeated excursions from the swamps and marshes in which he concealed himself, and skirmished successfully with the militia who had joined the British standard, and the small parties of regulars by whom they were occasionally supported.

His talents as a partisan, added to his knowledge of the country, enabled him to elude every attempt to seize him; and such was his humanity as well as respect for the laws, that no violence

CHAP. IX 1780 or outrage was ever attributed to the party under his command.

The interval between the victory of the 16th of August, and the expedition into North Carolina, was employed in quelling what was termed the spirit of revolt in South Carolina. The efforts of the people to recover their independence were considered as new acts of rebellion, and were met with a degree of severity which policy was supposed to dictate, but which gave a keener edge to the resentments which civil discord never fails to engender. Several of the most active militia men who had taken protections as British subjects, and entered into the British militia, having been afterwards found in arms, and made prisoners at Camden, were executed as traitors. Orders were given to officers commanding at different posts to proceed in the same manner against persons of a similar description; and these orders were, in many instances, carried into execution. A proclamation was issued for sequestering the estates of all those inhabitants of the province, not included in the capitulation of Charleston, who were in the service, or acting under the authority of Congress, and of all those who, by an open avowal of what were termed rebellious principles, or by other notorious acts should manifest a wicked and desperate perseverance in opposing the re-establishment of royal authority. *

* Rem.

1780

While taking these measures to break the spirit of independence, Lord Cornwallis was indefatigable in urging his preparations for the expedition into North Carolina.

The day after the battle near Camden, emissaries had been despatched into that state for the purpose of inviting the friends of the British government to take up arms. Meanwhile the utmost exertions were continued to embody the people of the country as a British militia; and Major Ferguson was employed in the district of Ninety Six, to train the most loyal inhabitants, and to attach them to his own corps.† After being employed for some time in Ninety Six, he was directed to enter the western parts of North Carolina, for the purpose of embodying the royalists in that quarter.

The route marked out for the main army was from Camden, through the settlement of the Waxhaws to Charlottestown, in North Carolina. On the 8th of September Lord Cornwallis moved from Camden, and reached Charlotte late in that month, where he expected to be joined by Ferguson. But in attempting to meet him, Ferguson was arrested by an event as important as it was unexpected.

Colonel Clarke, a refugee from Georgia, had formed a plan for the reduction of Augusta, which was defended only by a few provincials, under the command of Lieutenant Colonel

† Sted.

CHAP. IX

1780

September.

Brown. About the time Lord Cornwallis commenced his march from Camden, Clarke advanced against Augusta, at the head of a body of irregulars whom he had collected in the frontiers of North and South Carolina, and invested that place. Brown made a vigorous defence; and the approach of Lieutenant Colonel Cruger with a reinforcement from Ninety Six, compelled Clarke to relinquish the enterprise, and to save himself by a rapid retreat. Intelligence of the transactions at Augusta was given to Ferguson, who, to favour the design of intercepting Clarke, moved nearer the mountains, and remained longer in that country than had been intended. This delay proved fatal to him. It gave an opportunity to several volunteer corps to unite, and to constitute a formidable force. The hardy mountaineers inhabiting the extreme western parts of Virginia and North Carolina, assembled on horseback with their rifles, under Colonels Campbell, M'Dowell, Cleveland, Shelby, and Sevier, and moved with their accustomed velocity towards Ferguson. On receiving notice of their approach, that officer commenced his march for Charlotte, despatching, at the same time, different messengers to Lord Cornwallis with information of his danger. These messengers being intercepted, no movement was made to favour his retreat.

When within about sixteen miles of Gilberttown, where Ferguson was then supposed to lie,

1780

Colonel M'Dowell deputed to Gates with a request that he would appoint a general officer to command them; and, in the mean time, Colonel Campbell of Virginia was chosen for that purpose. On reaching Gilbert-town, and finding that the British had commenced their retreat, it was determined to follow them with the utmost celerity. At the Cowpens, this party was joined by Colonels Williams, Tracy, and Branan, of South Carolina, with about four hundred men, who also gave information respecting the distance and situation of their enemy. About nine hundred choice men were selected, by whom the pursuit was continued through the night, and through a heavy rain; and, the next day, about three in the afternoon, they came within view of Ferguson, who, finding that he must be overtaken, had determined to await the attack on King's mountain, and was encamped on its summit,—a ridge five or six hundred yards long, and sixty or seventy wide.

October 7.

The Americans, who had arranged themselves into three columns, the right commanded by Colonel Sevier and Major Winston, the centre by Colonels Campbell and Shelby, and the left by Colonels Cleveland and Williams, immediately rushed to the assault. The attack was commenced by the centre, while the two wings gained the flanks of the British line; and, in about five minutes, the action became general. Ferguson made several impetuous charges with

CHAP. IX
1780

the bayonet, which, against riflemen, were necessarily successful. But, before any one of them could completely disperse the corps against which it was directed, the heavy and destructive fire of the others, who pressed him on all sides, called off his attention to other quarters, and the broken corps was rallied, and brought back to the attack.

In the course of these successive repulses, the right and centre had become intermingled, and were both, by one furious charge of the bayonet, driven almost to the foot of the mountain. With some difficulty they were rallied and again brought into the action; upon which the British, in turn, gave way, and were driven along the summit of the ridge, on Cleveland and Williams, who still maintained their ground on the left.

Defeat of Ferguson.

In this critical state of the action, Ferguson received a mortal wound, and instantly expired. The courage of his party fell with him, and quarter was immediately demanded.* The action continued rather more than an hour.

In this sharp action one hundred and fifty of Ferguson's party were killed on the spot, and about the same number were wounded. Eight hundred and ten, of whom one hundred were British troops, were made prisoners, and fifteen hundred stand of excellent arms were taken.

* The details of this battle are chiefly taken from a paper signed by Colonels Campbell, Shelby, and Cleveland, and published in the Virginia Gazette of the 18th of November, 1780.

The Americans fought under cover of trees, and their loss was inconsiderable; but among the slain was Colonel Williams, who was greatly and justly lamented. As cruelty generally begets cruelty, the example set by the British at Camden was followed, and ten of the most active of the royalists were selected from the prisoners, and hung upon the spot. The victorious mountaineers, having accomplished the object for which they assembled, returned to their homes.

Lord Cornwallis retreats out of North Carolina.

The destruction of this party arrested the progress of Lord Cornwallis in North Carolina, and inspired serious fears for the posts in his rear. He retreated to Wynnsborough, between Camden and Ninety Six, where he waited for reinforcements from New York.

The victory obtained on the 16th of August having suggested views of more extensive conquest in the south, Sir Henry Clinton had determined to send a large reinforcement to the southern army. In the opinion that Lord Cornwallis could meet with no effectual resistance in the Carolinas, he had ordered the officer commanding this reinforcement to enter the Chesapeake in the first instance, and to take possession of the lower parts of Virginia, after which he was to obey the orders he should receive from Lord Cornwallis, to whom a copy of his instructions had been forwarded.

The detachment amounted to near three thousand men, under the command of General Les-

CHAP. IX
1780

lie. It sailed on the 6th of October, and, entering James River after a short passage, took possession of the country on the south side as high as Suffolk. After a short time, Leslie drew in his out-posts, and began to fortify Portsmouth. At this place he received orders from Lord Cornwallis to repair to Charleston by water.

While Cornwallis waited at Wynnsborough for this reinforcement, the light corps of his army were employed in suppressing the parties which were rising in various quarters of the country, in opposition to his authority. Marion had become so formidable as to endanger the communication between Camden and Charleston. Tarlton was detached against him, and Marion was under the necessity of concealing himself in the swamps. From the unavailing pursuit of him through marshes which were scarcely penetrable, Tarlton was called to a different quarter, where an enemy supposed to be entirely vanquished, had reappeared in considerable force.

Sumpter had again assembled a respectable body of mounted militia, at the head of which he advanced towards the posts occupied by the British. On receiving intelligence of his approach, Earl Cornwallis formed a plan for surprising him in his camp on Broad River, the execution of which was committed to Major Wemyss. That officer marched from Wynnsborough at the head of a regiment of infantry and about forty dragoons, reached the camp of Sumpter several hours before day, and immediately charged the out piquet, which made but a slight resistance. Only five shots are said to have been fired, but from these Wemyss received two dangerous wounds which disabled him from the performance of his duty. The assailants fell into confusion, and were repulsed with the loss of their commanding officer and about twenty men. After this action, Sumpter crossed Broad River, and, having formed a junction with Clarke and Branan, threatened Ninety Six.

Major Wemyss attacks and is defeated by Sumpter.

Alarmed for the safety of that post, Earl Cornwallis recalled Tarlton, and ordered him to proceed against Sumpter. So rapid was his movement that he had nearly gained the rear of his enemy before notice of his return was received. In the night preceding the day on which he expected to effect his purpose, a deserter apprised Sumpter of the approaching danger, and that officer began his retreat. Tarlton, pursuing with his usual rapidity, overtook the rear guard at the ford of the Ennoree, and cut it to pieces; after which, fearing that Sumpter would save himself by passing the Tyger, he pressed forward, with, as he states, about two hundred and eighty cavalry and mounted infantry, and, in the afternoon, came within view of the Americans, who were arranged in order for battle.

Sumpter had reached the banks of the Tyger, when the firing of his videttes announced the

CHAP. IX 1780

approach of his enemy. He immediately posted his troops to great advantage on a steep eminence, having their rear and part of their right flank secured by the river, and their left covered by a barn of logs, into which a considerable number of his men were thrown.

Tarlton, without waiting for his infantry, or for a field piece left with them in his rear, rushed to the charge with his usual impetuosity. After several ineffectual attempts to dislodge the Americans, he retired from the field with great precipitation and disorder, leaving ninety-two dead, and one hundred wounded.

After remaining in possession of the ground for a few hours, Sumpter, who was severely wounded in the action, crossed the Tyger, after which his troops dispersed. His loss was only three killed, and four wounded.

Availing himself of the subsequent retreat and dispersion of the American militia, Tarlton denominated this severe check a victory; while congress, in a public resolution, voted their thanks to General Sumpter and the militia he commanded, for this and other services which had been previously rendered.

The shattered remains of the army defeated near Camden, had been slowly collected at Hillsborough, and great exertions were made to reorganize and reinforce it. The whole number of continental troops in the southern army amounted to about fourteen hundred men.

On receiving intelligence that Lord Cornwallis had occupied Charlotte, Gates detached Smallwood to the Yadkin, with directions to post himself at the ford of that river, and to take command of all the troops in that quarter of the country. The more effectually to harass the enemy, a light corps was selected from the army and placed under the command of Morgan, now a brigadier general.

As Lord Cornwallis retreated, Gates advanced to Charlotte, Smallwood encamped lower down the Catawba on the road to Camden; and Morgan was pushed forward some distance in his front. In the expectation that farther active operations would be postponed until the spring, Gates intended to pass the winter in this position. Such was the arrangement of the troops when their general was removed.

November 5.

On the 5th of November, without any previous indications of dissatisfaction, congress passed a resolution requiring the Commander-in-chief to order a court of inquiry on the conduct of General Gates as commander of the southern army, and to appoint some other officer to that command, until the inquiry should be made.

Greene appointed to the command of the southern army.

Washington, without hesitation, selected Greene for that important and difficult service. In a letter to congress recommending him to their support, he mentioned General Greene as "an officer in whose abilities, fortitude, and integrity, from a long and intimate experience of

CHAP. IX

1780

them, he had the most entire confidence." To Mr. Matthews, a delegate from South Carolina, he said, "You have your wish in the officer appointed to the southern command. I think I am giving you a general; but what can a general do without men, without arms, without clothing, without stores, without provisions?" About the same time the legion of Lee was ordered into South Carolina.

Arrives in camp.

Greene hastened to the army he was to command; and, on the second of December, reached Charlotte, then its head quarters. Soon after his arrival in camp, he was gratified with the intelligence of a small piece of good fortune obtained by the address of Lieutenant Colonel Washington.

Smallwood, having received information that a body of royal militia had entered the country in which he foraged, for the purpose of intercepting his wagons, detached Morgan and Washington against them. Intelligence of Morgan's approach being received, the party retreated; but Colonel Washington, being able to move with more celerity than the infantry, resolved to make an attempt on another party, which was stationed at Rugely's farm, within thirteen miles of Camden. He found them posted in a logged barn, strongly secured by abattis, and inaccessible to cavalry. Force being of no avail, he resorted to the following stratagem. Having painted the trunk of a pine, and mounted it on a carriage so as to resemble a field piece, he paraded it in front of the enemy, and demanded a surrender. The whole party, consisting of one hundred and twelve men, with Colonel Rugely at their head, alarmed at the prospect of a cannonade, surrendered themselves prisoners of war.*

Detaches Morgan over the Catawba.

To narrow the limits of the British army, and to encourage the inhabitants, Greene detached Morgan west of the Catawba, with orders to take a position near the confluence of the Pacolet with the Broad River. His party consisted of rather more than three hundred chosen continental troops, commanded by Lieutenant Colonel Howard, of Maryland, of Washington's regiment of light dragoons, amounting to about eighty men, and of two companies of militia from the northern and western parts of Virginia commanded by Captains Triplet and Taite, which were composed almost entirely of old continental soldiers. He was also to be joined on Broad River by seven or eight hundred volunteers and militia commanded by General Davidson, and by Colonels Clarke and Few.

After making this detachment, Greene, for the purpose of entering a more plentiful country, advanced lower down the Pedee, and encamped on its east side, opposite the Cheraw hills. Lord Cornwallis remained at Wynnsborough, pre-

* The author received this account both from General Morgan and Colonel Washington.

CHAP. IX paring to commence active operations, so soon

1780 as he should be joined by Leslie.

The position he occupied on the Pedee was about seventy miles from Wynnsborough, and towards the north of east from that place. The detachment commanded by Morgan had taken post at Grindal's ford on the Pacolet, one of the south forks of Broad River, not quite fifty miles north-west of Wynnsborough. The active courage of his troops, and the enterprising temper of their commander, rendered him extremely formidable to the parties of royal militia who were embodying in that quarter of the country.

Supposing Morgan to have designs on Ninety Six, Lord Cornwallis detached Lieutenant Colonel Tarlton with his legion, part of two regiments of infantry, and a corps of artillery with two field pieces, consisting altogether of about one thousand men, across the Broad River, to cover that important post. As he lay between Greene and Morgan, he was desirous of preventing their junction, and of striking at one of them while unsupported by the other. To leave it uncertain against which division his first effort would be directed, he ordered Leslie to halt at Camden until the preparations for entering North Carolina should be completed. Having determined to penetrate into that state by the upper route, he put his army in motion and directed his course northwestward, between the Catawba and Broad Rivers. Leslie was directed

1780

to move up the banks of the former, and to join him on the march; and Tarlton was ordered to strike at Morgan. Should that officer escape Tarlton, the hope was entertained that he might be intercepted by the main army.*

High waters delayed Cornwallis and Leslie longer than had been expected; but Tarlton overcame the same obstacles, and reached Morgan before a correspondent progress was made by the other divisions.*

1781
January 14.

The combined movements of the British army were communicated to General Morgan on the 14th of January. Perceiving the insecurity of his own position, he retired across the Pacolet, the fords over which he was desirous of defending.

Sixteenth.

But a passage of that river being effected at a ford about six miles below him, he made a precipitate retreat; and, on the evening of the same day, his pursuers occupied the camp he had abandoned. Morgan retired to the Cowpens, where he determined to risk a battle. It was believed that he might have crossed the Broad River, or have reached a mountainous country which was also near him, before he could have been overtaken; and the superiority of his adversary was so decided as to induce his best officers to think that every effort ought to be made to avoid an engagement. But Morgan had great and just confidence in himself and in his troops; he was unwilling to fly from an enemy

* Letter of Lord Cornwallis.—*Stedman.*

CHAP. IX

1781

not so decidedly his superior as to render it madness to fight him; and he also thought that, if he should be overtaken while his men were fatigued and retreating, the probability of success would be much less than if he should exhibit the appearance of fighting from choice.

These considerations determined him to halt earlier than was absolutely necessary.*

Battle of the Cowpens.

Tarlton, having left his baggage under a strong guard, with orders not to move until break of day, recommenced the pursuit at three in the morning.

Before day, Morgan was informed of his approach, and prepared to receive him.

Although censured by many for having determined to fight, and by some for the ground he chose, all admit the judgment with which his disposition was made.

On an eminence, in an open wood, he drew up his continental troops, and Triplet's corps, deemed equal to continentals, amounting to between four and five hundred men, who were commanded by Lieutenant Colonel Howard. In their rear, on the descent of the hill, Lieutenant Colonel Washington was posted with his cavalry, and a small body of mounted Georgia militia commanded by Major M'Call, as a corps de reserve. On these two corps rested his hopes of victory, and with them he remained in person.

* These reasons for his conduct were given to the author by General Morgan soon after his return from the southern campaign.

The front line was composed entirely of militia, under the command of Colonel Pickens. Major M'Dowell, with a battalion of North Carolina volunteers, and Major Cunningham, with a battalion of Georgia volunteers, were advanced about one hundred and fifty yards in front of this line, with orders to give a single fire as the enemy approached, and then to fall back into the intervals, which were left for them in the centre of the first line. The militia, not being expected to maintain their ground long, were ordered to keep up a retreating fire by regiments, until they should pass the continental troops, on whose right they were directed again to form. His whole force, as stated by himself, amounted to only eight hundred men.

Soon after this disposition was made, the British van appeared in sight. Confident of a cheap victory, Tarlton formed his line of battle, and his troops rushed forward with great impetuosity, shouting as they advanced.

After a single well directed fire, M'Dowell and Cunningham fell back on Colonel Pickens, who, after a short but warm conflict, retreated into the rear of the second line.* The British pressed forward with great eagerness; and, though received by the continental troops with a firmness unimpaired by the rout of the front line, continued to advance. Soon after the action

* Some of them formed afterwards, and renewed the action on Howard's right.

with the continental troops had commenced, Tarlton ordered up his reserve. Perceiving that the enemy extended beyond him both on the right and left, and that, on the right especially, his flank was on the point of being turned, Howard ordered the company on his right to change its front, so as to face the British on that flank. From some mistake in the officer commanding this company, it fell back, instead of fronting the enemy, upon which the rest of the line, supposing a change of ground for the whole to have been directed, began to retire in perfect order. At this moment General Morgan rode up, and directed the infantry to retreat over the summit of the hill, about one hundred yards to the cavalry. This judicious but hazardous movement was made in good order, and extricated the flanks from immediate danger. Believing the fate of the day to be decided, the British pressed on with increased ardour, and in some disorder; and when the Americans halted, were within thirty yards of them. The orders then given by Howard to face the enemy were executed as soon as they were received; and the whole line poured in a fire as deadly as it was unexpected. Some confusion appearing in the ranks of the enemy, Howard seized the critical moment, and ordered a charge with the bayonet. These orders were instantly obeyed, and the British line was broken.

At the same moment the detachment of cavalry on the British right was routed by Washington. The militia of Pickens, who rode to the ground, had tied their horses in the rear of Howard's left. When the front line was broken, many of them fled to their horses, and were closely pursued by the cavalry, who, while the continental infantry were retiring, passed their flank, and were cutting down the scattered militia in their rear. Washington, who had previously ordered his men not to fire a pistol, now directed them to charge the British cavalry with drawn swords. A sharp conflict ensued, but it was not of long duration. The British were driven from the ground with considerable slaughter, and were closely pursued. Both Howard and Washington pressed the advantage they had respectively gained, until the artillery, and great part of the infantry had surrendered. So sudden was the defeat, that a considerable part of the British cavalry had not been brought into action; and, though retreating, remained unbroken. Washington, followed by Howard with the infantry, pursued them rapidly, and attacked * them with great spirit; but, as they

* In the eagerness of pursuit, Washington advanced near thirty yards in front of his regiment. Three British officers, observing this, wheeled about, and made a charge upon him. The officer on his right aimed a blow to cut him down as an American sergeant came up, who intercepted the blow by disabling his sword arm. The officer on his left was about to make a stroke at him at the same instant, when a waiter, too small to wield a sword, saved him by wounding the officer with a ball from a pistol. At this moment, the officer in the

CHAP. IX

1781

were superior to him in numbers, his cavalry received a temporary check; and in this part of the action he sustained a greater loss than in any other. But the infantry coming up to support him, Tarlton resumed the retreat.†

In this engagement upwards of one hundred British, including ten commissioned officers, were killed; twenty-nine commissioned officers, and five hundred privates were made prisoners. Eight hundred muskets, two field pieces, two standards, thirty-five baggage wagons, and one hundred dragoon horses, fell into the hands of the conquerors.

Tarlton retreated towards the headquarters of Lord Cornwallis, then about twenty-five miles from the Cowpens.

This complete victory cost the Americans less than eighty men in killed and wounded.

Seldom has a battle in which greater numbers were not engaged, been so important in its consequences as that of the Cowpens. Lord Cornwallis was not only deprived of a fifth of his numbers, but lost a most powerful and active part of his army. Unfortunately, Greene was not in a condition to press the advantage. The whole southern army did not much exceed two

centre, who was believed to be Tarlton, made a thrust at him which he parried; upon which the officer retreated a few paces, and then discharged a pistol at him, which wounded his horse.

† The author has received statements of this action from General Morgan and from Colonels Howard and Washington.

1781

thousand men, a great part of whom were militia.

The camp of Lord Cornwallis at Turkey Creek on the east side of Broad River, was as near as the Cowpens to the fords at which Morgan was to cross the Catawba. Of consequence, that officer had much cause to fear that, encumbered as he was with prisoners and military stores, he might be intercepted before he could pass that river. Comprehending the full extent of his danger, he abandoned the baggage he had taken, and leaving his wounded under the protection of a flag, detached the militia as an escort to his prisoners, and brought up the rear in person with his regulars. Passing Broad River on the evening of the day on which the battle was fought, he hastened to the Catawba, which he crossed on the 23d, at Sherald's ford, and encamped on its eastern bank.

Pursuit of the American army through North Carolina into Virginia.

Lord Cornwallis employed the 18th in forming a junction with Leslie. Early next morning he put his army in motion, and, on the 25th, reached Ramsay's mills, where the roads taken by the two armies unite. At this place, to accelerate his future movements, he destroyed his baggage; and, after collecting a small supply of provisions, resumed the pursuit. He reached Sherald's ford in the afternoon of the 29th; and, in the night, an immense flood of rain rendered the river impassable.

January.

CHAP. IX

1781

January 31.

While Morgan remained on the Catawba, watching the motions of the British army, and endeavouring to collect the militia, General Greene arrived, and took command of the detachment.

In his camp on the Pedee, opposite the Cheraw hills, Greene had been joined by Lee's legion, amounting to about one hundred cavalry, and one hundred and twenty infantry. The day after his arrival, he was ordered to join Marion for the purpose of attempting to carry a British post at Georgetown, distant about seventy-five miles from the American army. The fort was surprised, but the success was only partial.

On receiving intelligence of the victory at the Cowpens, Greene detached Stevens' brigade of Virginia militia, whose terms of service were on the point of expiring, to conduct the prisoners to Charlottesville in Virginia, and turned his whole attention to the effecting of a junction between the two divisions of his army. It was principally with a view to this object that he hastened to the detachment under Morgan, leaving the other division to be commanded by General Huger.

February 1.

Early in the morning of the first of February, Lord Cornwallis forced a passage over the Catawba, at a private ford which was defended by General Davidson, with about three hundred North Carolina militia. Davidson was killed, and his troops dispersed. They were followed by Tarlton, who, hearing in the pursuit, that several bodies of militia were assembling at a tavern about ten miles from the ford, hastened to the place of rendezvous, and charging them with his usual impetuosity, broke their centre, killed some, and dispersed the whole party.

It was found impracticable to bring the militia into the field, and Huger, who had been directed to march to Salisbury, was ordered to effect a junction between the two divisions of the army at some place farther north.

Greene retreated along the Salisbury road, and, in the evening of the third, crossed the Yadkin at the trading ford. His passage of the river, then already much swollen by the rain of the preceding day, was facilitated by boats which had been previously collected. The rear guard, which, being impeded by the baggage of the whigs who fled from Salisbury did not cross till midnight, was overtaken by the van of the British army, and a skirmish ensued in which some loss was sustained, but the Americans effected the passage of the river.

February 3.

The rains having rendered the Yadkin unfordable, and the boats being collected on the opposite side, the pursuit was necessarily suspended; but Greene continued his march to Guilford court house where he was joined by Huger.

Ninth.

After some delay, and apparent hesitation respecting his movements, Lord Cornwallis

CHAP. IX 1781 marched up the Yadkin, which he crossed near its source on the morning of the eighth.

After the junction between the divisions of Huger and Morgan, the infantry of the American army, including six hundred militia, amounted to about two thousand effectives; and the cavalry to between two and three hundred. Lord Cornwallis lay twenty-five miles above them at Salem, with an army estimated from twenty-five hundred to three thousand men, including three hundred cavalry. Having failed in his attempt to prevent the junction of the two divisions of the American army, his object was to place himself between Greene and Virginia, and force that officer to a general action before he could be joined by the reinforcements which were known to be preparing for him in that state. His situation favoured the accomplishment of this object.

Greene, on the other hand, was indefatigable in his exertions to cross the Dan without exposing himself to the hazard of a battle. To effect this object, the whole of his cavalry, with the flower of his infantry, amounting together to rather more than seven hundred men, were formed into a light corps, for the purpose of harassing and impeding the advance of the enemy, until the less active part of his force, with the baggage and military stores should be secured. Morgan being rendered incapable of duty by severe indisposition, the command of this corps was conferred on Colonels Otho and Williams.

Lord Cornwallis had been informed that it would be impossible to obtain boats at the ferries on the Dan in sufficient numbers for the transportation of the American troops before he could overtake them. And, as the river could not be forded below, he calculated with confidence on succeeding in his object by keeping above Greene, and prevent his reaching those shallow fords by which alone it was thought possible to escape into Virginia.

Dix's ferry is about fifty miles from Guilford court house, and was almost equidistant from the two armies. Considerably below, and more than seventy miles from Guilford court house, were two other ferries, Boyd's and Irwin's, which were only four miles apart. By directing their march towards the lower and more remote ferries, the distance from Lord Cornwallis was so much ground gained; and by despatching an officer with a few men to Dix's, the boats at that, and at an intermediate ferry, might be brought down the river in time to meet the army at the intended crossing place. These facts being suggested by Lieutenant Colonel Carrington, quartermaster general for the southern department, the proposition was instantly adopted, and an officer despatched to bring the boats from above down to Boyd's ferry.*

* The author received this fact from Colonel Carrington.

CHAP. IX

1781

The next day both armies resumed their line of march. While General Greene pressed forward to Boyd's, Williams gained an intermediate road leading to Dix's ferry, and thus placed himself between the two armies, a small distance in front of the one, and considerably in rear of the other. Such was the boldness and activity of this corps that Lord Cornwallis found it necessary to temper the eagerness of his pursuit with caution. Yet he moved with great rapidity;—marching nearly thirty miles each day. On the morning of the third day, he attempted to surprise the Americans by marching from the rear of his column into the road which had been taken by them, while his van proceeded slowly on its original route. Information of this movement was received, and Lieutenant Colonel Lee charged his advanced cavalry with such impetuosity, as to cut a company nearly to pieces. A captain and several privates were made prisoners. The whole British army turned into this road and followed in the rear of Williams, who used every effort to delay their march.

February 14.

The measures adopted by Greene for collecting the boats were successful; and, on the fourteenth, he effected the passage of his troops and stores.

When Williams supposed that the American army had reached the Dan, he left the road leading to Dix's ferry, and entering that which Greene had taken, urged his march to the lower ferries with the utmost celerity. Lord Cornwallis, being at length informed that Greene had taken the lower road, turned into it about the same time by a nearer way, and his front was in sight of the rear of Williams. So rapid were the movements of both armies that, in the last twenty-four hours, the Americans marched forty miles; and the rear had scarcely touched the northern bank, when the van of the enemy appeared on the opposite shore.

That General Greene was able to effect this retreat without loss, evidences the judgment with which he improved every favourable circumstance.

The exertions, the fatigues, the sufferings, and the patience of both armies, during this long, toilsome, and rapid pursuit, were extreme. Without tents, without spirits, often without provisions, and always scantily supplied with them; through deep and frozen roads, high waters, and frequent rains; each performed, without a murmur, the severe duties assigned to it. The difference between them consists only in this,—the British troops were well clothed; the Americans were almost naked, and many of them barefooted.

Great praise was bestowed by the general on his whole army; but the exertions of Colonel Williams, and of Lieutenant Colonel Carrington were particularly noticed.

CHAP. IX

1781

Although that part of North Carolina through which the armies had passed, was well affected to the American cause, such was the rapidity with which they moved, and such the terror inspired by the presence of the enemy, that no aid was drawn from the militia. Indeed, those who had joined the army from the more remote parts of the country could not be retained; and, when it reached the Dan, the militia attached to it did not exceed eighty men.

Having driven Greene out of North Carolina, Lord Cornwallis turned his attention to the re-establishment of regal authority in that state. For this purpose, he proceeded by easy marches to Hillsborough, at that time its capital, where he erected the royal standard, and issued a proclamation inviting the inhabitants to repair to it, and to assist him in restoring the ancient government.

Lord Cornwallis retires to Hillsborough.

As soon as it was known that General Greene had entered Virginia, he was reinforced by six hundred militia drawn from the neighbouring counties, the command of which was given to General Stevens.

Apprehension that Lord Cornwallis, if left in the undisturbed possession of North Carolina, would succeed, to the extent of his hopes, in recruiting his army and procuring the submission of the people, General Greene determined, on receiving this small reinforcement, to re-enter that state; and, avoiding a general engagement, to keep the field against a superior enemy, who had demonstrated his capacity for rapid movement and hardy enterprise.

February.

On the 18th, while Lord Cornwallis remained on the opposite shore, the legion of Lee had passed the Dan. On the 21st, the light infantry also recrossed it; and, on the 23d, they were followed by the main body of the army.

Greene recrosses the Dan.

The light infantry hung round the quarters of the enemy, while the main body advanced slowly, keeping in view the roads to the western parts of the country, from which a considerable reinforcement of militia was expected.*

General Greene was not mistaken in the consequences of leaving Lord Cornwallis in the peaceable possession of North Carolina. He was informed that seven independent companies were raised in one day. A large body of royalists had begun to embody themselves on the branches of the Haw River; and Colonel Tarlton, with the cavalry of his legion and some infantry, was detached from Hillsborough to favour their rising, and to conduct them to the British army.

Intelligence of the movements of the loyalists and of Tarlton being received, Greene ordered

* The western militia had been engaged in a war with the Cherokee Indians, who, neglected by the United States, and incited by the British, had determined once more to take up the hatchet. The militia from the western parts of Virginia and North Carolina entered their country, burnt their towns, containing near one thousand houses, destroyed fifty thousand bushels of grain, killed twenty-nine men, took several prisoners, and compelled the nation to sue for peace.

CHAP. IX

1781

Lieutenant Colonel Lee with the cavalry of his legion, and General Pickens with between three and four hundred militia, who had just formed a junction near Hillsborough, to move against both parties.

In a long lane, Lee, whose cavalry was in front of the whole detachment, came up with the royalists. He was mistaken by them for Tarlton, whom they had not yet seen, to whose encampment they were proceeding, and whose corps was then taking refreshment, not much more than a mile distant from them. Perceiving their mistake, Lee received their expressions of joy and attachment, and had just reached their colonel, to whom he was about to make communications which might have enabled him to proceed on his design of surprising Tarlton, when the infantry who followed close in his rear, were recognized by the insurgents; and a firing took place between them. It being apparent that this circumstance must give the alarm to the British, Lee changed his plan, and turning on the royalists, who still supposed him to be a British officer, cut them to pieces while they were making protestations of loyalty, and asserting that they were "the very best friends of the king." More than one hundred, among whom was Colonel Pyle, their leader, fell under the swords of his cavalry. This terrible but unavoidable carnage broke, in a great measure, the spirits of the tories in that part of the country. Some

Party of loyalists commanded by Colonel Pyle, cut to pieces.

who were on their march to join the British standard, returned, determined to await the issue of events before they went too far to recede.

The hope of surprising Tarlton being thus disappointed, Pickens and Lee determined to postpone the attack till the morning; and took a position for the night between him and a corps of militia which was advancing from the western counties of Virginia under Colonel Preston. Tarlton had meditated an attempt on this corps; but at midnight, when his troops were paraded to march on this design, he received an express from Lord Cornwallis, directing his immediate return to the army. In obedience to this order, he began his retreat long before day, and crossed the Haw, just as the Americans, who followed him, appeared on the opposite bank. Two pieces of artillery commanded the ford and stopped the pursuit.

To approach more nearly the great body of the loyalists, who were settled between Haw and Deep Rivers, and to take a position in a country less exhausted than that around Hillsborough, Lord Cornwallis crossed the Haw, and encamped on Allimance creek.

As the British army retired, General Greene advanced. Not being yet in a condition to hazard an engagement, he changed his ground every night. In the course of the critical movements, which were made in order to avoid an action, and at the same time to overawe the loyalists, and maintain a position favourable to a junction with the several detachments who were marching from different quarters to his assistance, he derived immense service from a bold and active light infantry, and from a cavalry which, though inferior in numbers, was rendered superior in effect to that of his enemy, by being much better mounted. They often attacked boldly and successfully, and made sudden incursions into the country, which so intimidated the royalists, that Lord Cornwallis found it difficult to obtain intelligence. By these means, all his attempts to bring the American general to action were frustrated; and his lordship was under the necessity of keeping his men close in their quarters.

During this hazardous trial of skill, Lord Cornwallis moved out in full force towards Rudy fork, where the light infantry lay, in the hope of surprising that corps under cover of a thick fog; and probably with ulterior views against General Greene. His approach was perceived, and a sharp skirmish ensued between a part of the light infantry, and a much superior body of British troops commanded by Lieutenant Colonel Webster, in which the loss was supposed to be nearly equal. The advance of the British army obliged Williams to retire; and General Greene, by recrossing the Haw and uniting with the light infantry on its north-eastern bank at the Rocky ford, disappointed any farther designs which might have been formed against the army then under his command, or against the reinforcements which were approaching. Being thus foiled, Lord Cornwallis withdrew to Deep River, and General Greene fell back to the iron works on Troublesome creek.

At length his reinforcements, though much inferior to the number he had been taught to expect, were received, and Greene, in his turn, sought a battle. With this view, he dissolved the corps of light infantry, advanced towards his enemy, and encamped within eight miles of him, at Guilford court house.

His army, including officers, amounted to about four thousand five hundred men, of whom not quite two thousand were continental troops and the residue consisted of Virginia and North Carolina militia. Those of Virginia were commanded by Generals Stevens and Lawson, and by Colonels Preston, Campbell, and Lynch; and those of North Carolina, by Generals Butler and Eaton.

Of the four regiments which composed the continental infantry, only one, the first of Maryland, was veteran. The other three consisted of new levies, with a few old continental soldiers interspersed among them. The legion of Lee, and the cavalry of Washington, like the first regiment of Maryland, added every advantage of experience to approved courage; and nearly

CHAP. IX
1781

all the officers commanding the new levies were veteran.

March 15.

Having determined to risk an action, Greene chose his ground with judgment. Early in the morning of the 15th, the fire of his reconnoitring parties announced the approach of the enemy on the great Salisbury road, and his army was immediately arranged in order of battle. It was drawn up in three lines, on a large hill, surrounded by other hills, chiefly covered with trees and underwood.

Battle of Guilford.

The front line was composed of the two brigades of North Carolina militia, who were posted to great advantage on the edge of the wood, behind a strong rail fence, with an extensive open field in front.

The two brigades of Virginia militia formed the second line. They were drawn up entirely in the wood, about three hundred yards in rear of the first, and on either side of the great Salisbury road.

The third line was placed about three hundred yards in rear of the second, and was composed of continental troops. The Virginia brigade, commanded by General Huger, was on the right; that of Maryland, commanded by Colonel Williams, was on the left. They were drawn up obliquely, with their left diverging from the second line, and partly in open ground.

The first and third regiments of dragoons, amounting to one hundred and two troopers,

Kirkwood's company of light infantry, and a regiment of militia riflemen under Colonel Lynch, formed a corps of observation for the security of the right flank, which was commanded by Lieutenant Colonel Washington. The legion, consisting of one hundred and sixty-eight horse and foot, and a body of riflemen commanded by Colonels Campbell and Preston, formed a corps of observation for the security of the left flank, which was placed under Lieutenant Colonel Lee. The artillery was in the front line, in the great road leading through the centre, with directions to fall back as the occasion should require.

Though Lord Cornwallis was sensible that the numbers of the American army were greatly augmented by troops whose continuance in service would be of short duration, he deemed it so important to the interests of his sovereign to maintain the appearance of superiority in the field, that he was unwilling to decline the engagement now offered him.

March 14.

On the advance of Greene, therefore, he prepared for action; and early in the morning moved from his ground, determined to attack the adverse army wherever it should be found. About four miles from Guilford court house, the advance, led by Lieutenant Colonel Tarlton, fell in with Lee, and a sharp skirmish ensued, which was terminated by the appearance of such large bodies of British troops, as rendered it prudent

Fifteenth.

CHAP. IX
1781

for Lee to retire. His lordship continued to advance until he came within view of the American army. His disposition for the attack was then made in the following order.

The seventy-first British regiment, with the German regiment of Bose, led by General Leslie, and supported by the first battalion of the guards under Colonel Norton, formed the right, and the twenty-third and thirty-third regiments, led by Lieutenant Colonel Webster, and supported by Brigadier General O'Hara with the grenadiers and second battalion of the guards, formed the left. The light infantry of the guards and the Yagers, posted in the wood on the left of the artillery, and the cavalry in column behind it in the road, formed a corps of observation.*

This disposition being made, the British troops advanced to the charge, with the cool intrepidity which discipline inspires.

The North Carolina militia were not encouraged by the great advantages of their position to await the shock. They broke instantly; and, throwing away their arms and flying through the woods, sought their respective homes.

The British then advanced on the second line, which received them with more firmness; and maintained their ground for some time with great resolution. Lord Cornwallis perceiving the corps on his flanks, brought the whole of his

* Letter of Lord Cornwallis.—*Stedman.*

reserved infantry into the line. On the right, General Leslie brought up the guards to oppose Lee; and, on the left, Webster changed his front to the left, and attacked Washington, while the grenadiers and second battalion of guards moved forward to occupy the place which he had just quitted.*

The ground being unfavourable to the action of horse, Washington had posted Lynch's riflemen, with whom he remained in person, on a height covered with thick woods; and had drawn up his cavalry and continental infantry about one hundred yards in their rear. On being attacked by Webster, the riflemen broke; and Washington, finding it impossible to rally them, rejoined his cavalry.

The British continuing to advance, and it being well understood that the militia could not stand the bayonet, General Stevens, who had received a ball in his right thigh, ordered his brigade to retreat. Lawson's brigade having given way a short time before, the second line was entirely routed; and the enemy advanced boldly on the third.

The several divisions of the British army had been separated from each other by extending themselves to the right and left in order to encounter the distinct corps which threatened their flanks; and by advancing in regiments at different times, as the different parts of the second

* Letter of Lord Cornwallis.—*Stedman.*

CHAP. IX 1781 line had given way. The thickness of the wood increased the difficulty of restoring order. They pressed forward with great eagerness, but with a considerable degree of irregularity.

Greene, in this state of the action, entertained the most sanguine hopes of a complete victory. His continental troops were fresh, in perfect order, and upon the point of engaging an enemy, broken into distinct parts, and probably supposing the severity of the action to be over. This fair prospect was blasted by the misconduct of a single corps. The second regiment of Maryland was posted at some distance from the first, in open ground; its left forming almost a right angle with the line, so as to present a front to any corps which might attack on that flank. The British in advancing, inclined to the right; and the second battalion of guards entered the open ground immediately after the retreat of Stevens, and rushed on the second regiment of Maryland while the first was engaged with Webster. Without waiting to receive the charge, that regiment broke in confusion. By pursuing them, the guards were thrown into the rear of the first regiment, from which they were concealed by the unevenness of the ground, and by a skirt of wood.

Greene was himself on the left, and witnessed the misfortune without being able to remedy it. His militia being entirely routed, the flight of one-fourth of his continental troops would most probably decide the fate of the day. Unwilling to risk his remaining three regiments, only one of which could be safely relied on, without a man to cover their retreat should the event prove unfortunate, he ordered Colonel Greene of Virginia to withdraw his regiment from the line, and to take a position in the rear, for the purpose of affording a rallying point, and of covering the retreat of the two regiments which still continued in the field.

The guards were soon called from the pursuit of the second Maryland regiment, and led by Lieutenant Colonel Stuart against the first. About this time Webster, finding himself overpowered by the first Maryland regiment, then commanded by Colonel Gunby, and by Kirkwood's company and the remaining regiment of Virginia, with whom he was engaged at the same time, had in a great measure withdrawn from the action, and retired across a ravine into an adjoining wood. This critical respite enabled Gunby to provide for the danger in his rear. Facing about, he met the guards, and a very animated fire took place on both sides, during which the Americans continued to advance.

In this critical moment, Lieutenant Colonel Washington, who was drawn to this part of the field by the vivacity of the fire, made a furious charge upon the guards and broke their ranks. At this juncture, Gunby's horse was killed under him, and the command devolved on Lieutenant

CHAP. IX
1781

Colonel Howard. The regiment advanced with such rapidity that Gunby could not overtake it, and was within thirty yards of the guards when they were charged by the cavalry. Almost at the same instant the Maryland infantry rushed upon them with the bayonet, and following the horse through them, were masters of the whole battalion. In passing through it, Captain Smith of the infantry killed its commanding officer.

After passing through the guards into the open ground where the second regiment had been originally posted, Howard perceived several British columns, with some pieces of artillery. Believing his regiment to be the sole infantry remaining in the field, he retreated in good order, and brought off some prisoners. The cavalry also retreated.*

About the same time the remaining Virginia regiment commanded by Colonel Hawes, and Kirkwood's infantry, who were still engaged with Webster, were directed by General Greene to retreat. The artillery was unavoidably abandoned; the horses which drew the pieces being killed, and the woods too thick to admit of their

* After passing through the guards into the cleared ground, Washington, who always led the van, perceived an officer surrounded by several persons who appeared to be aids-de-camp. Believing this to be Lord Cornwallis, he rushed forward in the hope of making him a prisoner, but was arrested by an accident. His cap fell from his head, and, as he leaped to the ground to recover it, the officer leading the column was shot through the body, and rendered incapable of managing his horse. The animal wheeled round with his rider, and galloped off the field. He was followed by all the cavalry, who supposed that this movement had been directed.

being dragged elsewhere than along the great road. The retreat was made in good order, and Greene, in person, brought up the rear.

Though the action was over on the right and centre, Campbell's riflemen still maintained their ground on the extreme of the American left, against General Leslie with the regiment of Bose and the first battalion of guards.

After the guards had routed the brigade commanded by Lawson, they were attacked on their right flank by the infantry of Lee's legion and by Campbell's riflemen, and were driven behind the regiment of Bose, which having moved with less impetuosity, was advancing in compact order.

This regiment sustained the American fire until Lieutenant Colonel Norton was able to rally the guards and to bring them back to the charge; after which the action was maintained with great obstinacy on both sides until the battle was decided on the right. Lieutenant Colonel Tarlton was then ordered to the support of Leslie. The legion infantry had retreated, and only a few resolute marksmen remained in the rear of Campbell who continued firing from tree to tree. Being unable to resist a charge of cavalry, they were quickly driven from the field.

Two regiments of infantry and a detachment of cavalry pursued the right wing and centre of the Americans for a short distance, but were soon ordered to return. On examining his situation,

CHAP. IX

1781

Lord Cornwallis found himself too much weakened, and his troops too much fatigued by the action, to hazard its renewal, or to continue the pursuit. General Greene halted about three miles from the field of battle, behind Rudy fork creek, for the purpose of collecting his stragglers; after which he retired about twelve miles, to the iron works on Troublesome creek, the place appointed for the rendezvous of his army in the event of its being defeated.

The returns made immediately after the action, exhibited a loss in killed, wounded and missing in the continental troops, of fourteen commissioned officers, and three hundred and twelve non-commissioned officers and privates. Major Anderson, a valuable officer of Maryland, was killed; and General Huger, who commanded the continental troops of Virginia, was wounded.

The same return states the loss of the militia at four captains and seventeen privates killed; and, in addition to General Stevens, one major, three captains, eight subalterns, and sixty privates, were wounded. A great proportion of this part of the army was missing; but it seems to have been expected that they would either rejoin their corps, or be found at their homes.

The victory at Guilford was dearly purchased. Official accounts state the loss of the British army at five hundred and thirty-two men, among whom were several officers of high rank and distinguished merit. Lieutenant Colonel Stuart of the guards was killed, and Lieutenant Colonel Webster, who was ranked by his enemies among the best officers in the British service, was mortally wounded. This loss, when compared with the numbers brought by Lord Cornwallis into the field, was very considerable. The Americans did not compute his troops at more than two thousand rank and file, but his own accounts state them at only fourteen hundred and forty-five.

No battle in the course of the war reflects more honour on the courage of the British troops, than that of Guilford. On no other occasion have they fought with such inferiority of numbers, or disadvantage of ground. Estimating his first line at nothing, General Greene's army consisted of three thousand two hundred men, posted on ground chosen by himself; and his disposition was skilfully made.

The American general, expecting to be again attacked, prepared for another engagement. But the situation of Lord Cornwallis had become too desperate to hazard a second battle, or to maintain his position. He found himself under the necessity of retreating to a place of greater security, where provisions might be obtained.

When the expedition into North Carolina was originally meditated, Major Craig, at the head of a small military and naval force, took possession of Wilmington, a town near the mouth

CHAP. IX

1781

of Cape Fear, and extended his authority several miles up the river. Lord Cornwallis now looked to a communication with this post for aids which had become indispensable to the farther operations of the campaign.

On the third day after the battle, he broke up his encampment, and proceeded by slow and easy marches towards Cross creek.

Greene advances to Ramsay's mills with a determination to enter South Carolina.

General Greene, on hearing that the British army was retreating, resolved to follow it. The difficulty of subsisting the troops in an exhausted and hostile country; and the necessity of waiting for a supply of ammunition, impeded the march of his army so much that he did not reach Ramsay's mills until the 28th of March.

At this place Lord Cornwallis had halted, and here General Greene expected to overtake and attack him. But, on the approach of the American army, his lordship resumed his march to

April 7.

Cross creek, and afterwards to Wilmington, where he arrived on the 7th of April.

General Greene gave over the pursuit at Ramsay's mills. So excessive had been the sufferings of his army from the want of provisions, that many of the men fainted on the march, and it had become absolutely necessary to allow them some repose and refreshment. The expiration of the time for which the Virginia militia had been called into service, furnished an additional motive for suspending the pursuit.

At this place, the bold and happy resolution was taken to carry the war into South Carolina. CHAP. IX 1781

The motives which induced the adoption of this measure were stated by himself in a letter communicating his determination to the Commander-in-chief. It would compel Lord Cornwallis to follow him, and thus liberate North Carolina, or to sacrifice all his posts in the upper parts of South Carolina and Georgia.

The Southern army amounted to about seventeen hundred effectives. That of Lord Cornwallis is understood to have been still less numerous. So impotent were the means employed for the conquest and defence of states which were of immense extent and value.

This unexpected movement gave a new aspect to affairs, and produced some irresolution in the British general respecting his future operations. After weighing the probable advantages and disadvantages of following Greene into South Carolina, he decided against this retrograde movement and determined to advance into Virginia.

CHAPTER X.

Virginia invaded by Arnold....He destroys the stores at Westham and at Richmond....Retires to Portsmouth ....Mutiny in the Pennsylvania line....Sir H. Clinton attempts to negotiate with the mutineers....They compromise with the civil government....Mutiny in the Jersey line....Mission of Colonel Laurens to France.... Propositions to Spain....Recommendations relative to a duty on imported and prize goods....Reform in the Executive departments....Confederation adopted.... Military transactions....Lafayette detached to Virginia ....Cornwallis arrives....Presses Lafayette....Expedition to Charlottesville, to the Point of Fork....Lafayette forms a junction with Wayne....Cornwallis retires to the lower country....General Washington's letters are intercepted....Action near Jamestown.

1781

Virginia invaded by Arnold.

THE evacuation of Portsmouth by Leslie afforded Virginia but a short interval of repose. So early as the 9th of December, 1780, a letter from General Washington announced to the governor that a large embarkation, supposed to be destined for the south, was about taking place at New York. On the 30th, a fleet of transports under convoy, having on board between one and two thousand men, commanded by General Arnold, anchored in Hampton road. The troops were embarked the next day on board vessels adapted to the navigation, and proceeded up James' River under convoy of two small ships of war. On the fourth of January they reached Westover, which is distant about twenty-five miles from Richmond, the capital of Virginia.

On receiving intelligence that a fleet had entered the capes, General Nelson was employed in raising the militia of the lower country; and on the 2d of January orders were issued to call out those above the metropolis and in its neighbourhood. January 2.

On reaching Westover, Arnold landed with the greater part of his army, and commenced his march towards Richmond. The few continental troops at Petersburg were ordered to the capital; and between one and two hundred militia, who had been collected from the town and its immediate vicinity, were directed to harass the advancing enemy.

This party was too feeble for its object; and, the day after landing at Westover, Arnold entered Richmond, where he halted with about five hundred men. The residue, amounting to about four hundred, including thirty horse, proceeded under Lieutenant Colonel Simcoe to Westham, where they burnt a valuable foundry, boring mill, powder magazine, and other smaller buildings, with military stores to a considerable amount, and many valuable papers belonging to the government, which had been carried thither as to a place of safety.

He destroys valuable stores at Richmond.

This service being effected, Lieutenant Colonel Simcoe rejoined Arnold at Richmond; where the public stores, and a large quantity of rum and salt, the property of private individuals, were entirely destroyed.

CHAP. X
1781
January.

Leaving Richmond the next day, the army returned to Westover * on the seventh; and, re-embarking on the morning of the tenth, proceeded down the river. It was followed by the Baron Steuben, who commanded in Virginia; and, near Hoods, Colonel Clarke drew a party of them into an ambuscade, and gave them one fire with some effect; but, on its being partially returned, the Americans broke and fled in the utmost confusion.†

Arnold proceeded slowly down the river; and on the twentieth reached Portsmouth, where he manifested the intention of establishing a permanent post.

The loss of the British in this expedition, was stated in the gazette of New York, at seven killed, including one subaltern, and twenty-three wounded, among whom was one captain. This small loss was sustained almost entirely in the ambuscade near Hoods.

In the north, the year commenced with an event, which, for a time, threatened the American cause with total ruin.

The accumulated sufferings and privations of the army constitute a large and interesting part of the history of that war which gave independence to the United States. Winter, without

* While the army lay at Westover, Lieutenant Colonel Simcoe, at the head of less than fifty horse, attacked and dispersed a body of militia at Charles City court house, with the loss of only one man killed, and three wounded.

† The author witnessed this skirmish.

much lessening their toils, added to those sufferings. The soldiers were perpetually on the point of starving, were often entirely without food; were exposed without proper clothing to the rigours of the season, and had now served almost twelve months without pay.

This state of things had been of such long continuance that scarcely the hope of a change could be indulged. It produced, unavoidably, some relaxation of discipline; and the murmurs, occasionally escaping the officers, sometimes heard by the soldiers, were not without their influence.

In addition to the general causes of dissatisfaction, the Pennsylvania line complained of a grievance almost peculiar to itself.

When congress directed enlistments to be made for three years, or during the war, the recruiting officers of Pennsylvania, in some instances, instead of engaging their men, definitively, for the one period or the other, engaged them generally for three years, or the war. This ambiguity in the terms of enlistment produced its natural effect. The soldier claimed his discharge at the expiration of three years, and the officer insisted on retaining him in service during the war. The soldier submitted with the more reluctance to the supposed imposition, as he constantly witnessed the immense bounties given to those who were not bound by a former enlistment.

CHAP. X

1781

Mutiny in the Pennsylvania line.

The discontents which these various causes had been long fomenting, broke out on the night of the 1st of January, in an open and almost universal revolt of the line.

On a signal given, the great body of the non-commissioned officers and privates paraded under arms, avowing the determination to march to the seat of congress, and either obtain redress of their complicated grievances, or serve no longer. In the attempt to suppress the mutiny, six or seven of the mutineers were wounded on the one side; and on the other, Captain Billing was killed, and several other officers were dangerously wounded. The authority of General Wayne availed nothing. On cocking his pistol, and threatening some of the most turbulent, the bayonet was presented to his bosom; and he perceived that strong measures would produce his own destruction, and perhaps the massacre of every officer in camp. A few regiments who did not at first join the mutineers, were paraded by their officers; but, had they even been willing to proceed to extremities, they were not strong enough to restore order. Infected quickly with the general contagion, or intimidated by the threats of the mutineers, they joined their comrades; and the whole body, consisting of about thirteen hundred men, with six field pieces, marched, under the command of their sergeants, towards Princeton.

The next day, General Wayne, accompanied by Colonels Butler and Stewart, officers possessing, in a high degree, the affections of the soldiery, followed them, in the hope of bringing them back to their duty, or at least of dividing them. They were overtaken near Middlebrook, and invited by a written message from General Wayne, to appoint one man from each regiment to state the grievances of which they complained.

In consequence of this invitation, a sergeant from each regiment met the officers at their quarters, and some verbal communications were made, from the complexion of which sanguine hopes were entertained that the affair might be terminated without farther hazard, or much injury to the service.

On the following day, the line of march was resumed, and the soldiers proceeded to Princeton. The propositions of the general and field officers were reported to them, and a committee of sergeants, to whom they were referred, stated their claims. These were,

1st. A discharge for all those who had served three years under their original engagements, whatever those engagements might have been, and who had not taken the increased bounty, and re-enlisted for the war.

2nd. An immediate payment of all their arrears of pay and clothing, as well to those who should be discharged, as to those who should continue in service.

3rd. The residue of their bounty, and future real pay to those who should continue in the army.

General Wayne being unwilling to discharge all those who had not re-enlisted for the war, the subject was referred to the civil power.

On receiving intelligence of the mutiny, congress appointed a committee to confer with the executive of Pennsylvania respecting it. The result of this conference was that both the committee, and the governor with some members of the executive council, left Philadelphia for the purpose of endeavouring to accommodate this dangerous commotion.

At his head quarters, at New Windsor, on the North River, General Washington received intelligence of this alarming mutiny. Accustomed as he had been to contemplate hazardous and difficult situations, it was not easy, under existing circumstances, to resolve instantly on the course it was most prudent to pursue. His first impression—to repair to the camp of the mutineers—soon gave place to opinions which were formed on more mature reflection.

It was almost certain that the business was already in the hands of the civil government, with whose arrangements it might be improper for him to interfere. Independent of this consideration, other motives of irresistible influence detained him on the North River.

The most important among those subjects of complaint which were alleged as the causes of the mutiny, were true in fact, were common to the whole army, and were of a nature to disseminate too generally those seeds of disquiet, which had attained their full growth and maturity in the Pennsylvania line. Strong symptoms of discontent had already been manifested; and it was, therefore, impossible to say with confidence, how far the same temper existed among the other troops; or how far the contagion of example had or would spread.

The danger arising from this state of things was much increased by the circumstance that the river was perfectly open, and afforded Sir Henry Clinton an easy and rapid transportation for his army to West Point, should the situation of its garrison invite an enterprise against that post.

It was an additional consideration of great weight, that it might have a most pernicious influence on the discipline of the whole army, should the authority of the Commander-in-chief be disregarded. He ought not to place himself in a situation where his orders might be disobeyed with impunity; an event much to be apprehended, should he repair to the camp of the mutineers, unattended by a military force adequate to the occasion.

CHAP. X

1781

Such a force could not be immediately commanded. His effectives in the Highlands amounted only to thirteen hundred and seventy-six men; and that whole division of the army, dispersed at various and distant stations, excluding the sick and those on furlough, did not exceed four thousand. Assuming therefore the fidelity of the troops, it was impracticable to march immediately with a force sufficient to reduce the Pennsylvania line, without leaving the Highlands undefended. Nor was it unworthy of consideration that, in the actual situation of the mutineers, the probability of their being attacked by such a force might drive them to the enemy, or disperse them, events, either of which would deprive the army of a valuable part of its strength.

It was therefore thought adviseable to leave the negotiation with the civil power, and to prepare for those measures which ought to be adopted in the event of its failure. The disposition of the troops on the North River was sounded, and found to be favourable; after which, a detachment of eleven hundred men was ordered to be in readiness to move on a moment's warning. On the first notice of the mutiny, the militia of Jersey took the field under General Dickenson, and measures were taken to call out those of New York should the occasion require it.

To avail himself of an event appearing so auspicious to the royal cause, Sir Henry Clinton ordered a large body of troops to be in readiness to move on the shortest notice; and despatched three emissaries with tempting offers to the revolters; and instructions to invite them, while the negotiation should be depending, to take a position behind the South River, where they should be effectually covered by detachments from New York. While these measures were taking, Sir Henry kept his eye on West Point, and held himself in readiness to strike at that place, should any movement on the part of General Washington open to him a prospect of success.*

Sir Henry Clinton attempts to negotiate with the mutineers.

His emissaries were immediately seized by the revolters, and their proposals communicated to General Wayne, with assurances of the utter detestation in which every idea of going over to the common enemy was held.

This favourable symptom, however, was accompanied by suspicious circumstances. They retained the British emissaries in their own possession; and could not be induced to cross the Delaware, or to march from Princeton. They would not permit any of their former officers, other than those already mentioned, to enter their camp; and General St. Clair, the Marquis de Lafayette, and Lieutenant Colonel Laurens, were ordered to leave Princeton.

Such was the state of things when the committee of congress, and President Read with a

* Letter of Sir Henry Clinton.

CHAP. X

1781

part of his executive council, arrived in the neighbourhood of the revolters. The former having delegated their power to the latter, a conference was held with the sergeants who now commanded, after which proposals were made and distributed among the troops for consideration.

In these proposals the government offered,

1st. To discharge all those who had enlisted indefinitely for three years or during the war, the fact to be examined into by three commissioners, to be appointed by the executive; and to be ascertained, when the original enlistment could not be produced, by the oath of the soldier.

2dly. To give immediate certificates for the depreciation on their pay, and to settle the arrearages as soon as circumstances would admit.

3dly. To furnish them immediately with certain specified articles of clothing which were most wanted.

They compromise with the civil authority.

On receiving these propositions, the troops agreed to march to Trenton. At that place the terms were accepted, with the addition that three commissioners should also be deputed by the line, who, conjointly with those of the executive should constitute the board authorized to determine on the claims of the soldiers to be discharged; and thereupon the British emissaries were surrendered, who were tried, condemned, and executed as spies.

Until the investigation should be made, and discharges given to those who should be found entitled to them, the sergeants retained their command. In consequence of the irksomeness of this state of things, the business was pressed with so much precipitation, that before the enlistments themselves could be brought from the huts, almost the whole of the artillery, and of the five first regiments of infantry, were liberated on the testimony of their own oaths. The enlistments being then produced, it was found that not many of the remaining regiments had engaged on the terms which, under the compact, would entitle them to leave the service; and that, of those actually dismissed, far the greater number had been enlisted absolutely for the war. The discharges given, however, were not cancelled; and the few who were to remain in service received furloughs for forty days.

Thus ended, in a temporary dissolution of the whole line of Pennsylvania, a mutiny, which a voluntary performance of much less than was extorted, would have prevented; and which, in the actual condition of the army, was of a nature and extent to inspire the most serious alarm.

Mutiny in the Jersey line.

The dangerous policy of yielding even to the just demands of soldiers made with arms in their hands, was soon illustrated. The success of the Pennsylvania line inspired that of Jersey, many of whom were also foreigners, with the hope of obtaining similar advantages. On the night of

CHAP. X 1781 the 20th, a part of the Jersey brigade, which had been stationed at Pompton, rose in arms; and, making precisely the same claims which had been yielded to the Pennsylvanians, marched to Chatham, where a part of the same brigade was cantoned, in the hope of exciting them also to join in the revolt.

General Washington, who had been extremely chagrined at the issue of the mutiny in the Pennsylvania line, and who was now assured of the confidence to be placed in the fidelity of the eastern troops, who were composed of natives, determined, by strong measures, to stop the farther progress of a spirit which threatened the destruction of the army, and ordered a detachment to march against the mutineers, and to bring them to unconditional submission. General Howe, who commanded this detachment, was instructed to make no terms with the insurgents while in a state of resistance; and, as soon as they should surrender, to seize a few of the most active leaders, and to execute them on the spot. These orders were promptly obeyed, and the Jersey mutineers returned to their duty.

In the hope of being more successful with the revolters of Jersey than he had been with those of Pennsylvania, Sir Henry Clinton offered them the same terms which had been proposed to the mutineers at Princeton; and General Robertson, at the head of three thousand men, was detached to Staten Island with the avowed purpose of crossing over into Jersey, and covering any movement which they might make towards New York. The emissary, being in the American interest, delivered his papers to the officer commanding at the first station to which he came. Other papers were dispersed among the mutineers; but the mutiny was crushed too suddenly to allow time for the operation of these propositions.

The vigorous measures taken in this instance were happily followed by such an attention on the part of the states, to the actual situation of the army, as checked the progress of discontent. Influenced by the representations of the Commander-in-chief, they raised three months' pay in specie, which they forwarded to the soldiers, who received it with joy, considering it as evidence that their fellow citizens were not entirely unmindful of their sufferings.

Although the army was thus reduced to such extreme distress, the discontents of the people were daily multiplied by the contributions which they were required to make, and by the irritating manner in which those contributions were drawn from them. Every article for public use was obtained by impressment; and the taxes were either unpaid, or collected by coercive means. Strong remonstrances were made against this system; and the dissatisfaction which pervaded the mass of the community, was scarcely less

CHAP. X

1781

dangerous than that which had been manifested by the army.

To the judicious patriots throughout America, the necessity of giving greater powers to the federal government became every day more apparent; but the efforts of enlightened individuals were too feeble to correct that fatal disposition of power which had been made by enthusiasm uninstructed by experience.

Mission of Colonel Laurens to France.

To relieve the United States from their complicated embarrassments, a foreign loan seemed an expedient of indispensable necessity, and from France they hoped to obtain it. Congress selected Lieutenant Colonel Laurens, a gentleman whose situation in the family of the Commander-in-chief had enabled him to take a comprehensive view of the military capacities and weaknesses of his country, for this interesting service; and instructed him also to urge the advantage of maintaining a naval superiority in the American seas. Before his departure, he passed some days at headquarters, and received from General Washington in the form of a letter, the result of his reflections on the existing state of things.

In this paper he detailed the pecuniary embarrassments of the government, and represented, with great earnestness, the inability of the nation to furnish a revenue adequate to the support of the war. He dwelt on the discontents which the system of impressment had excited among the people, and expressed his fears that the evils felt in the prosecution of the war, might weaken the sentiments which began it.

From this state of things, he deduced the vital importance of an immediate and ample supply of money, which might be the foundation for substantial arrangements of finance, for reviving public credit, and giving vigour to future operations; as well as of a decided effort of the allied arms on the continent to effect the great objects of the alliance, in the ensuing campaign.

Next to a supply of money, he considered a naval superiority in the American seas, as an object of the deepest interest.

To the United States, it would be of decisive importance, and France also might derive great advantages from transferring the maritime war to the coast of her ally.

The future ability of the United States to repay any loan which might now be obtained was displayed; and he concluded with assurances that there was still a fund of inclination and resource in the country, equal to great and continued exertions, provided the means were afforded of stopping the progress of disgust, by changing the present system, and adopting another more consonant with the spirit of the nation, and more capable of infusing activity and energy into public measures; of which a powerful succour in money must be the basis. "The

CHAP. X

1781

people were discontented, but it was with the feeble and oppressive mode of conducting the war, not with the war itself."

With reason did the Commander-in-chief thus urge on the cabinet of Versailles, the policy of advancing a sum of money to the United States which might be adequate to the exigency. Deep was the gloom with which their political horizon was overcast. The British, in possession of South Carolina and of Georgia, had overrun the greater part of North Carolina also; and it was with equal hazard and address that Greene maintained himself in the northern frontier of that state.

A second detachment from New York was making a deep impression on Virginia, where the resistance had been neither so prompt nor so vigorous * as the strength of that state and the unanimity of its citizens had given reason to expect.

The perplexities and difficulties in which the affairs of America were involved, were estimated by the British government even above their real value. Intercepted letters of this date from the minister, expressed the most sanguine hopes that the great superiority of force at the disposal of Sir Henry Clinton, would compel Washington with his feeble army to take refuge on the eastern side of the Hudson.

* A slave population must be unfavourable to great and sudden exertions by militia.

Even congress relaxed for an instant from its habitual firmness; and, receding from the decisive manner in which that body had insisted on the territorial and maritime rights of the nation, directed the American minister at Madrid to relinquish, if it should be absolutely necessary, the claims of the United States to navigate the Mississippi below the thirty-first degree of north latitude, and to a free port on the banks of that river within the Spanish territory. It is remarkable that only Massachusetts, Connecticut, and North Carolina, dissented from this resolution; New York was divided.† On a subsequent day, the subject was again brought forward, and a proposition was made for still farther concessions to Spain; but this proposition was negatived by all the states.*

Propositions to Spain.

Happily for the United States, Mr. Jay, their minister at the court of Madrid, required as the price of the concessions he was instructed to make, that the treaty he was labouring to negotiate should be immediately concluded.

The establishment of a revenue subject to the exclusive control and direction of the continental government, was connected inseparably with the restoration of credit. The efforts therefore to negotiate a foreign loan were accompanied

† Secret journals of Congress, v. 2, pp. 393, 396, 407. This measure was moved by the delegation from Virginia, in consequence of instructions of 2d Jan. 1781. Sec. 10, H. at large, 538.

* Secret journals of Congress, v. 2, p. 468.

CHAP. X

1781

by resolutions requesting the respective states to place a fund under the control of congress, which should be both permanent and productive. A resolution was passed, recommending to the respective states to vest a power in congress to levy for the use of the United States a duty of five *per centum ad valorem* on all goods imported into any of them; and also on all prizes condemned in any of the American courts of admiralty.

Recommendations relative to a duty on imported and prize goods.

This fund was to be appropriated to the payment of both the principal and interest of all debts contracted in the prosecution of the war; and was to continue until those debts should be completely discharged.

Congress, at that time, contained several members who perceived the advantages which would result from bestowing on the government of the nation the full power of regulating commerce, and, consequently, of increasing the import as circumstances might render adviseable; but state influence predominated, and they were overruled by great majorities. Even the inadequate plan which they did recommend was never adopted. Notwithstanding the greatness of the exigency, and the pressure of the national wants, never, during the existence of the confederation, did all the states unite in assenting to this recommendation; so unwilling are men possessed of power, to place it in the hands of others.

Reform in the organization of the executive departments.

About the same time a reform was introduced into the administration, the necessity of which had been long perceived. From a misplaced prejudice against institutions sanctioned by experience, all the great executive duties had been devolved either on committees of congress, or on boards consisting of several members. This unwieldy and expensive system had maintained itself against all the efforts of reason and public utility. But the scantiness of the national means at length prevailed over prejudice, and the several committees and boards yielded to a secretary for foreign affairs, a superintendent of finance, a secretary of war, and a secretary of marine. But so miserably defective was the organization of congress, as an executive body, that the year had far advanced before this measure, the utility of which all acknowledged, could be carried into complete operation by making all the appointments.

Confederation adopted.

About this time the articles of confederation were ratified. Much difficulty was encountered in obtaining the adoption of this instrument. The numerous objections made by the states yielded successively to the opinion that a federal compact would be of vast importance in the prosecution of the war. One impediment it was found peculiarly difficult to remove. Within the chartered limits of several states, were immense tracts of vacant territory, which, it was supposed, would constitute a large fund of fu-

CHAP. X

1781

ture wealth; and the states not possessing that advantage insisted on considering this territory as a joint acquisition. At length this difficulty also was surmounted; and, in February, 1781, to the great joy of America, this interesting compact was rendered complete.* Like many other human institutions, it was productive, neither in war nor in peace, of all the benefits which its sanguine advocates had expected. Had peace been made before any agreement for a permanent union was formed, it is far from being improbable that the different parts might have fallen asunder, and a dismemberment have taken place.

* The secret journals of congress, published under the resolutions of March 27th, 1818, and April 21st, 1820, contain "A History of the Confederation." The course of public opinion on a most important point—the nature of the connexion which ought to be maintained between these United States—may be in some degree perceived in the progress of this instrument, and may not be entirely uninteresting to the American reader.

So early as July, 1775, Doctor Franklin submitted "Articles of Confederation and perpetual union" to the consideration of congress, which were to continue in force until a reconciliation with Great Britain should take place on the terms demanded by the colonies. Into this confederation, not only all the British colonies on the continent, but Ireland and the West India islands were to be admitted.

Congress was to consist of members chosen by each colony in proportion to its numbers, and was to sit in each successively. Its powers were to embrace the external relations of the country, the settling of all disputes between the colonies, the planting of new colonies; and were to extend to ordinances on such general subjects as, though necessary to the general welfare, particular assemblies can not be competent to, viz. "Those that may relate to our general commerce, or general currency; the establishment of ports; and the regulation of our common forces."

The executive was to consist of a council of twelve, selected by congress from its own body, one-third of whom were to be changed annually.

Amendments were to be proposed by congress; and, when approved by a majority of the colonial assemblies, were to become a part of the constitution.

If the confederation really preserved the idea of union until the good sense of the nation adopted a more efficient system, this service alone entitles that instrument to the respectful recollection of the American people, and its framers to their gratitude.

Military transactions.

Such was the defensive strength of the positions taken by the adverse armies on the Hudson, and such their relative force, that no decisive blow could be given by either in that quarter of the continent. The anxious attentions of General Washington, therefore, were unremittingly directed to the south. One of

---

In June, 1776, a committee was appointed to prepare and digest the form of a confederation to be entered into between the United Colonies, which brought in a draft (in the hand writing of Mr. John Dickinson) on the 12th of the succeeding month.

This report was under debate until the 14th of November, 1777, on which day congress agreed on the articles afterwards adopted by the states.

In the scheme supposed to be prepared by Mr. Dickinson, the confederation is considered as an alliance of sovereign states, who meet as equals by their deputies assembled to deliberate on their common concerns, each sovereign having a voice. This principle was retained; but several modifications in the language and principle of the original scheme were made, which indicate a watchful and growing jealousy of the powers of congress.

In each, an article is introduced reserving the rights of the states. That which is found in the report, "reserves to each state the sole and exclusive regulation and government of its internal police, in all matters that *shall not interfere with the articles of this confederation.*"

This article was so modified as to declare that "each state retains its sovereignty," "and every power, jurisdiction and right, which is not by this confederation *expressly* delegated to the United States in congress assembled."

This denial of all incidental powers had vast influence on the affairs of the United States. It defeated, in many instances, the granted powers, by rendering their exercise impracticable.

The report permits the states to impose duties on imports

CHAP. X
1781

those incidents which fortune occasionally produces, on the seizing or neglect of which the greatest military events frequently depend, presented, sooner than was expected, an opportunity which he deemed capable of being improved to the destruction of the British army in Virginia.

The French fleet, from its arrival on the American coast, had been blocked up in the harbour of Newport; and the land forces of that nation had been reduced to a state of inactivity by the necessity of defending their ships. Late in January, a detachment from the British fleet

and exports; provided they "do not interfere with any stipulations in treaties hereafter entered into by the United States."

The confederation confines this restriction on the power of the state to such duties as interfere with the stipulations in treaties entered into "in pursuance of any treaties already proposed by congress to the courts of France and Spain."

Each plan assigns to the state in which troops shall be raised for the common defence, the power of appointing the field and inferior officers. The confederation adds the power of filling up such vacancies as may occur.

The report inhibits a state from endeavouring by force to obtain compensation for advances made or injuries suffered during the war, which shall not be allowed by congress.

The confederation omits this inhibition.

The report gives to congress the power of making treaties.

The confederation adds a proviso, "that no treaty of commerce shall be made whereby the legislative power of the respective states shall be restrained from imposing such imports and duties on foreigners as their own people are subjected to, or from prohibiting the exportation or importation of any species of goods or commodities whatever."

The report authorizes congress to appoint "courts for the trial of all crimes, frauds, and piracies committed on the high seas, or on any navigable river not within a county or parish."

The confederation limits the jurisdiction to "piracies and felonies committed on the high seas."

Both empower congress to appoint courts for the trial of appeals in cases of capture; but the confederation provides that no member of congress shall be appointed a judge of any such court.

Both empower congress to settle differences between the

was encountered on the east end of Long Island by a furious storm, in which such damage was sustained as to destroy for a time the naval superiority which Arbuthnot had uniformly preserved.

To turn this temporary superiority to advantage, Monsieur Destouches resolved to detach a ship of the line, with two frigates, to the Chesapeake; a force which the delegation from Virginia had assured him would be sufficient for the purpose.

On receiving certain accounts of the loss sustained in the storm, General Washington con-

states. The confederation prescribes minutely the manner in which this power shall be exercised.

Both empower congress "to regulate the trade and manage all affairs with the Indians." The confederation provides "that the legislative right of any state within its own limits be not infringed or violated."

The report gives the power of "establishing and regulating post offices throughout all the United Colonies (states) *on the lines of communication* from one colony (state) to another."

The confederation varies the phraseology and adds, "and exacting such postage on the papers passing through the same as may be requisite to defray the expenses of the said office."

The report places many important portions of the executive power in a council of state, to consist of one delegate from each state to be named annually by the delegates of that state.

The confederation empowers congress to appoint a committee to sit in the recess of congress, to be denominated "a committee of the states," and to consist of one delegate from each state, to exercise such powers as congress might from time to time vest them with.

A few of the states agreed to ratify the confederation unconditionally. By many, amendments were proposed which were steadily rejected by congress. It was obvious that the delays would be almost interminable should congress relax this determination, because every change would make it necessary again to submit the instrument as amended to the several states. It is remarkable that Jersey alone proposed an enlargement of the powers of congress. That state was desirous of investing the representatives of the state with the power of regulating commerce.

The states possessing no vacant lands, or an inconsiderable

CHAP. X 1781

ceived the design of improving that circumstance by immediate and powerful operations against Arnold. Confident that the critical moment must be seized, or the enterprise would fail, he ordered a detachment of twelve hundred men, under the command of the Marquis de Lafayette, to the head of the Chesapeake; there to embark for that part of Virginia which was to become the theatre of action, under convoy of a French frigate, for which he applied to the admiral. He immediately communicated this measure to the Count de Rochambeau, and to Monsieur Destouches, to whom he also stated his conviction that no serious advantage could be expected from a few ships, unaided by land troops. "There were," he said, "a variety of positions to be taken by Arnold, one of which was Portsmouth, his present station, where his ships might be so protected by his batteries on the shore as to defy a mere naval attack; and

quantity within their chartered limits, pressed earnestly and perseveringly their claim to participate in the advantages of territory, which was, they said, acquired by the united arms of the whole; and Maryland refused, on this account, to accede to the confederation. At length, several of the states empowered their members in congress to ratify that instrument as forming a union between the twelve states who had assented to it. Maryland, alarmed at the prospect of being excluded from the union, gave her reluctant consent to the confederation, accompanied by a protest, in which she still asserted her claim to her interest in the vacant territory which should be acknowledged at the treaty of peace, to be within the United States.

It required the repeated lessons of a severe and instructive experience to persuade the American people that their greatness, their prosperity, their happiness, and even their safety, imperiously demanded the substitution of a government for their favourite league.

where he would certainly be able to maintain himself until the losses sustained in the late storm should be repaired, and the superiority at sea recovered, when he would unquestionably be relieved."

To insure the success of the expedition, he recommended that the whole fleet should be employed on it, and that a detachment of one thousand men should be embarked for the same service.

These representations did not prevail. The original plan had already been put in execution. February 9. On the 9th of February, a sixty-four gun ship with two frigates, under Monsieur de Tilley, had sailed for the Chesapeake; and, as some of the British ships had been repaired, the French admiral did not think it prudent to put to sea with the residue of his fleet.

As had been foreseen by General Washington, de Tilley found Arnold in a situation not to be assailed with any prospect of success. After showing himself therefore in the bay, and making an ineffectual attempt to enter Elizabeth River, he returned to Newport. At the capes, he fell in with the Romulus, a fifty gun ship, coming from Charleston to the Chesapeake, which he captured.

Both the Count de Rochambeau, and the Chevalier Destouches, being well disposed to execute the plans suggested by General Washington, they determined, on the return of Mon-

CHAP. X 1781 sieur de Tilley, to make a second expedition to the Chesapeake with the whole fleet, and eleven hundred men. General Washington, therefore, hastened to Newport, that in a personal conference with them, he might facilitate the execution of an enterprise from which he still entertained sanguine hopes.

March 6. Early on the 6th of March he reached Newport, and went instantly on board the Admiral, where he was met by the Count de Rochambeau. It was determined that a detachment from the army, then in perfect readiness, should be embarked under the Count de Viominil; and that the fleet should put to sea as soon as possible. The wind was favourable to the French, and adverse to the British. Yet the fleet did not sail until the evening of the eighth. It appears from a letter of Monsieur Destouches, that this delay was in some measure attributable to a disaster which befel one of his frigates in getting out of port; and there is reason to suppose that it may be ascribed to a want of supplies. Whatever may have been the cause, Arnold is most probably indebted to it for his escape from the fate which his treason merited.

Two days after Destouches had sailed, he was followed by Arbuthnot, who overtook him off the capes of Virginia. A partial engagement ensued which continued about an hour, when the fleets were separated.

The French admiral called a council of war the next day, in which it was declared unadviseable to renew the action, and he returned to Newport.

March 26.

The arrival of two thousand men commanded by General Philips, gave the British a decided superiority in Virginia, and changed the destination of Lafayette, who had been ordered to join the southern army, but to whom the defence of that state was now committed. The troops under his command being taken chiefly from the eastern regiments, had imbibed strong prejudices against a southern climate; and desertions became so frequent as to threaten the dissolution of the corps.

This unpromising state of things was completely changed by a happy expedient adopted by Lafayette. Appealing to the generous principles of his soldiers, principles on which the feelings of his own bosom taught him to rely, he proclaimed in orders, that he was about to enter on an enterprise of great danger and difficulty, in which he persuaded himself his soldiers would not abandon him. If, however, any individual of the detachment was unwilling to accompany him, a permit to return should most assuredly be granted him.

This measure had the desired effect, and put an end to desertion.* To keep up the good dis-

* The author was assured by General Lafayette that this was true. Such was the enthusiasm of the moment, that a lame sergeant hired a place in a cart to keep up with the army.

CHAP. X 1781 positions of the moment, this ardent young nobleman, who was as unmindful of fortune as he was ambitious of fame, borrowed from the merchants of Baltimore, on his private credit, a sum of money sufficient to purchase shoes, linen, spirits, and other articles of immediate necessity for the detachment.†

Having made these preparations for the campaign, he marched with the utmost celerity to the defence of Virginia. That state was in great need of assistance. The enemy had penetrated deep into its bosom, and was committing those excesses on its inhabitants to which a country unable to repel invasion must always be exposed.

General Philips, on his arrival, took command of all the British troops in Virginia; and, after completing the fortification of Portsmouth, commenced offensive operations.

About two thousand five hundred men were embarked on board some small vessels, and landed at various places in the neighbourhood of Williamsburg. Different detachments spread themselves over the lower part of that neck of land which is made by York and James Rivers; and, after destroying, without opposition, a ship yard belonging to the state, with some armed vessels and public stores, re-embarked and pro-

† It is not unworthy of notice, that the ladies of Baltimore charged themselves with the toil of immediately making up the summer clothing for the troops. Innumerable instances of their zeal in the common cause of their country were given in every state in the union.

ceeded to City Point, where they landed in the afternoon of the 24th. The next day they marched against Petersburg, at which place, immense quantities of tobacco and other stores were deposited.

April 24.

Baron Steuben was not in a situation to check their progress. The levies of Virginia had marched to the aid of General Greene; and the whole number of militia, at that time in the field, did not much exceed two thousand men. Unwilling to abandon so important a place as Petersburg without the semblance of fighting, the baron posted about one thousand men a mile below the town with orders to skirmish with the enemy. The British troops, without being able to bring him to a close engagement, were two or three hours employed in driving him across the Appomattox, the bridge over which being taken up as soon as the militia had passed it, farther pursuit became impracticable.

This skirmish having terminated with scarcely any loss on either side, the baron retreated towards Richmond, and Philips took quiet possession of Petersburg; where he destroyed a considerable quantity of tobacco, and all the vessels lying in the river.

This service being accomplished, Arnold was detached through Osbornes to Warwick, between which place and Richmond, a respectable naval force, consisting of small armed vessels, had been collected with the intention of co-operating with

CHAP. X
1781

the French fleet against Portsmouth; and a few militia were stationed on the northern bank of the river to assist in defending the flotilla.

The crews of the vessels, on receiving a fire from a few field pieces ordered by Arnold to the bank, scuttled them, escaped to the opposite shore, and dispersed with the militia. Philips marched with the residue of the army to Chesterfield court house, the place of rendezvous for the new levies of Virginia, where he destroyed the barracks with a few public stores; after which he joined Arnold in the neighbourhood of Warwick, and marched without interruption to Manchester, a small town on the southern bank

April 30.

of James River, immediately opposite to Richmond; where, as was the general practice, the warehouses were set on fire, and all the tobacco consumed.

On the preceding evening, the Marquis de Lafayette, who had made a forced march from Baltimore, arrived with his detachment at Richmond; and that place, in which a great proportion of the military stores of the state were then collected, was saved, for the time, from a visit which was certainly designed.

The regular troops composing this detachment were joined by about two thousand militia, and sixty dragoons. Not thinking it adviseable to attempt the passage of the river in the presence of so respectable an army, General Philips retired to Bermuda Hundred, a point of land in the confluence of the James and Appomatox, at which place he re-embarked his troops, and fell down the river to Hog Island.

The Marquis fixed his head quarters on the north of Chiccahominy, about eighteen miles from Richmond; where he remained until a letter from Lord Cornwallis called Philips again up James River.

When that nobleman determined on marching from Wilmington into Virginia, he signified his wish that the British troops in that state, should take their station at Petersburg.

On receiving this letter, Philips proceeded to comply with the request it contained. As soon as the fleet moved up the river, Lafayette returned to the defence of Richmond. Having, on his arrival, received intelligence that Lord Cornwallis was marching northward, and finding Philips landed at Brandon on the south side of the river, he was persuaded that a junction of the two armies must be intended, and hastened to take possession of Petersburg * before Philips could reach that place. In this however he was anticipated by the British general; upon which he recrossed James River, and, encamping a few miles below Richmond, used his utmost exertions to remove the military stores in that town to a place of greater security.

* General Lafayette states that this movement also facilitated the transportation of some military stores to the southern army, which were greatly needed.

CHAP. X

1781

Cornwallis arrives.

In this position his army was permitted to repose itself but a few days. Lord Cornwallis, after passing through North Carolina and the southern parts of Virginia without encountering much opposition, and effecting a junction with Arnold, who had succeeded by the death of Philips to the command of the army in Virginia,† found himself at the head of a force which nothing in that state could resist; and determined on a vigorous plan of offensive operations. His immediate object was to bring the Marquis to an action; for which purpose he crossed James River at Westover, where he was joined by a reinforcement from New York, and attempted, by turning the left flank of the American army, to get into its rear. Lafayette was not in a condition to risk an engagement. His objects were the security of the public stores, the preservation of his small army for future services, and a junction with the Pennsylvania line which was on its march southward, under the command of General Wayne. As Lord Cornwallis crossed James River, he retired towards the upper country, inclining his route to the north in order to favour a junction with Wayne.

The fine horses found in the stables of private gentlemen, gave to the British general an effi-

† General Philips died the day on which the army entered Petersburg. Arnold on succeeding to the command addressed a letter to Lafayette, which the American general refused to receive, informing the officer who brought it, and whom he treated in other respects with great politeness, that he would receive no letter from Arnold.—*Cor. of Lafayette.*

cient cavalry; and enabled him to mount so many infantry, as to move large detachments with unusual rapidity. With these advantages, he was so confident of overtaking and destroying his enemy, as to say exultingly in a letter which was intercepted, "the boy can not escape me." His sanguine hopes, however, were disappointed. Lafayette moved with so much celerity and caution as to convince Cornwallis of the impracticability of overtaking him, or of preventing his junction with Wayne.

After marching some distance up the northern side of Northanora, his lordship relinquished the pursuit, and turned his attention to other objects which were more attainable.

Military stores had been collected in various parts of the middle country, and, among others, at the Point of Fork, a point of land made by the confluence of the Rivanna and Fluvanna, the two branches of James' River. Colonel Simcoe was detached with five hundred men against this post, which was protected by between five and six hundred new levies, and a few militia. Tarlton, with two hundred and fifty cavalry and mounted infantry, was ordered at the same time against Charlottesville, where the general assembly was in session. So rapid were his movements that a mere accident prevented his entering the town before any notice of his approach was given. A private gentleman, Mr. Jouiette, who was acquainted with a nearer route than the

CHAP. X
1781

great road, hastened to Charlottesville on a fleet horse with the interesting intelligence, and entered the town about two hours before the British cavalry. Nearly all * the members of the legislature made their escape, and reassembled at Staunton, on the western side of the Blue Ridge. Tarlton, after destroying the stores at Charlottesville, proceeded down the Rivanna to the Point of Fork.

The detachment commanded by Simcoe, being composed chiefly of infantry, could not move with equal celerity. That officer, however, conducted his march with so much secrecy and address, that Steuben seems to have been either unapprized of his approach, or to have had no accurate information of his numbers. Intelligence of the expedition to Charlottesville had reached him, and he had prudently employed himself in removing his stores from the Point of Fork to the south side of the Fluvanna.

The river was at the time unfordable; and the boats were all secured on the southern bank. Yet Steuben, suspecting the detachment of Simcoe to be the van of the British army, or apprehending that Tarlton might get into his rear, withdrew precipitately in the night, and marched near thirty miles, leaving behind him such stores as could not be removed. These were destroyed next morning by a small detach-

* Seven fell into the hands of Tarlton.

ment of men who crossed the river in a few canoes.

Presses Lafayette over the Rapidan.

To secure his junction with Wayne, and to keep open his communication towards the north, Lafayette had crossed the Rapidan.

Lafayette forms a junction with Wayne.

These movements of the two armies had thrown Lord Cornwallis between Lafayette and the military stores which had been transported from Richmond up James' River, and deposited at different places, but principally at Albemarle old court house, high up that river. To this place Lord Cornwallis directed his march.

The Marquis, having effected a junction with the Pennsylvania line consisting of eight hundred men, recrossed the Rapidan, and advanced with so much celerity towards the British army, that he encamped within a few miles of it, while upwards of a day's march from its point of destination.

Confident that the object of the American general must be to protect the magazines on the Fluvanna, Lord Cornwallis encamped at Elk Island, and advanced his light troops to a position commanding the road, by which it was supposed the Americans must pass.

Lafayette, however, discovered in the night a nearer road which had long been disused; and the next morning the British general had the mortification to perceive that the American army had crossed the Rivanna, and taken a strong

CHAP. X

1781

position behind the Mechunk creek, which, in a great measure, commanded the route leading from the camp of his lordship to Albemarle old court house. At this place a considerable reinforcement of mountain militia was received.

Cornwallis retires to the lower country.

Apprehending the force opposed to him to be greater than it was in reality, and probably desirous of transferring the war to the lower country, Lord Cornwallis abandoned the objects he had pursued, and retired first to Richmond, and afterwards to Williamsburg.

June 18.

The Marquis followed with cautious circumspection. On the 18th of June, he was reinforced by four or five hundred new levies under the Baron Steuben, which augmented his army to four thousand men, of whom two thousand were regulars. That of Lord Cornwallis was, probably, rather more numerous.

As the British army retreated to Williamsburg, Lafayette, who sought a partial, though he avoided a general engagement, pressed its rear with his light parties. Colonel Simcoe, who covered the retreat, was overtaken by Colonel Butler about six miles from Williamsburg, and a sharp action ensued. The Americans claimed the advantage; but were compelled to retire by the approach of the whole British army.

In the bold and rapid course taken by Lord Cornwallis through the lower and central parts of Virginia, much private as well as public property * was destroyed; and the resources of the state were considerably diminished; but no solid advantage was obtained. Although, from various causes, especially from a want of arms, and from that general repugnance which a harassed, unpaid militia, will universally manifest to military service, less resistance was encountered than was to be expected from the strength and population of the state; no disposition was openly manifested to join the royal standard, or to withdraw from the contest. The Marquis complained of "much slowness, and much carelessness in the country; but the dispositions of the people," he said, "were good, and they required only to be awakened." This,

* While the British army overran the country, their ships sailed up the rivers, pillaged the farms, received the slaves who fled from their masters, and, in some instances, reduced the houses to ashes. While they were in the Potowmac, a flag was sent on shore at Mount Vernon, requiring a supply of fresh provisions. The steward of General Washington, believing it to be his duty to save the property of his principal, and entertaining fears for the magnificent buildings of the Commander-in-chief, went on board with the flag, carried a supply of fresh provisions, asked the restoration of the slaves who had taken refuge in the fleet, and requested that the buildings might be spared. Mr. Lund Washington, to whom the general had entrusted the management of his estate, communicated these circumstances to him, and informed him that he too had sustained considerable losses. "I am sorry," said the general, in reply, "to hear of your loss; I am a little sorry to hear of my own. But that which gives me most concern is, that you should have gone on board the vessels of the enemy and furnished them with refreshments. It would have been a less painful circumstance to me to have heard, that in consequence of your non-compliance with their request, they had burnt my home and laid the plantation in ruins. You ought to have considered yourself as my representative, and should have reflected on the bad example of communicating with the enemy, and making a voluntary offer of refreshment to them, with a view to prevent a conflagration."

CHAP. X
1781

he thought, would be best effected by the presence of General Washington, an event for which he expressed the most anxious solicitude. But Washington deemed it of more importance to remain on the Hudson, for the purpose of digesting and conducting a grand plan of combined operations then meditated against New York, by the execution of which he counted more certainly on relieving the southern states, than by any other measure it was in his power to adopt.

General Washington's letters are intercepted.

An express carrying letters, communicating to congress the result of his consultations on this subject, with the commanders of the land and naval forces of France, was intercepted in Jersey. The interesting disclosure made by these letters, alarmed Sir Henry Clinton for the safety of New York, and determined him to require the return of a part of the troops in Virginia. Supposing himself too weak, after complying with this requisition, to remain at Williamsburg, Lord Cornwallis took the resolution of retiring to Portsmouth.

In pursuance of this resolution, he marched from Williamsburg and encamped in such a manner as to cover the ford into the island of Jamestown. On the same evening, the Queen's rangers crossed over into the island; and the two succeeding days were employed in passing over the baggage.

The morning after the evacuation of Williamsburg, Lafayette changed his position, and pushed his best troops within nine miles of the British camp, with the intention of attempting their rear, when the main body should have passed into Jamestown.

Suspecting his design, Lord Cornwallis encamped the greater part of his army on the main land as compactly as possible, and displayed a few troops on the island in such a manner as, in appearance, to magnify their numbers. All the intelligence received by Lafayette concurred in the representation that the greater part of the British army had passed over to the island in the night. Believing this to be the fact, he detached some riflemen to harass their outposts, while he advanced at the head of the continental troops in order to cut off the rear.

July 6.

Every appearance was calculated to countenance the opinion he had formed. The British light parties were drawn in, and the piquets were forced by the riflemen without much resistance, but an advanced post which covered the encampment from the view of the Americans, was perseveringly maintained, though three of the officers commanding it were successively picked off by the riflemen. Lafayette, who arrived a little before sunset, suspected from the obstinacy with which this post was maintained, that it covered more than a rear guard, and determined to reconnoitre the camp, and judge of its strength from his own observation.* It was

* Correspondence with Lafayette.

CHAP. X
1781

in a great measure concealed by woods; but from a tongue of land stretching into the river, he perceived the British force to be much more considerable than had been supposed, and hastened to call off his men.

Action near Jamestown.

He found Wayne closely engaged. A piece of artillery had been left weakly defended, which Wayne determined to seize. Scarcely was the attempt made, when he discovered the whole British army, arranged in order for battle, moving out against him. To retreat was impossible, and the boldest had become the safest measure. Under this impression he advanced rapidly, and, with his small detachment, not exceeding eight hundred men, made a gallant charge on the British line. A warm action ensued, which was kept up with great spirit until the arrival of Lafayette, who, perceiving Wayne to be out-flanked both on the right and left, ordered him to retreat and form in a line with the light infantry, who were drawn up about half a mile in his rear. The whole party then saved itself behind a morass.

Fortunately for Lafayette, Lord Cornwallis did not improve the advantage he had gained. Suspecting this to be a stratagem of the American general to draw him into an ambuscade, a suspicion equally favoured by the hardiness and time of the attack, Lord Cornwallis, who supposed his enemy to be stronger than he was in reality, would allow no pursuit; and, in the course of the night, crossed over into the island, whence he, soon afterwards, proceeded to Portsmouth.

In this action, the Americans lost one hundred and eighteen men, among whom were ten officers; and two pieces of artillery were left on the field, the horses attached to them being killed. The British loss was less considerable.

All active operations were now suspended; and the harassed army of Lafayette was allowed some repose.

Although no brilliant service was performed by that young nobleman, the campaign in Virginia enhanced his military reputation, and raised him in the general esteem. That with so decided an inferiority of effective force, and especially of cavalry, he had been able to keep the field in an open country, and to preserve a considerable proportion of his military stores, as well as his army, was believed to furnish unequivocal evidence of the prudence and vigour of his conduct.

CHAPTER XI.

Farther state of affairs in the beginning of the year 1781....Measures of Mr. Morris, the superintendent of finances....Designs of General Washington against New York....Count Rochambeau marches to the North River....Intelligence from the Count de Grasse....Plan of operations against Lord Cornwallis....Naval engagement....The combined armies march for the Chesapeake....Yorktown invested....Surrender of Lord Cornwallis.

1781

State of affairs at the beginning of the year 1781.

THE deep gloom which had enveloped the prospects of America in the commencement of the year, which darkened for a time in the south, had also spread itself over the north. The total incompetency of the political system adopted by the United States to their own preservation, became every day more apparent. Each state seemed fearful of doing too much, and of taking upon itself a larger portion of the common burden than was borne by its neighbour.

The resolutions of congress had called for an army of thirty-seven thousand men, to be in camp by the first of January. Had this requisition been made in time, it is not probable that so large a force could have been brought into the field; but it was made late, and then the difficulties and delays on the part of the several states, exceeded every reasonable calculation. The regular force drawn from Pennsylvania to

Georgia inclusive, at no time, during this active and interesting campaign, amounted to three thousand effective men; and the states from New Hampshire to New Jersey inclusive, so late as the month of April, had furnished only five thousand infantry. Of these, the returns for that month exhibit, in the northern department, less than three thousand effectives. The cavalry and artillery, at no time, amounted to one thousand men. This small army was gradually and slowly augmented so as, in the month of May, to exhibit a total of near seven thousand men, of whom rather more than four thousand might have been relied on for action.

The prospects for the campaign were rendered still more unpromising by the failure of supplies for the support of the troops. The long expected clothing from Europe had not arrived; and the want of provisions * furnished a still more serious cause of alarm.

After congress had come to the resolution of emitting no more bills on the credit of the continent, the duty of supplying the army with provisions necessarily devolved on the states, who were required to furnish certain specified articles for the subsistence of the troops, according to a ratio established by the federal government. These requisitions had been neglected to such a degree as to excite fears that the soldiers must be disbanded from the want of food.

* See note No. V. at the end of the volume.

CHAP. XI

1781

To increase the general embarrassment, the quartermaster department was destitute of funds, and unable to transport provisions or other stores from place to place, but by means of impressment supported by a military force. This measure had been repeated, especially in New York, until it excited so much disgust and irritation among the people, that the Commander-in-chief was under serious apprehensions of actual resistance to his authority.

While in this state of deplorable imbecility, intelligence from every quarter announced increasing dangers.

Information was received that an expedition was preparing in Canada against Fort Pitt, to be conducted by Sir John Johnston, and Colonel Conelly; and it was understood that many, in the country threatened with invasion, were ready to join the British standard. The Indians too had entered into formidable combinations, endangering the whole extent of the western frontier.

In addition to these alarming circumstances, some vessels had arrived at Crown Point from Canada, with information that three thousand men had been assembled on the lakes, for the purpose of attempting, once more, an invasion from that quarter.

This information, though unfounded, was believed to be true, and was, at that critical moment, the more alarming, because a correspondence of a criminal nature had just been discovered between some persons in Albany and in Canada. A letter intercepted by Generals Schuyler and Clinton, stated the disaffection of particular settlements, the provision made in those settlements for the subsistence of an invading army, and their readiness to join such army.

This intelligence from the northern frontier derived increased interest from the ambiguous conduct observed by the inhabitants of that tract of country which now constitutes the state of Vermont. They had settled lands within the chartered limits of New York, under grants from the governor of New Hampshire; and had, early in the war, declared themselves independent, and exercised the powers of self-government. The state of New York, however, still continuing to assert her claim of sovereignty, the controversy on this delicate subject had become so violent as to justify the apprehension that, in the opinion of the people of Vermont, the restoration of British authority was an evil not of greater magnitude, than the establishment of that of New York. The declaration was openly made that, if not admitted into the union as an independent state, they held themselves at liberty to make a separate peace; and some negotiations had been commenced, which were believed to manifest a disposition in Vermont, to abandon the common cause of America.

Accustomed to contemplate all public events which might grow out of the situation of the United States, and to prepare for them while at a distance, the American chief was not depressed by this state of American affairs. With a mind happily tempered by nature, and improved by experience, those fortunate events which had occasionally brightened the prospects of his country, never relaxed his exertions, or lessened his precautions; nor could the most disastrous state of things drive him to despair. Although entirely uncertain what operation he might be enabled to undertake during the approaching campaign, he had adopted such preparatory steps as might enable him to turn to advantage any fortunate incident which might occur. In consequence of conferences previously held with the Count de Rochambeau, for the purpose of digesting a system adapted to contingent events, orders were transmitted to that officer, directing him to be in readiness to march as large a body of the French troops to the North River, as could be spared from the protection of the fleet.

Early in May, the Count de Barras, who had been appointed to the command of the French fleet stationed on the American coast, arrived in Boston accompanied by the Viscount de Rochambeau, and brought the long expected information from the cabinet of Versailles, respecting the naval armament designed to act in the American seas. Twenty ships of the line, to be commanded by the Count de Grasse, were destined for the West Indies, twelve of which were to proceed to the continent of America, and might be expected to arrive in the month of July.

Designs of General Washington against New York.

An interview between General Washington and the Count de Rochambeau immediately took place at Weathersfield, in which it was determined to unite the troops of France to those of America on the Hudson, and to proceed against New York. The regular army at that station was estimated at four thousand five hundred men,* and though it was understood that Sir Henry Clinton would be able to reinforce it with five or six thousand militia, it was believed that the post could not be maintained without recalling a considerable part of the troops from the south; in which event, the allied army might be employed advantageously in that part of the union.

The prospect of expelling the British from New York roused the northern states from that apathy into which they appeared to be sinking, and vigorous measures were taken to fill their regiments. Yet those measures were not completely successful. In the month of June, when

* Sir H. Clinton in a letter to Lord Cornwallis, dated June 11, 1781, states his effective force at ten thousand nine hundred and thirty-one.

CHAP. XI 1781 the army took the field, and encamped at Peekskill, its effective numbers did not exceed five thousand men.

Such was the American force in the north, with which the campaign of 1781 was opened. It fell so far short of that on which the calculations had been made at Weathersfield, as to excite serious doubts respecting the propriety of adhering to the plan there concerted, although some compensation was made for this deficiency on the part of the states by the arrival of a reinforcement of fifteen hundred men to the army of Rochambeau under convoy of a fifty gun frigate.

To supply even this army with provisions, required much greater exertions than had ever been made since the system of requisitions had been substituted for that of purchasing. The hope of terminating the war produced these exertions. The legislatures of the New England states took up the subject in earnest, and passed resolutions for raising the necessary supplies. But until these resolutions could be executed, the embarrassments of the army continued; and, for some time after the troops had taken the field, there was reason to apprehend, either that the great objects of the campaign must be relinquished for want of provisions, or that coercive means must still be used.

New England not furnishing flour, this important article was to be drawn from New York,

New Jersey, and Pennsylvania. The two first states were much exhausted; and the application to Pennsylvania did not promise to be very successful. On this subject, therefore, serious fears existed.

These were removed, in a great degree, by the activity and exertions of an individual.

Superintendent of finances appointed.

The management of the finances had been lately committed to Mr. Robert Morris, a delegate to congress from the state of Pennsylvania. This gentleman united considerable political talents to a degree of mercantile enterprise, information, and credit, seldom equalled in any country. He had accepted this arduous appointment on the condition of being allowed the year 1781 to make his arrangements; during which time, the department was to be conducted by those already employed, with the resources which government could command. But the critical state of public affairs, and the pressing wants of the army, furnished irresistible motives for changing his original determination, and entering immediately on the duties of his office. The occasion required that he should bring his private credit in aid of the public resources, and pledge himself personally and extensively, for articles of absolute necessity which could not be otherwise obtained. Condemning the system of violence and of legal fraud, which had too long been practised, as being calculated to defeat its own object, he sought the gradual

CHAP. XI restoration of confidence by the only means
1781 which could restore it:—a punctual and faithful compliance with his engagements. Herculean as was this task in the existing derangement of American finances, he entered upon it courageously; and, if not completely successful, certainly did more than could have been supposed possible with the means placed in his hands. It is, in no inconsiderable degree, to be attributed to him, that the very active and decisive operations of the campaign were not impeded, perhaps defeated, by a failure of the means for transporting military stores, and feeding the army.

On determining to enter on the duties of his office, Mr. Morris laid before congress the plan of a national bank, whose notes were to be receivable from the respective states as specie, into the treasury of the United States. Congress gave its full approbation to this beneficial institution; and passed an ordinance for its incorporation.

Important as was this measure to the future operations of the army, a contract entered into with the state of Pennsylvania was of still more immediate utility.

After furnishing flour to relieve the wants of the moment on his private credit, Mr. Morris proposed to take on himself the task of complying with all the specific requisitions made on Pennsylvania, and to rely for reimbursement on the taxes imposed by law, to be collected under his direction. This proposition being accepted, the contract was made; and supplies which the government found itself unable to furnish, were raised by an individual.

Count Rochambeau marches to the North River.

As the French troops approached the North River, intelligence was received that a large detachment from New York had made an incursion into Jersey, under appearances indicating an intention not to return immediately. This being thought a favourable moment for gaining the posts on the north end of York Island, a plan was formed for seizing them by a *coup de main.* General Washington fixed on the night of the second of July for making the attempt; it being supposed that the Count de Rochambeau might join the American army at Kingsbridge by that time. An aid-de-camp was therefore despatched to meet that officer with letters explaining the enterprise, and requesting him to meet the Commander-in-chief at the time and place appointed.

With the proposed attack on these works, an attempt to cut off some light troops stationed on the outside of Kingsbridge at Morrissania, under the command of Colonel Delaney, was to be combined. This part of the plan was to be executed by the Duke de Lauzun, to whose legion Sheldon's dragoons, and a small body of continental troops dispersed on the lines, under

CHAP. XI 1781

the command of General Waterbury, were to be added.

On the part of the Americans, all that could contribute to the success of this enterprise was done. A strong detachment commanded by General Lincoln, which fell down the river in boats with muffled oars, reached its ground undiscovered on the night of the first of July; and the army, conducted by General Washington, marched to Valentine's hill. The next day, Lincoln perceived that the detachment had returned from Jersey, that the British were encamped in great force on the north end of the island, and that a ship of war watched the landing place. These unexpected obstacles having defeated the design upon the works, he proceeded to execute his eventual orders of co-operation with the Duke de Lauzun. These were, after landing above Spiken Devil Creek, to march to the high ground in front of Kingsbridge, and there conceal his detachment, until the attack on Delaney's corps should commence.

The Duke de Lauzun did not arrive, and the return of day betrayed Lincoln. A British corps advanced upon him; on hearing which, General Washington put his troops in motion, and, on his approach, the British troops retired into the island.

Both parts of the plan having thus failed, the army retreated to Dobbs' ferry, where it was joined by the Count de Rochambeau on the sixth of July.

The thanks of the Commander-in-chief were given to that officer in general orders, for the unremitting zeal with which he had proceeded to form his so long wished for junction with the American army; and he was requested to convey to the officers and soldiers under his command, the grateful sense which the general entertained of the cheerfulness with which they had performed so long and laborious a march at so hot a season.

The utmost exertions were made for the grand enterprise against New York. But as the execution of any plan that could be formed, depended on events which were uncertain, the Commander-in-chief directed his attention to other objects, to be pursued if that which was most desirable should prove unattainable. Should the siege of New York become unadviseable, his views were turned to Virginia, the Carolinas, and Georgia.

Early in August, the apprehension that he should be unable to accomplish his favourite object, began to influence his conduct. Letters from the Marquis de Lafayette announced that a large portion of the troops in Virginia were embarked, and that their destination was believed to be New York. This intelligence induced him to turn his attention more seriously to the south; but, to conceal from Sir Henry

CHAP. XI

1781

Clinton this eventual change of plan, his arrangements were made secretly, and the preparations for acting against New York were continued. A reinforcement from Europe of near three thousand men, induced Sir Henry Clinton to countermand the orders he had given to Lord Cornwallis to detach a part of the army in Virginia to his aid; and also to direct that nobleman to take a strong position on the Chesapeake, from which he might execute the designs meditated against the states lying on that bay, so soon as the storm which threatened the British power for the moment, should blow over. In a few days after the arrival of this reinforcement, the Count de Barras gave General Washington the interesting information, that De Grasse was to have sailed from Cape Francis for the Chesapeake, on the third of August, with from twenty-five to twenty-nine ships of the line, having on board three thousand two hundred soldiers; and that he had made engagements with the officers commanding the land and naval forces of Spain in the West Indies, to return to those seas by the middle of October.

Intelligence from the Count de Grasse.

This intelligence manifested the necessity of determining immediately, and positively, on the object against which the combined forces should be directed. The shortness of the time appropriated by De Grasse for his continuance on the American coast, the apparent unwillingness of the naval officers to attempt to force a passage into the harbour of New York, and the failure of the states to comply with the requisitions which had been made on them for men, decided in favour of operations to the south; and Lafayette was requested to make such a disposition of his army as should be best calculated to prevent Lord Cornwallis from saving himself by a sudden march to Charleston.*

Conformably to the intelligence communicated by the Count de Barras, the Count de Grasse arrived in the Chesapeake late in August with twenty-eight ships of the line and several frigates. At Cape Henry he found an officer despatched by Lafayette with full intelligence of the situation of the armies in Virginia. Lord Cornwallis had collected his whole force at Yorktown and Gloucester Point, which he was fortifying assiduously; and the Marquis had taken a position on James River.

In consequence of this information, four ships of the line and several frigates were detached to block up the mouth of York River, and convey the land forces brought from the West Indies, under the command of the Marquis de St. Simon, up the James to join Lafayette, who, on receiving this reinforcement, took post at

* In pursuance of these orders, Wayne was detached to the south side of James River, under the pretext of reinforcing Greene, but was ordered to maintain a position which would enable him to intercept and oppose the march of Lord Cornwallis, should he attempt to force his way to Charleston. Lafayette was on the alert to co-operate with Wayne in the event of such a movement.—*Cor. with Lafayette.*

CHAP. XI 1781

Williamsburg. In the mean time, the fleet lay at anchor just within the capes. On the 25th of August the Count de Barras * sailed from Newport for the Chesapeake.

Rodney was apprized of the destination of De Grasse, but seems not to have suspected that the whole fleet would sail for the continent of America. Supposing therefore that a part of his squadron would be sufficient to maintain an equality of naval force in the American seas, he detached Sir Samuel Hood to the continent with only fourteen sail of the line. That officer arrived at Sandy Hook on the twenty-eighth of August.

Admiral Greaves, who had succeeded Arbuthnot in the command of the fleet on the American station, lay in the harbour of New York with seven ships of the line, only five of which were fit for service. On the day that Hood appeared and gave information that De Grasse was probably on the coast, intelligence was also received that De Barras had sailed from Newport.

The ships fit for sea were ordered out of the harbour; and Greaves, with the whole fleet, consisting of nineteen sail of the line, proceeded in quest of the French.

* This admiral was the senior of De Grasse, to whom the command of the expedition had been entrusted, and was therefore authorized by the minister of marine, to cruise on the coast of Newfoundland while his ships should join the grand fleet. He preferred serving under his junior officer.—*Cor. of Lafayette.*

Not suspecting the strength of De Grasse, he hoped to fall in with one or the other of their squadrons, and to fight it separately.

Early in the morning of the 5th of September, while the French fleet lay at anchor just within the Chesapeake, the British squadron was descried. Orders were immediately given by De Grasse to form the line, and put to sea. About four in the afternoon, the action commenced between the headmost ships, and continued until sunset. Several ships were much damaged, but neither admiral could claim the victory. For five successive days the hostile fleets continued within view of each other. After which, De Grasse returned to his former station within the capes. At his anchorage ground he found De Barras with the squadron from Newport, and fourteen transports laden with heavy artillery, and military stores proper for carrying on a siege. The British admiral approaching the capes, found the entrance of the Chesapeake defended by a force with which he was unable to contend, and therefore bore away for New York.

Plan of operations against Lord Cornwallis.

General Washington had determined to entrust the defence of the Hudson to General Heath, and to command the southern expedition in person. All the French, and a detachment amounting to upwards of two thousand men from the continental army, were destined for this service. On the 19th of August, Hazen's

CHAP. XI
1781

regiment and the Jersey line, were directed to pass the Hudson at Dobbs' ferry, and take a position between Springfield and Chatham, where they were to cover some bake-houses to be constructed in the neighbourhood, for the purpose of veiling the real designs of the American chief, and of exciting fears for Staten Island. On the same day, the whole army was put in motion; and on the twenty-fifth the passage of the river was completed.

The combined armies march for the Chesapeake.

To conceal as long as possible the real object of this movement, the march of the army was continued until the thirty-first, in such a direction as to keep up fears for New York; and a considerable degree of address was used to countenance the opinion that the real design was against that place. The letters which had been intercepted by Sir Henry Clinton favoured this deception; and so strong was the impression they made that, even after it became necessary for the combined army to leave the route leading down the Hudson, he is stated to have retained his fears for New York, and not to have suspected the real object of his adversary until he had approached the Delaware; * and it had become too late to obstruct the progress of the allied army towards Virginia. He then resolved to make every exertion in his power to

* The first indication given by Sir Henry Clinton of suspecting the southern expedition, is in his letter to Lord Cornwallis of the 2nd of September, in which he says, "By intelligence I have this day received, it would seem that Washington is moving southward."

relieve Lord Cornwallis, and in the mean time to act offensively in the north. An expedition was planned against New London, in Connecticut, and a strong detachment, under the command of General Arnold, was embarked on board a fleet of transports, which landed early in the morning of the 6th of September on both sides the harbour, about three miles from the town.

September 6.

New London is a seaport town on the west side of the Thames. A fort called fort Trumbull, and a redoubt had been constructed just below it, on the same side of the river; and opposite to it, on Groton hill, was fort Griswold, a strong square fortification, but not fully manned. General Arnold, who commanded in person the troops that landed on the western side of the harbour, advanced immediately against the posts on that side. These being untenable, were evacuated on his approach; and he took possession of them with inconsiderable loss. To prevent the escape of the vessels up the river, Lieutenant Colonel Eyre, who commanded the division which landed on the Groton side of the harbour, had been ordered to storm fort Griswold, which had been represented to Arnold as too incomplete to make any serious resistance. But the place being of some strength, and the approach to it difficult, Colonel Ledyard, who commanded it with a garrison of one hundred and sixty men, determined to defend it. On his

CHAP. XI
1781

refusing to surrender, the British assaulted it on three sides, and overcoming the difficulties opposed to them, made a lodgement on the ditch and fraized work, and entered the embrasures with charged bayonets. Further resistance being hopeless, the action ceased on the part of the Americans, and Colonel Ledyard delivered his sword to the commanding officer of the assailants. Irritated by the obstinacy of the defence, and the loss sustained in the assault, the British officer on whom the command had devolved, tarnished the glory of victory by the inhuman use he made of it. Instead of respecting, with the generous spirit of a soldier, the gallantry which he had subdued, he indulged the vindictive feelings which had been roused by the slaughter of his troops. In the account given of this affair by Governor Trumbull to General Washington, he says, "The sword presented by Colonel Ledyard was immediately plunged into his bosom, and the carnage was kept up until the greater part of the garrison was killed or wounded."

In this fierce assault, Colonel Eyre was killed, and Major Montgomery, the second in command, also fell, as he entered the American works. The total loss of the assailants was not much less than two hundred men.

The town of New London, and the stores contained in it, were consumed by fire. To escape the odium which invariably attends the wanton destruction of private property, this fire was attributed to accident; but all the American accounts unite in declaring it to have been intentional.

September 6.

The march of General Washington was not arrested by this excursion into New England. Having made the arrangements for the transportation of his army down the Chesapeake, he proceeded in person to Virginia, attended by the Count de Rochambeau, and the Chevalier de Chatelleux; and, on the 14th of September, reached Williamsburg * accompanied by Rochambeau, Chatelleux, Knox, and Du Portail, he immediately repaired to the fleet, and a plan of co-operation was adjusted on board the Ville de Paris, conforming to his wish in every respect, except that the Count de Grasse declined complying with a proposition to station some of his

* While the American troops were encamped at Williamsburg and the French fleet lay in the bay, the Count de Grasse, circumscribed in point of time, and therefore, unwilling to await the arrival of the army from the north, urged Lafayette to attack the British in Yorktown; offering to aid him not only with all the marines of the fleet, but with as many seamen as he should require. The Marquis de St. Simon, an officer of great experience, united himself with the admiral in pressing this measure. He stated that, the works of Cornwallis being incomplete, Yorktown and Gloucester might, in all probability, be carried by storm, if attacked by superior numbers. The temptation was great for a young general scarcely twenty-four years of age. A full excuse for the attempt was found in the declaration of De Grasse, that he could not wait for the arrival of the troops from the north. Success would have given unrivaled brilliancy to the reputation of Lafayette, but would necessarily have cost much blood. Lafayette refused to sacrifice the soldiers which were confided to him to his personal glory, and persuaded De Grasse to await the arrival of Washington and Rochambeau, when the capture of Cornwallis would be certainly made without the waste of human life.—*Cor. with Lafayette.*

CHAP. XI 1781 ships in the river above Yorktown, thinking it too hazardous.

While the close investment of the British army was delayed, only until the troops from the north should arrive, serious apprehensions were excited that the brilliant results confidently anticipated from the superiority of the land and naval forces of the allies, would be put in imminent hazard.

Information was received that a reinforcement of six ships of the line under Admiral Digby had reached New York. Confident that the British fleet, thus augmented, would attempt every thing for the relief of Lord Cornwallis, De Grasse expected to be attacked by a force not much inferior to his own. Thinking his station within the Chesapeake unfavourable for a naval combat, he designed to change it, and communicated to General Washington his intention to leave a few frigates to block up the mouths of James and York Rivers, and to put to sea with his fleet in quest of the British. If they should not have left the harbour of New York, he purposed to block them up in that place; supposing that his operations in that quarter would be of more service to the common cause, than his remaining in the bay, an idle spectator of the siege of York.

The Commander-in-chief was much alarmed at this communication. Should the admiral put to sea, the winds and many accidents might prevent his return to the Chesapeake. During his absence, a temporary naval superiority might be acquired by the British in those waters, and the army of Lord Cornwallis might be placed in perfect security. The movement would expose to the caprice of fortune, an object of vast importance, which was now reduced almost to certainty. The admiral was therefore entreated to preserve his station.

Fortunately, the wishes of the general prevailed, and the admiral consented to relinquish those plans of active enterprise which his thirst for military glory had suggested, and to maintain a station which the American general deemed so conducive to the interests of the allies.

September 25.

On the 25th of September, the last division of the allied troops arrived in James River, and were disembarked at the landing near Williamsburg; soon after which, the preparations for the siege were completed.

Yorktown invested.

York is a small village on the south side of the river which bears that name, where the long peninsula between the York and the James, is only eight miles wide. In this broad and bold river, a ship of the line may ride in safety. Its southern banks are high, and, on the opposite shore, is Gloucester Point, a piece of land projecting deep into the river, and narrowing it, at that place, to the space of one mile. Both these posts were occupied by Lord Cornwallis.

The communication between them was commanded by his batteries, and by some ships of war which lay under his guns.

The main body of his army was encamped on the open grounds about Yorktown, within a range of outer redoubts and field works, calculated to command the peninsula, and impede the approach of the assailants; and Lieutenant Colonel Dundass, with a small detachment consisting of six or seven hundred men, held the post at Gloucester Point. He was afterwards reinforced by Lieutenant Colonel Tarlton.

The legion of Lauzun, and a brigade of militia under General Weedon, the whole commanded by the French General de Choisé, were directed to watch the enemy on the side of Gloucester; and, on the twenty-eighth, the grand combined army moved down on the south side of the river, by different roads, towards Yorktown. About noon, the heads of the columns reached the ground assigned them respectively; and, after driving in the piquets and some cavalry, encamped for the evening. The next day, the right wing, consisting of Americans, extended farther to the right, and occupied the ground east of Beverdam creek; while the left wing, consisting of French, was stationed on the west side of that stream. In the course of the night, Lord Cornwallis withdrew from his outer lines; and the works he had evacuated were, the next day, occupied by the besieging army, which now invested the town completely on that side.

Two thousand men were stationed on the Gloucester side for the purpose of keeping up a rigorous blockade. On approaching the lines, a sharp skirmish took place which terminated unfavourably for the British; after which they remained under cover of their works, making no attempt to interrupt the blockade.

October 6.

On the night of the sixth of October, until which time the besieging army was incessantly employed in disembarking their heavy artillery and military stores, and drawing them to camp, the first parallel was commenced within six hundred yards of the British lines. This operation was conducted with so much silence, that it appears not to have been perceived until the return of daylight disclosed it to the garrison; by which time the trenches were in such forwardness as to cover the men. By the evening of the ninth, several batteries and redoubts were completed, and the effect of their fire was soon perceived. New batteries were opened the next day, and the fire became so heavy that the besieged withdrew their cannon from the embrasures, and scarcely returned a shot. The shells and red hot balls from the batteries of the allied army reached the ships in the harbour, and, in the evening, set fire to the Charon of forty-four guns, and to three large transports, which were entirely consumed. Reciprocal esteem, and a

CHAP. XI

1781

October.

spirit of emulation between the French and Americans, being carefully cultivated by the Commander-in-chief, the siege was carried on with great rapidity. The second parallel was opened, on the night of the eleventh, within three hundred yards of the British lines. The three succeeding days were devoted to the completion of this parallel, during which the fire of the garrison, which had opened several new embrasures, became more destructive than at any previous time. The men in the trenches were particularly annoyed by two redoubts advanced three hundred yards in front of the British works, which flanked the second parallel of the besiegers. Preparations were made, on the fourteenth, to carry them both by storm. The attack of one was committed to the Americans, and of the other to the French. The Marquis de Lafayette commanded the American detachment, and the Baron de Viominel the French. Towards the close of the day, the two detachments marched with equal firmness to the assault. Colonel Hamilton, who had commanded a battalion of light infantry throughout this campaign, led the advanced corps of the Americans; and Colonel Laurens turned the redoubt at the head of eighty men, in order to take the garrison in reverse, and intercept their retreat. The troops rushed to the charge without firing a gun and without giving the sappers time to remove the abattis and palisades.

Passing over them, they assaulted the works with irresistible impetuosity on all sides at the same time, and entered them with such rapidity that their loss was inconsiderable.* This redoubt was defended by Major Campbell, with some inferior officers, and forty-five privates. The major, a captain, a subaltern, and seventeen privates, were made prisoners, and eight privates were killed while the assailants were entering the works.

The redoubt attacked by the French was defended by a greater number of men; and the resistance, being greater, was not overcome so quickly, or with so little loss. One hundred and twenty men, commanded by a lieutenant colonel, were in this work, eighteen of whom were killed, and forty-two, including a captain and two subaltern officers, were made prisoners.

* One sergeant and eight privates were killed; and one lieutenant colonel, four captains, one subaltern, one sergeant, and twenty-five rank and file, were wounded.

The irritation produced by the recent carnage in fort Griswold had not so far subdued the humanity of the American character as to induce retaliation. Not a man was killed except in action. "Incapable," said Colonel Hamilton in his report, "of imitating examples of barbarity, and forgetting recent provocation, the soldiery spared every man that ceased to resist." Mr. Gordon, in his History of the American War, states the orders given by Lafayette, with the approbation of Washington, to have directed that every man in the redoubt, after its surrender, should be put to the sword. These sanguinary orders, so repugnant to the character of the Commander-in-chief and of Lafayette, were never given. There is no trace of them among the papers of General Washington; and Colonel Hamilton, who took a part in the enterprise, which assures his perfect knowledge of every material occurrence, has publicly contradicted the statement. It has been also contradicted by Lafayette.

CHAP. XI

1781

The assailants lost, in killed and wounded, near one hundred men.

The Commander-in-chief was highly gratified with the active courage displayed in this assault. Speaking of it in his diary, he says—"The bravery exhibited by the attacking troops was emulous and praiseworthy. Few cases have exhibited greater proofs of intrepidity, coolness, and firmness, than were shown on this occasion." The orders of the succeeding day, congratulating the army on the capture of these important works, expressed a high sense of the judicious dispositions and gallant conduct of both the Baron de Viominel and the Marquis de Lafayette, and requested them to convey to every officer and man engaged in the enterprise, the acknowledgments of the Commander-in-chief for the spirit and rapidity with which they advanced to the attack, and for the admirable firmness with which they supported themselves under the fire of the enemy without returning a shot. "The general reflects," concluding the orders, "with the highest degree of pleasure, on the confidence which the troops of the two nations must hereafter have in each other. Assured of mutual support, he is convinced there is no danger which they will not cheerfully encounter, no difficulty which they will not bravely overcome." *

* General Lafayette states a fact which proves in an eminent degree the good feelings of the American soldiers towards their allies. While encamped together under his command at

CHAP. XI

1781

During the same night, these redoubts were included in the second parallel; and, in the course of the next day, some howitzers were placed in them, which, by five in the afternoon, were opened on the besieged.

The situation of Lord Cornwallis was becoming desperate. His works were sinking, in every quarter, under the fire of the besiegers. The batteries already playing on him had silenced nearly all his guns, and the second parallel was about to open, which must in a few hours render the town untenable. To suspend a catastrophe which appeared almost inevitable, he resolved on attempting to retard the completion of the second parallel, by a vigorous sortie against two batteries which appeared to be in the greatest forwardness, and were guarded by French troops. The party making this sortie was led by Lieutenant Colonel Abercrombie, who attacked the two batteries with great impetuosity about four in the morning, and carried both with inconsiderable loss; but the guards from the trenches immediately advancing on the assailants, they retreated without being able to effect any thing of importance.

October 16.

Williamsburg, the Americans, who were *bivouacked,* saw their allies under tents without a murmur; and saw them supplied regularly with rations of flour for three days from the American magazines, while corn meal was measured out very irregularly to themselves. The superior officers lent their horses to those of France and walked themselves. Although their general was himself a Frenchman, the Americans saw not only without jealousy, but with pleasure, every preference given to their allies.

CHAP. XI

1781

About four in the afternoon the besiegers opened several batteries in their second parallel; and it was apparent that, in the course of the ensuing day, the whole line of batteries in that parallel would be ready to play on the town. The works of the besieged were not in a condition to sustain so tremendous a fire. In this extremity, Lord Cornwallis formed the bold design of forcing his way to New York.

He determined to leave his sick and baggage behind, and, crossing over in the night with his effectives to the Gloucester shore, to attack De Choisé. After cutting to pieces or dispersing the troops under that officer, he intended to mount his infantry on the horses taken from that detachment, and on others to be seized on the road, and, by a rapid march to gain the fords of the great rivers, and, forcing his way through Maryland, Pennsylvania, and Jersey, to form a junction with the army in New York.*

This desperate attempt would be extremely hazardous; but the situation of the British general had become so hopeless, that it could scarcely be changed for the worse.

Boats prepared under other pretexts were held in readiness to receive the troops at ten in the evening, and convey them over the river. The arrangements were made with such secrecy that the first embarkation arrived at the point unperceived, and part of the troops were landed,

* Stedman, Annual Register, letter of Lord Cornwallis.

when a sudden and violent storm interrupted the execution of this hazardous plan, and drove the boats down the river. The storm continued till near daylight, when the boats returned. But the plan was necessarily abandoned, and the boats were sent to bring back the soldiers, who were relanded on the southern shore in the course of the forenoon without much loss.

CHAP. XI

1781

In the morning of the seventeenth, several new batteries were opened in the second parallel, which poured in a weight of fire not to be resisted. The place being no longer tenable, Lord Cornwallis, about ten in the forenoon, beat a parley, and proposed a cessation of hostilities for twenty-four hours, that commissioners might meet at Moore's house, which was just in the rear of the first parallel, to settle terms for the surrender of the posts of York and Gloucester. To this letter General Washington returned an immediate answer declaring his "ardent desire to spare the further effusion of blood, and his readiness to listen to such terms as were admissible;" but as in the present crisis he could not consent to lose a moment in fruitless negotiations, he desired that "previous to the meeting of the commissioners, the proposals of his lordship might be transmitted in writing, for which purpose a suspension of hostilities for two hours should be granted. The general propositions * stated by Lord Cornwallis as forming the basis

October 17.

* See note No. VI. at the end of the volume.

CHAP. XI

1781

of the capitulation, though not all admissible, being such as led to the opinion that no great difficulty would occur in adjusting the terms, the suspension of hostilities was prolonged for the night. In the mean time, to avoid the delay of useless discussion, the Commander-in-chief drew up and proposed such articles † as he would be willing to grant. These were transmitted to Lord Cornwallis with the accompanying declaration that, if he approved them, commissioners might be immediately appointed to digest them into form. In consequence of this message, the Viscount de Noailles, and Lieutenant Colonel Laurens, were met next day by Colonel Dundass and Major Ross; but, being unable to adjust the terms of capitulation definitively, only a rough draught of them could be prepared, which was to be submitted to the consideration of the British general. Determined not to expose himself to those accidents which time might produce, General Washington could not permit any suspense on the part of Lord Cornwallis. He therefore immediately directed the rough articles which had been prepared by the commissioners to be fairly transcribed, and sent them to his lordship early next morning, with a letter expressing his expectation that they would be signed by eleven, and that the garrison would march out by two in the afternoon. Finding all attempts to obtain better terms un-

October 18.

† See note No. VII. at the end of the volume.

1781

Surrender of Lord Cornwallis.

availing, Lord Cornwallis submitted to a necessity no longer to be avoided, and, on the 19th of October, surrendered the posts of Yorktown and Gloucester Point, with their garrisons, and the ships in the harbour with their seamen, to the land and naval forces of America and France.

Nineteenth.

The army, artillery, arms, military chest, and public stores of every denomination, were surrendered to General Washington; the ships and seamen, to the Count de Grasse. The total number of prisoners,* excluding seamen, rather exceeded seven thousand men. The loss sustained by the garrison during the siege, amounted to five hundred and fifty-two men, including six officers.

Lord Cornwallis endeavoured to introduce an article into the capitulation, for the security of those Americans who had joined the British army; but the subject was declared to belong to the civil department, and the article was rejected. Its object, however, was granted without appearing to concede it. His lordship was permitted to send the Bonetta sloop of war untouched, with despatches to Sir Henry Clinton;

* The return of prisoners contained two generals, thirty-one field officers, three hundred and twenty-six captains and subalterns, seventy-one regimental staff, six thousand five hundred and twenty-seven non-commissioned officers and privates, and one hundred and twenty-four persons belonging to the hospital, commissary, and wagon departments, making in the whole seven thousand and seventy-three prisoners. To this number are to be added six commissioned, and twenty-eight non-commissioned officers and privates made prisoners in the two redoubts which were stormed, and in the sortie made by the garrison.

CHAP. XI
1781

and the Americans whose conduct had been most offensive to their countrymen were embarked on board this vessel.

The allied army may be estimated, including militia, at sixteen thousand men. In the course of this siege, they lost, in killed and wounded, about three hundred. The treaty was opened on the eleventh day after the ground was broken by the besiegers, and the capitulation was signed on the thirteenth. The whole army merited great approbation; but, from the nature of the service, the artillerists and engineers were enabled to distinguish themselves particularly. Generals du Portail and Knox were each promoted to the rank of Major General; and Colonel Govion, and Captain Rochfontaine, of the corps of engineers, were each advanced a grade by brevet. In addition to the officers belonging to those departments, Generals Lincoln, De Lafayette, and Steuben, were particularly mentioned by the Commander-in-chief, in his orders issued the day after the capitulation; and terms of peculiar warmth were applied to Governor Nelson, who continued in the field during the whole siege, at the head of the militia of Virginia; and also exerted himself, in a particular manner, to furnish the army with those supplies which the country afforded. The highest acknowledgments were made to the Count de Rochambeau; and several other French officers were named with distinction. So many disasters had attended the former efforts of the United States to avail themselves of the succours occasionally afforded by France, that an opinion not very favourable to the alliance appears to have gained some ground in the country, and to have insinuated itself into the army. The Commander-in-chief seized this occasion to discountenance a course of thinking from which he had always feared pernicious consequences, and displayed the great value of the aids lately received, in language highly flattering to the French monarch, as well as to the land and naval forces of that nation.

Knowing the influence which the loss of the army in Virginia must have on the war, Sir Henry Clinton determined to hazard much for its preservation. About seven thousand of his best troops sailed for the Chesapeake, under convoy of a fleet augmented to twenty-five ships of the line. This armament left the Hook the day on which the capitulation was signed at Yorktown, and appeared off the capes of Virginia on the 24th of October. Unquestionable intelligence being there received that Lord Cornwallis had surrendered, the British general returned to New York.

The exultation manifested throughout the United States at the capture of this formidable army was equal to the terror it had inspired. In congress, the intelligence was received with joy proportioned to the magnitude of the event;

CHAP. XI 1781

and the sense of that body on this brilliant achievement was expressed in various resolutions, returning the thanks of the United States to the Commander-in-chief, to the Count de Rochambeau, to the Count de Grasse, to the officers of the allied army generally, and to the corps of artillery, and engineers particularly. In addition to these testimonials of gratitude, it was resolved that a marble column should be erected at Yorktown, in Virginia, with emblems of the alliance between the United States and his Most Christian Majesty, and inscribed with a succinct narrative of the surrender of Earl Cornwallis to his Excellency General Washington, the Commander-in-chief of the combined forces of America and France; to his Excellency the Count de Rochambeau, commanding the auxiliary troops of his Most Christian Majesty in America; and to his Excellency Count de Grasse, commanding in chief the naval army of France in the Chesapeake. Two stand of colours taken in Yorktown were presented to General Washington; two pieces of field ordnance to the Count de Rochambeau; and application was made to his Most Christian Majesty, to permit the Admiral to accept a testimonial of their approbation similar to that presented to the Count de Rochambeau. Congress determined to go in solemn procession to the Dutch Lutheran church, to return thanks to Almighty God for crowning the allied arms with success, by the surrender of the whole British army under Lord Cornwallis; and also issued a proclamation, appointing the 13th day of December for general thanksgiving and prayer, on account of this signal interposition of Divine Providence.

It was not by congress only that the public joy at this great event, and the public approbation of the conduct of General Washington were displayed. The most flattering and affectionate addresses of congratulation were presented from every part of the union; and state governments, corporate towns, and learned institutions, vied with each other in the testimonials they gave of their high sense of his important services, and of their attachment to his person and character.

The superiority of the allied force opened a prospect of still farther advantages. The remaining posts of the British in the southern states were too weak to be defended against the army which had triumphed over Lord Cornwallis; and the troops which occupied them could neither escape nor be reinforced, if the Count de Grasse could be prevailed on to co-operate against them. Although, in his first conference, he had explicitly declared his inability to engage in any enterprise to be undertaken subsequent to that against Yorktown,* the siege of that place had employed so much less time than the admiral had consented to appropriate to it, that the general resumed his plan

* See note No. VIII. at the end of the volume.

CHAP. XI 1781 of southern operations. In a letter addressed to De Grasse, he used every argument which might operate on his love of fame, or his desire to promote the interests of the allies, to prevail on him to co-operate in an expedition against Charleston. If this object should be unattainable, his attention was next turned to Wilmington, in North Carolina, which was still occupied by a small detachment of British troops who kept that state in check. The capture of this detachment, though not an object of much consequence in itself, was supposed to derive some importance from the influence which the complete liberation of North Carolina might have on the future military operations of the United States, and on their negotiations. General Washington proposed to send a detachment intended to reinforce General Greene, as far as Wilmington, under convoy. The reduction of that place, he supposed, would detain the fleet but a few days, after which it might proceed to the West Indies.

To enforce the representations contained in his letter, as well as to pay his respects to the admiral, and to express in person the high sense entertained of his important services, the Commander-in-chief repaired on board the Ville de Paris. The Count acknowledged his conviction

October 23. of the advantages to be expected from an expedition against Charleston; but said, that "the orders of his court, ulterior projects, and his engagements with the Spaniards, rendered it impossible for him to remain on the coast during the time which would be required for the operation." As he also declined taking on board the troops designed to reinforce General Greene, preparations were made for their march by land; and Major General St. Clair, who commanded the detachment, was ordered to take Wilmington in his route, and to gain possession of that post.

The Count de Grasse having consented to remain in the bay a few days for the purpose of covering the transportation of the eastern troops, and of the ordnance to the Head of Elk, they were embarked in the beginning of November, November. under the command of General Lincoln, who was directed to march them into New Jersey and New York, and to canton them for the winter in those states.* The French troops remained in Virginia, not only for the protection of that state, but to be in readiness to march southward or northward, as the exigencies of the ensuing campaign might require.

The transportation of the troops and ordnance to the Head of Elk being effected, the Count de Grasse sailed for the West Indies, and the Commander-in-chief proceeded to Philadelphia.

* See note No. IX. at the end of the volume.

NOTES.

NOTE—No. I. *See Page* 3

The following petition addressed to Governor Livingston, will furnish some evidence of the situation to which that part of Jersey was reduced.

To his excellency William Livingston, esquire, governor, captain general, and commander-in-chief in and over the state of New Jersey and the territories thereunto belonging in America, chancellor and ordinary in the same—the humble petition of the officers, civil and military, whose names are hereunto subscribed,

Showeth,—That a large detachment of the British army, a few weeks ago, made an invasion into the lower counties of this state on Delaware, and plundered a few of the inhabitants. That at present a large detachment are invading them a second time. That the enemy in this second incursion, have, as we have been credibly informed, by the express orders of Colonel Mawhood, the commanding officer, bayoneted and butchered in the most inhuman manner, a number of the militia who have unfortunately fallen into their hands. That Colonel Mawhood immediately after the massacre, in open letters, sent to both officers and privates by a flag, had the effrontery to insult us with a demand, that we should lay down our arms, and if not, threatened to burn, destroy, and lay the whole country waste, and more especially the property of a number of our most distinguished men, whom he named. That he has since put his threat into execution, in one instance, by burning one of the finest dwelling houses in Salem county, and all the other buildings on the same farm, the property of Colonel Benjamin Home. That plunder, rapine, and devastation in the most fertile and populous parts of these counties, widely mark their footsteps wherever they go. That they are spreading disaffection, they are using every possible means to corrupt the minds of the people, who, within their lines, have so little virtue as to purchase from them.

That we are in no state of defence. That we are so exposed by reason of our situation, that some of our officers, civil and military, have moved out of the counties for safety. That our militia, during the last winter, have been so fatigued out by repeated calls and continued service, and disaffection is now so widely diffused, that very few can be called out, in some places, none. That we have no troops of light horse regularly embodied, there is a scarcity of small arms among us, and no field pieces. That in these two incursions, we have very sensibly felt the want of field pieces and artillery men, that the number of us assembled is so small, that though we should use the greatest conduct and bravery, we could only provoke, not injure our enemy.

That the extent of our country is so great, that our small number of men fatigued out, indifferently armed and without field pieces, can not defend it. That, as Delaware runs all along those counties, we are liable to be attacked in numberless places.

That the acquisition of these counties would be of great advantage to the enemy. That they could nearly maintain their whole army a campaign by the plunder, forage, and assistance they could draw from them. That although the United States might not need them, yet it might perhaps be adviseable to defend them, to prevent the advantage the enemy might receive from them. That our riches, and former virtue, make us a prey to an enemy, whose tender mercies are cruelties.

That in short, our situation is beyond description deplorable. That the powers civil and military are daily relaxing, and disaffection prevailing. That we can neither stay at our houses, go out, nor come in with safety. That we can neither plough, plant, sow, reap nor gather. That we are fast falling into poverty, distress, and into the hands of our enemy. That unless there can be sent to our relief and assistance a sufficient body of standing troops, we must be under the disagreeable necessity of leaving the country to the enemy, and removing ourselves and families to distant places for safety. That although the present detachment may be fled and gone, before the relief reaches us, yet a body of troops are necessary for our protection, as long as the enemy possess Philadelphia. And these are the sentiments not only of us the subscribers, but of all the rest of the officers civil and military, and other the good subjects of this state in these counties.

NOTE—No. II. *See Page* 85

The following is the report made by the committee:

"January 1, 1779. The committee appointed to confer with the Commander-in-chief on the operations of the next campaign, report, that the plan proposed by congress for the emancipation of Canada, in co-operation with an army from France, was the principal subject of the said conference.

That, impressed with a strong sense of the injury and disgrace which must attend an infraction of the proposed stipulations, on the part of these states, your committee have taken a general view of our finances, of the circumstances of our army, of the magazines of clothes, artillery, arms and ammunition, and of the provisions in store, and which can be collected in season.

Your committee have also attentively considered the intelligence and observations communicated to them by the Commander-in-chief, respecting the number of troops and strong holds of the enemy in Canada; their naval force, and entire command of the water communication with that country—the difficulties, while they possess such signal advantages, of penetrating it with an army by land—the obstacles which are to be surmounted in acquiring a naval superiority —the hostile temper of many of the surrounding Indian tribes towards these states, and above all the uncertainty whether the enemy will not persevere in their system of harassing and distressing our sea-coast and frontiers by a predatory war.

That on the most mature deliberation, your committee can not find room for a well grounded presumption that these states will be able to perform their part of the proposed stipulations. That in a measure of such moment, calculated to call forth, and direct to a single object a considerable portion of the force of our ally, which may otherwise be essentially employed, nothing else than the highest probability of success could justify congress in making the proposition.

Your committee are therefore of opinion that the negotiation in question, however desirable, and interesting, should be deferred until circumstances render the co-operation of these states more certain, practicable, and effectual.

That the minister plenipotentiary of these states at the court of Versailles, the minister of France in Pennsylvania, and the minister of France, be respectively informed that the operations of the next campaign must depend on such a variety of contingencies to arise, as well from our own internal circumstances and resources, as the progress and movements of our enemy, that time alone can mature and point out the plan which ought to be pursued. That congress, therefore, can not, with a degree of confidence answerable to the magnitude of the object, decide on the practicability of their co-operating the next campaign, in an enterprise for the emancipation of Canada; that every preparation in our power will nevertheless be made for acting with vigour against the common enemy, and every favourable incident embraced with alacrity, to facilitate, and hasten the freedom and independence of Canada, and her union with these states—events which congress, from motives of policy with respect to the United States, as well as of affection for their Canadian brethren, have greatly at heart."

Mr. de Sevelinges in his introduction to Botta's History, recites the private instructions given to Mr. Girard on his mission to the United States. One article was, "to avoid entering into any formal engagement relative to Canada and other English possessions which congress proposed to conquer. Mr. de Sevelinges adds that "the policy of the cabinet of Versailles viewed the possession of those countries, especially of Canada by England, as a principle of useful inquietude and vigilance to the Americans. The neighbourhood of a formidable enemy must make them feel more sensibly the price which they ought to attach to the friendship and support of the king of France."

The author has reason to believe that this policy was known to the Marquis de Lafayette when his devotion to the interests of the United States induced him to add his influence to their solicitations for aid to this enterprise.

NOTE—No. III. *See Page* 233

A letter to President Reed of Pennsylvania from which the following extracts are taken, is selected from many others written with the same view.

Morristown, May 28th, 1780.

Dear Sir,—I am much obliged to you for your favour of the 23d. Nothing could be more necessary than the aid given by your state towards supplying us with provisions. I assure you, every idea you can form of our distresses, will fall short of the reality. There is such a combination of circumstances to exhaust the patience of the soldiery, that it begins at length to be worn out, and we see in every line of the army, the most serious features of mutiny and sedition: all our departments, all our operations are at a stand; and unless a system very different from that which has for a long time prevailed, be immediately adopted throughout the states, our affairs must soon become desperate beyond the possibility of recovery. If you were on the spot, my dear sir, if you could see what difficulties surround us on every side, how unable we are to administer to the most ordinary calls of the service, you would be convinced that these expressions are not too strong: and that we have every thing to dread: Indeed I have almost ceased to hope. The country in general is in such a state of insensibility and indifference to its interests, that I dare not flatter myself with any change for the better.

The committee of congress in their late address to the several states, have given a just picture of our situation. I very much doubt its making the desired impression; and if it does not, I shall consider our lethargy as incurable. The present juncture is so interesting, that if it does not produce correspondent exertions, it will be a proof, that motives of honour, public good, and even self-preservation, have lost their influence upon our minds. This is a decisive moment, one of the most, I will go further and say, the most important America has seen. The court of France has made a glorious effort for our deliverance, and if we disappoint its intentions by our supineness, we must become contemptible in the eyes of all mankind; nor can we, after that, venture to confide that our allies will persist in an attempt to establish what it will appear we want inclination or ability to assist them in.

Every view of our own circumstances ought to determine us to the most vigorous efforts; but there are considerations of another kind, that should have equal weight. The combined fleets of France and Spain last year were greatly superior to those of the enemy; the enemy nevertheless sustained no material damage, and at the close of the campaign gave a very important blow to our allies. This campaign, the difference between the fleets, from every account I have been able to collect, will be inconsiderable: indeed it is far from clear that there will be an equality. What are we to expect will be the case if there should be another campaign? In all probability the advantage would be on the side of the English, and then what would become of America? We ought not to deceive ourselves. The maritime resources of Great Britain are more substantial and real than those of France and Spain united. Her commerce is more extensive than that of both her rivals; and it is an axiom, that the nation which has the most extensive commerce will always have the most powerful marine. Were this argument less convincing, the fact speaks for itself: her progress in the course of the last year is an incontestable proof.

"It is true France in a manner created a fleet in a very short space, and this may mislead us in the judgment we form of her naval abilities. But if they bore any comparison with those of Great Britain, how comes it to pass, that with all the force of Spain added, she has lost so much ground in so short a time, as now to have scarcely a superiority. We should consider what was done by France, as a violent and unnatural effort of the government, which, for want of sufficient foundation, can not continue to operate proportionable effects.

"In modern wars, the longest purse must chiefly determine the event. I fear that of the enemy will be found to be so. Though the government is deeply in debt and of course poor, the nation is rich, and their riches afford a fund which will not be easily exhausted. Besides, their system of public credit is such, that it is capable of greater exertions than that of any other nation. Speculatists have been a long time foretelling its downfall; but we see no symptoms of the catastrophe being very near. I am persuaded it will at least last out the war.

"France is in a very different position. The abilities of the present financier, have done wonders; by a wise administration of the revenues, aided by advantageous loans, he has avoided the necessity of additional taxes. But I am well informed if the war continues another campaign, he will be obliged to have recourse to the taxes usual in time of war, which are very heavy, and which the people of France are not in a condition to endure for any length of time. When this necessity commences, France makes war on ruinous terms, and England, from her individual wealth, will find much greater facilities in supplying her exigencies.

"Spain derives great wealth from her mines, but it is not so great as is generally imagined. Of late years the profit to government is essentially diminished. Commerce and industry are the best mines of a nation; both which are wanted by her. I am told her treasury is far from being so well filled as we have flattered ourselves. She is also much divided on the propriety of the war. There is a strong party against it. The temper of the nation is too sluggish to admit of great exertions; and though the courts of the two kingdoms are closely linked together, there never has been in any of their wars, a perfect harmony of measures, nor has it been the case in this; which has already been no small detriment to the common cause.

"I mention these things to show that the circumstances of our allies, as well as our own, call for peace, to obtain which we must make one great effort this campaign. The present instance of the friendship of the court of France, is attended with every circumstance that can render it important and agreeable, that can interest our gratitude or fire our emulation. If we do our duty we may even hope to make the campaign decisive of the contest. But we must do our duty in earnest, or disgrace and ruin will attend us. I am sincere in declaring a full persuasion that the succour will be fatal to us if our measures are not adequate to the emergency.

"Now, my dear sir, I must observe to you, that much will depend on the state of Pennsylvania. She has it in her power to contribute, without comparison, more to our success, than any other state, in the two essential articles of flour and transportation. I speak to you in the language of frankness, and as a friend. I do not mean to make any insinuations unfavourable to the state. I am aware of the embarrassment the government labours under from the open opposition of one party and the underhand intrigues of another. I know that with the best dispositions to promote the public service, you have been obliged to move with circumspection. But this is a time to hazard, and to take a tone of energy and decision. All parties but the disaffected will acquiesce in the necessity and give their support.

"The matter is reduced to a point. Either Pennsylvania must give us all we ask, or we can undertake nothing. We must renounce every idea of co-operation, and must confess to our allies that we look wholly to them for our safety. This will be a state of humiliation and bitterness against which the feelings of every good American ought to revolt. Yours I am convinced will, nor have I the least doubt, but that you will employ all your influence to animate the legislature and the people at large. The fate of these states hangs upon it. God grant we may be properly impressed with the consequences.

"I wish the legislature could be engaged to vest the executive with plenipotentiary powers. I should then expect every thing practicable from your abilities and zeal. This is not a time for formality and ceremony. The crisis in every point of view is extraordinary, and extraordinary expedients are necessary. I am decided in this opinion."

NOTE—No. IV. *See Page* 261

André having been unquestionably a spy, and his sentence consequently just; and the plot in which he had engaged having threatened consequences the most fatal to America; his execution, had he been an ordinary person, would certainly have been viewed with cold indifference. But he was not an ordinary person. In a letter written at the time by Colonel Hamilton, who in genius, in candour, and in romantic heroism, did not yield to this unfortunate Englishman, the character of André is thus feelingly and eloquently drawn. "There was something singularly interesting in the character and fortunes of André. To an excellent understanding, well improved by education and travel, he united a peculiar elegance of mind and manners, and the advantages of a pleasing person. It is said he possessed a pretty taste for the fine arts, and had himself attained some proficiency in poetry, music, and painting. His knowledge appeared without ostentation, and embellished by a diffidence that rarely accompanies so many talents and accomplishments, which left you to suppose more than appeared. His sentiments were elevated and inspired esteem, they had a softness that conciliated affection. His elocution was handsome, his address easy, polite, and insinuating. By his merit he had acquired the unlimited confidence of his general, and was making rapid progress in military rank and reputation. But in the height of his career, flushed with new hopes from the execution of a project the most beneficial to his party that could be devised, he is at once precipitated from the summit of prosperity, sees all the expectations of his ambition blasted, and himself ruined. The character I have given of him is drawn partly from what I saw of him myself, and partly from information. I am aware that a man of real merit is never seen in so favorable a light as through the medium of adversity. The clouds that surround him are so many shades that set off his good qualities. Misfortune cuts down little vanities, that in prosperous times, serve as so many spots in his virtues; and gives a tone to humanity that makes his worth more amiable.

"His spectators, who enjoy a happier lot, are less prone to detract from it through envy; and are much disposed by compassion to give the credit he deserves, and perhaps even to magnify it."

NOTE—No. V. *See Page* 377

On the first of May, 1781, General Washington commenced a military journal. The following is a brief statement of the situation of the army at that time. "I begin at this epoch, a concise journal of military transactions, &c. I lament not having attempted it from the commencement of the war in aid of my memory: and wish the multiplicity of matter which continually surrounds me, and the embarrassed state of our affairs, which is momentarily calling the attention to perplexities of one kind or another, may not defeat altogether, or so interrupt my present intention and plan, as to render it of little avail.

"To have the clearer understanding of the entries which may follow, it would be proper to recite, in detail, our wants, and our prospects; but this alone would be a work of much time, and great magnitude. It may suffice to give the sum of them, which I shall do in a few words, viz:

"Instead of having magazines filled with provisions, we have a scanty pittance scattered here and there in the different states.

"Instead of having our arsenals well supplied with military stores, they are poorly provided, and the workmen all leaving them.—Instead of having the various articles of field equipage in readiness to deliver, the quartermaster general is but now applying to the several states (as the dernier ressort) to provide these things for their troops respectively. Instead of having a regular system of transportation established upon credit—or funds in the quartermaster's hands to defray the contingent expenses of it—we have neither the one or the other; and all that business, or a great part of it, being done by military impressment, we are daily and hourly oppressing the people, souring their tempers, and alienating their affections. Instead of having the regiments completed to the new establishments (and which ought to have been so by the of agreeably to the requisitions of congress, scarce any state in the union has, at this hour, one-eighth part of its quota in the field; and there is little prospect that I can see of ever getting more than half. In a word, instead of having every thing in readiness to take the field, we have nothing. And instead of having the prospect of a glorious offensive campaign before us, we have a bewildered and gloomy prospect of a defensive one; unless we should receive a powerful aid of ships, land troops and money from our generous allies: and these at present are too contingent to build upon."

NOTE—No. VI. *See Page* 405

York in Virginia, 17th October, 1781, half past four, P. M.

SIR,—I have this moment been honoured with your excellency's letter dated this day. The time limited for sending my answer will not admit of entering into the details of articles, but the basis of my proposals will be, that the garrisons of York and Gloucester shall be prisoners of war with the customary honours; and for the convenience of the individuals which I have the honour to command, that the British shall be sent to Britain, and the Germans to Germany, under engagements not to serve against France, America, or their allies, until released or regularly exchanged. That all arms and public stores shall be delivered up to you, but that the usual indulgence of side arms to officers and of retaining private property shall be granted to officers and soldiers; and the interests of individuals in civil capacities, and connected with us, shall be attended to. If your excellency thinks that a continuance of the suspension of hostilities will be necessary to transmit your answer, I shall have no objection to the hour that you propose. I have the honour to be,

Sir, your most obedient and most humble servant,

CORNWALLIS.

His excellency General Washington, &c. &c. &c.

NOTE—No. VII. *See Page* 406

Head quarters before York, 18th October, 1781.

MY LORD,—To avoid unnecessary discussions and delays, I shall at once, in answer to your lordship's letter of yesterday, declare the general basis upon which a definitive treaty of capitulation must take place. The garrison of York and Gloucester, including the seamen, as you propose, will be received prisoners of war. The condition annexed of sending the British and German troops to the parts of Europe to which they respectively belong, is inadmissible. Instead of this, they will be marched to such parts of the country as can most conveniently provide for their subsistence; and the benevolent treatment of prisoners, which is invariably observed by the Americans, will be extended to them. The same honours will be granted to the surrendering army, as were granted to the garrison of Charleston.

The shipping and boats in the two harbours, with all their guns, stores, tackling, furniture, and apparel, shall be delivered in their present state to an officer of the navy appointed to take possession of them.

The artillery, arms, accoutrements, military chest, and public stores of every denomination, shall be delivered unimpaired, to the heads of departments, to which they respectively belong.

The officers will be indulged in retaining their side arms, and the officers and soldiers may preserve their baggage and effects with this reserve, that property taken in the country will be reclaimed.

With regard to the individuals in civil capacities, whose interests your lordship wishes may be attended to, until they are more particularly described, nothing definitive can be settled.

I have to add, that I expect the sick and wounded will be supplied with their own hospital stores, and attended by British surgeons particularly charged with the care of them.

Your lordship will be pleased to signify your determination either to accept or reject the proposals now offered, in the course of two hours from the delivery of this letter, that commissioners may be appointed to digest the articles of capitulation, or a renewal of hostilities may take place.

I have the honour to be, my lord, &c.

GEORGE WASHINGTON.

Lieutenant General Earl Cornwallis.

York, in Virginia, 18th October, 1781.

Sir,—I agree to open a treaty of capitulation upon the basis of the garrisons of York and Gloucester, including seamen, being prisoners of war without annexing the condition of their being sent to Europe; but I expect to receive a compensation in arranging the articles of capitulation for the surrender of Gloucester in its present state of defence.

I shall in particular desire that the Bonetta sloop of war, may be left entirely at my disposal from the hour the capitulation is signed, to receive an aid-de-camp to carry my despatches to Sir Henry Clinton and such soldiers as I may think proper to send as passengers in her, to be manned with fifty men of her own crew, and to be permitted to sail without examination when my despatches are ready; engaging on my part that the ship shall be brought back and delivered to you, if she escapes the dangers of the sea; that the crew and soldiers sent as passengers shall be accounted for in future exchanges as prisoners; that she shall carry off no officer without your consent, nor public property of any kind; and I shall likewise desire that the traders and inhabitants may preserve their property, and that no person may be punished or molested for having joined the British troops.

If you choose to proceed to negotiation on these grounds, I shall appoint two field officers of my army to meet two officers from you at any time and place you think proper, to digest the articles of capitulation. I have the honour to be, sir,

Your most obedient and most humble servant,

CORNWALLIS.

His excellency General Washington, &c. &c. &c.

NOTE—No. VIII. *See Page* 411

Head quarters, 20th October, 1781.

Sir,—The surrender of York, from which so much glory and advantage are derived to the allies, and the honour of which belongs to your excellency, has greatly anticipated our most sanguine expectations. Certain of this event under your auspices, though unable to determine the time, I solicited your excellency's attention in the first conference with which you honoured me, to ulterior objects of decisive importance to the common cause. Although your excellency's answer on that occasion was unfavourable to my wishes, the unexpected promptness with which our operations have been conducted to their final success having gained us time, the defect of which was one of your excellency's principal objections, a perspective of the most extensive and happy consequences, engages me to renew my representations.

Charleston, the principal maritime port of the British in the southern parts of the continent, the grand deposite and point of support for the present theatre of the war, is open to a combined attack, and might be carried with as much certainty as the place which has just surrendered.

This capture would destroy the last hope which induces the enemy to continue the war; for having experienced the impracticability of recovering the populous northern states, he has determined to confine himself to the defensive in that quarter, and to prosecute a most vigorous offensive in the south, with a view of conquering states, whose spare population and natural disadvantages render them infinitely less susceptible of defence; although their productions render them the most valuable in a commercial view. His naval superiority, previous to your excellency's arrival, gave him decisive advantages in the rapid transport of his troops and supplies: while the immense land marches of our succours, too tardy and expensive in every point of view, subjected us to be beaten in detail.

It will depend upon your excellency, therefore, to terminate the war, and enable the allies to dictate the law in a treaty. A campaign so glorious and so fertile in consequences, could be reserved only for the Count de Grasse.

It rarely happens that such a combination of means, as are in our hands at present, can be seasonably obtained by the most strenuous of human exertions.—A decisively superior fleet, the fortune and talents of whose commander overawe all the naval force that the most incredible efforts of the enemy have been able to collect; an army flushed with success, and demanding only to be conducted to new attacks; and the very season which is proper for operating against the points in question.

If upon entering into the detail of this expedition, your excellency should still determine it impracticable, there is an object which though subordinate to that above mentioned, is of capital importance to our southern operations, and may be effected at infinitely less expense; I mean the enemy's post at Wilmington in North Carolina. Circumstances require that I should at this period reinforce the southern army under General Greene. This reinforcement transported by sea under your excellency's convoy, would enable us to carry the post in question with very little difficulty, and would wrest from the British a point of support in North Carolina, which is attended with the most dangerous consequences to us, and would liberate another state. This object would require nothing more than the convoy of your excellency to the point of operation, and the protection of the debarkation.

I intreat your excellency's attention to the points which I have the honour of laying before you, and to be pleased at the same time to inform me what are your dispositions for a maritime force to be left on the American station.

I have the honour to be, &c.

GEORGE WASHINGTON.

NOTE—No. IX. *See Page* 413

Late in October an irruption was made into the country on the Mohawk, by Major Ross, at the head of about five hundred men, composed of regulars, rangers, and Indians. Colonel Willet, with between four and five hundred men, partly of the troops denominated levies, and partly militia, immediately marched in quest of them, and fell in with them at Johnstown, where they were slaughtering cattle, apparently unapprehensive of an enemy. Before showing himself, he detached Major Rowley of Massachusetts with the left wing to fall on the rear, while he should engage the front. On his appearance the British party retired to a neighbouring wood, and the American advance was just beginning to skirmish with them, when that whole wing, without any apparent cause, suddenly fled from the field, leaving a field-piece posted on a height in order to cover a retreat, to fall into the hands of the enemy. Fortunately for the party, Rowley appeared in the rear at this critical juncture, and regained what the right wing had lost. Night soon coming on, Major Ross retired further into the wood, and encamped on the top of a mountain. He seems after this skirmish to have been only intent on repassing the dreary wilderness in his rear, and securing his party; an object not to be accomplished without immense fatigue and great suffering, as Colonel Willet had cut off their return to their boats, and they were to retreat by the way of Buck island, or Oswegatchie. With a select part of his troops who were furnished with five days provisions, and about sixty Indians who had just joined him, and who, he said, "are the best cavalry for the service of the wilderness," he commenced a rapid pursuit, and in the morning of the 30th, at a ford on Canada creek, fell in with about forty whites and some Indians who were left in the rear to procure provisions. These were attacked and the greater number of them killed or taken, upon which the main body fled with such rapidity that the pursuit proved ineffectual. In the party at Canada creek was Major Walter Butler, the person who perpetrated the massacre at Cherry-valley. His entreaties for quarter were disregarded, and he fell the victim of that vengeance which his own savage temper had directed against himself.

END OF VOLUME III.